What people are say

T0308617

The Not So Subtle Art of ~~Caring. Letters~~ on Leadership

I have always appreciated that Philip practices what he preaches. He delivers results with a servant leadership approach to unlock the power and capability of his people through engagement, enablement and empowerment. *The Not So Subtle Art of Caring* offers a great lesson for leaders looking to do just that.
Greg Smith, Executive Vice President, Global Operations & Supply Chain, Medtronics

With *Letters on Leadership* Phillip Kane masters to describe the key to leadership: To be dedicated to what you do and to care about what you do both for the business and, most important, not to forget the people involved. Caring about your people is the key.
Martin Pedersen, CEO/Owner at JP Group a/s, Denmark

No leadership book is more needed for today's world than Phillip Kane's *The Not So Subtle Art of Caring: Letters on Leadership*. It's time for CEO's, organizational leaders and boards to understand that kindness does not equal weakness. Phillip engages readers with story after inspirational story from over thirty years of transforming organizations; masterfully illustrating that leaders who value the well-being of their people are trusted and consistently deliver results. This is GOOD reading not only for how to lead, but also for how to live.
Kris Wittenberg, founder of Be Good to People, BeGoodtoPeople. com

Having had a front row seat to many of the stories contained in Phillip Kane's new book, *The Not So Subtle Art of Caring: Letters on*

i

Leadership, I saw firsthand that focusing on winning AND caring for others can deliver extraordinary results. This book is important reading for anyone searching for a different, better way to lead others.

Thomas J. Caracciolo, Dubin Clark & Company

Organizations are no more than collectives of individuals. Why, then, should we be surprised that the same thing that moves, nurtures, and inspires individuals – an open and caring heart - also works at the organizational level? Through lived experiences, illustrative stories, and a principle-based leadership model, Phillip Kane makes a compelling case that "winning" in the marketplace is completely compatible with, and even dependent upon, caring about others. This is a timely and much-needed addition to the leadership literature.

Dr Sarah Gardial, Dean, Jack C. Massey College of Business, Belmont University

Storytelling has been a part of Phillip Kane's life since he was a kid, and he carried over the family tradition into his business life. When you can write or tell a story about someone with whom your listeners can identify, they are much more likely to see themselves doing the same thing. People seldom tire of hearing stories about themselves and the people they know. These stories get repeated, and the lessons of the stories spread far and wide.

James M. Kouzes and **Barry Z. Posner**, authors of *The Leadership Challenge: How Extraordinary Things Happen in Organizations*

Having read my share of leadership books, Kane does a wonderful job of sharing some very practical lessons on how to care about your people. Afterall, no matter how much you know, your team won't even begin to listen and follow until they know that you care. This book is required reading for new and seasoned leaders.

Craige Stout, CEO, Stout Risius Ross, Advisors LLC

This thoughtful and experienced-based leadership book is based on weekly management letters that Mr. Kane sent to his staff during his long career as a C-suite leader and manager in corporate America. His letters highlight weekly outcomes and discuss how their results reflect one of the dozen qualities of the Not So Subtle Leader that form the core of his book. Mr. Kane's book provides a refreshing presentation of key factors leading to successful teams and has enormous value for new managers as well as for those who have been doing things the same way for a long time.
Robert A. "Bob" Kulinski, President United Way of Summit County, Ohio (Ret)

I've been studying leadership since I was a patrol leader in Boy Scouts. This book has it all; lots of real-life examples by a trailblazer in the business, validated by hundreds of specific references from notable authors. It will benefit leaders at any level. I plan to use *The Not So Subtle Art of Caring* in my leadership workshops
Captain J. Charles "Charlie" Plumb, U.S.Navy (Ret)

Phillip's very personal approach, in utilizing letters sent to his teams over many years, provides deep insights into the artistry demanded of a more caring leader who commits to deliver outstanding results.
Robert J. Keegan, Former Chairman & CEO, The Goodyear Tire & Rubber Company

I have had the opportunity to see firsthand, and I hope contribute to, Phillip Kane's caring leadership style. His book, Letters on Leadership, is a primer for delivering extraordinary results while putting others first. This very unique and real-life account of business successes offers those in search of a better way to lead a simple and proven way to win.
Brett Ponton, Chief Executive Officer, Terminix

The Not So Subtle Art of Caring: Letters on Leadership

Real stories from a real leader to real people about what really matters

The Not So Subtle Art of Caring: Letters on Leadership

Real stories from a real leader to real
people about what really matters

Phillip Kane

BUSINESS
BOOKS

Winchester, UK
Washington, USA

JOHN HUNT PUBLISHING

First published by Business Books, 2022
Business Books is an imprint of John Hunt Publishing Ltd., No. 3 East St., Alresford,
Hampshire SO24 9EE, UK
office@jhpbooks.com
www.johnhuntpublishing.com
www.johnhuntpublishing.com/business-books

For distributor details and how to order please visit the 'Ordering' section on our website.

Text copyright: Phillip Kane 2021

ISBN: 978 1 78904 908 4
978 1 78904 909 1 (ebook)
Library of Congress Control Number: 2021932914

A CIP catalogue record for this book is available from the British Library.

Design: Stuart Davies

UK: Printed and bound by CPI Group (UK) Ltd, Croydon, CR0 4YY
Printed in North America by CPI GPS partners

We operate a distinctive and ethical publishing philosophy in
all areas of our business, from our global network of authors to
production and worldwide distribution.

Contents

For my father – who told me stories … not nearly enough of them.

*"People often ask me what is enlightenment. I tell them caring –
that's all there is to enlightenment."*
Abhijit Naskar
1991-
Indian Neuroscientist

Foreword

Most people believe that getting a leadership position is an acknowledgment for the hard work performed until then. A sort of celebration for a good career.

This is exactly the starting point of any leadership failure.

What I learned throughout all the leadership positions I had in my career at Fiat Chrysler Automobiles, Iveco and Recordati, is that a call to lead is only a beginning.

Getting the chance to lead people marks the inception of one of the most challenging journeys any manager could possibly perform in his or her life, but moreover on behalf of the lives of others.

Leading is indeed a privilege. The most fascinating and luxurious of all because any action (good or bad), any decision (right or wrong), any behavior (righteous or cynical) will inevitably affect other people's current and future lives.

As in any journey, there will be good days and bad ones. The worst of all, and with Covid-19 there have been too many of these, is when as a leader you will be called to tell one or more of your mates the very difficult, "I'm going to have to let you go."

In any moment, including these worst moments, especially these worst moments, what separates leaders from managers is their care for other people.

True leaders care for those they have the privilege to lead.

Does this mean being perfect, or a saint or an angel? Not at all!

Caring is not about being nice to people all the time. Caring sometimes means delivering tough news or telling people they've let you down.

Caring simply means treating others ALWAYS with dignity, respect and love.

Caring about our people is not difficult, does not weaken our ego nor our public image and does not require extra-hours, it just requires a dedication and commitment to the notion that winning while caring for others is not only possible, it is absolutely essential.

Rewards for caring will outpace any sort of expectation one might have otherwise had for the investment they made in their position. Because they will be repaid by the hearts of others, something no amount of money can purchase.

When soldiers see their Commander-in-Chief standing on the battlefield with them, driving the action and ready to take decisions real-time, they know he is living their same fear to die, their same ambition to win, their same desire to succeed. And they will fight for him or her and be ready to pay the utmost price for that.

But when they know their leader is sitting, miles away, in a comfortable boardroom smoking cigars, checking details of the next football game and taking decisions after having read not less than 100 pages of PowerPoint presentations (instead of speaking with real people), they will feel they belong to a different world and they are playing a different game. At that point they will have no inclination to take risks or fight for their leader. They will get stuck by the fear of making mistakes and will embrace a "wait and see" attitude that will soon pervade the entire organization.

Caring while leading means standing alongside ready to support. It means spending time and effort to understand people's needs and putting them into the best possible condition to succeed.

The extreme opposite of caring is micro-management. Micromanagers are just that – managers – not leaders. They are holdovers from a time gone by. But it's not an outdated style. It's a style that never actually worked in the first place. People want the freedom to act and the ability to engineer a solution. They lose their self-confidence the minute their boss steps onto their shoes with a turn-key solution.

Many leaders have a tendency to confuse caring with compassion. True leaders are not the ultimate Father Confessor or an unconditional forgiver of any mistake. This is not caring. A leader who cares will be there to help explain the right way when others make a mistake but will not tolerate the same mistake twice nor will they forgive a lack of creativity and ingenuity to ultimately resolve a problem.

Smart people will always be thankful to leaders who have pushed them to become better managers and better human beings; only losers will complain. The difference though, is caring leaders push others in ways that encourage, in ways that protect their dignity, in ways that build up, not tear down.

Sometimes leadership can be lonely. The feeling of loneliness comes with the job and is actually one of the things that mark the difference between leaders and others. Great leaders can feel particularly alone when tough decisions must be made or when fire is headed toward their teams, because caring leaders insulate their teams from this sort of pain. But trust me when I tell you that the gratitude, trust and loyalty from those who follow you will more than offset the cost of caring while you lead.

Finally, in one of the hardest decisions they have to make, caring leaders also make the choice to leave detractors behind to strengthen the rest of the team. They dump the ballast to make the ship faster. They understand that no amount of negative energy or failure to fight for what the team is trying to accomplish can ever be tolerated.

But by making a choice to lead with care, these best-in-class leaders not only win more often, they build relationships that will last a lifetime.

That's why there is no better thing in life than leading people. Make the right use of that privilege and the rewards can exceed your wildest expectations. They have for me, mostly because I got the part about caring for others right more often than I got it wrong.

This book by Phillip Kane is a great tool for all leaders who believe, as I do, that growing one's leadership skills is an everlasting process. It is a perfect guide for leaders of any age searching for a better way to lead people. And the stories Phillip tells not only make it easy to relate to, but they offer proof that what he is saying actually works, because his stories are words he used in leading actual people to accomplish actual extraordinary feats.

Caring for others never goes out of style and it's a style that applies anywhere in the world. Phillip lived here in Milan for a while, so he knows that firsthand. Now we have his book to make sure the rest of us never forget it.

So, thanks Phillip for writing this book, for letting me be a part of it, and for making the world a more caring place.

Alfredo Altavilla
Milan, Italy
February 2021

Preface

The Family Business

"Der Apfel nicht gerne weit vom Baum."
"The apple does not like to fall far from the tree."
German proverb - 1585

In September of 2010, I was asked if I would move to Fort Smith to lead a wholly owned subsidary of the Goodyear Tire & Rubber Company which was underperforming expectations. My first question was, "Where's Fort Smith?" Upon learning it was in Arkansas, my second question was, "Where in Arkansas?" I'd soon find out.

On my first day, I was loaded on one of Goodyear's three corporate planes, and flown from Akron, Ohio to Arkansas by a group of executives on their way further west. As the plane circled tiny Fort Smith, looking out my window on that beautiful Fall day, I had my own sort of Princess Diaries moment. But instead of having my footman welcome me to Genovia, one of our pilots announced that we were about to land in Fort Smith, population 86,297. As my escorts left, one of Goodyear's VPs clapped me on the back and encouraged me by suggesting that I "don't eff this up." Then I was on my own.

I was about to meet around 100 of our 2,700 employees for the first time. Our business didn't have a conference room. So, I addressed the assembled body of HQ associates in the rear parking lot by standing on the loading dock. I'm not so tall, so the loading dock part was a bonus. I'm not a boisterous extrovert, so the parking lot part wasn't. My speech was short: a story about Moses; that things were about to become very different; that I was intent on helping them win; that they were the most important thing in our business; and that when we'd win, their lives would improve. It felt good to finally be able to say these things.

It was the first time in my career I had complete and total responsibility for anything. Until then, I had led large groups of human beings. But never had I been given the opportunity to set not only the strategy and budget for a business, but most importantly for me, the culture as well. It was finally my chance to prove that what I believed, knew in my heart, about leading others was correct.

I knew it because I had seen it work for most of my life. I'd also seen what didn't work, as recently as the day before – namely top-down, command and control management by apathetic, extroverted narcissists concerned almost entirely with their own incomes, and whose last interaction with a customer or front-line associate probably involved a photographer and a self-serving press release.

Despite multiple research projects including a 10-year study called the CEO Genome Project, from the leadership advisory firm ghSmart and published in the Harvard Business Review (Botelho, 2017) which have concluded that despite America's predilection for hiring loud, outgoing managers as CEOs, their introverted counterparts actually perform better well more than half the time, US boards continue to hire to the loud, back-slapper formula, never seeming to conclude that these folks have a fundamental leadership flaw. They're not the right person for the job. They're not wired to do it the right way.

I had seen it done the right way since I was a boy, watching my father, a truck dealer and leader of men, inspire others. My father was a servant leader before there was a name for it. My father was also a storyteller. He'd tell stories to make a point. And you'd remember both – the story and the point. And you'd follow him anywhere. I grew up not wanting to be a doctor, lawyer, or an Indian chief. I wanted to be my dad. I went to a college 30 minutes away from home so I could skip school on a near daily basis to be with my father, to learn from him. Eventually, after finishing school and hoping to start work for my father, I learned that he had a rule – same as his dad – that I could go to work for him, but I had to go to work somewhere else first.

So, I did … for another servant and storyteller by the name of Tony Kaskocsak. Tony believed that his one role in life was to give those he led whatever they needed to win, then pretty much spend the rest of his time on vacation, telling stories about human kindness and winning. Which he did. And I learned about both.

Later, along my way, I met a Catholic priest from Nigeria by the name of Father Casmir Maduakor who used stories to bridge his language gap while making a point and touching my life in the process.

And so, standing there on that loading dock that day, having just recently seen another American board fall for the tall, dark, and handsome extrovert trick, I was determined to prove there was a better way.

And I did. We did. In just 15 months we drove a dramatic turn in the business. We did so by fundamentally changing the way people were spoken to and treated. We told stories for sure. More than anything we cared more about others than we did for ourselves.

That's what this book is about after all. It's about a better way to lead others. It's about winning, by choosing to put others first. It's about making a case for introverted stewards. It's about listening to those closest to the work. It's about investing, not cutting. It's about integrity, gratitude, and trust.

It's about The Not So Subtle Art of Caring.

Caring is hard. Caring requires personal investment. Caring requires ensuring that those one has the privilege to lead have whatever they need to be successful. Sometimes that means having difficult and critical conversations with others when they let you down. Caring requires recognizing that the needs of others are primary to your own, and that there exists something or someone somewhere which is a greater power than you. Caring requires taking the time to ensure that those you lead understand exactly what they are being asked to do, why they are being asked to do it, how to do it, and most importantly that their lives will improve when they do it. Accomplishing that requires reaching every single person in your organization. And that requires talking to them, a lot – in terms they can understand, relate to, believe in and fight for. Fortunately, people relate to stories, making the task a great deal easier.

I learned that first from my father, a few heroes I met out in the world and from my own 30 years in business. I'd also learned it from arguably the most notable man to have ever lived.

Using stories that connect to a point about how we should choose to do what we do has enabled me to create winning cultures and teams that have delivered extraordinary results throughout my career. It's because stories help people better grasp the point, then better internalize the message. When this happens the chance of people acting on the message increases factorially. According to a well-known Stanford study by Bower and Clark, those informed through stories were seven times more likely than those informed via list to recall the information presented - 93% v. 13%. (Bower, G., 1969)

But this isn't just about storytelling. Storytelling is merely a tool or a means, albeit a tremendously impactful one, to effect change. It is the change itself told by the stories that matters most – a change in the way that we think about treating, caring for and leading, others. Behind the stories is the fundamental truth that there exists a kinder, more effective way to lead people. Stories have simply been a way to prove the point.

I used stories in the form of a letter that I wrote to my team in Arkansas, and other teams I've been fortunate to lead, before and after, every Friday throughout my career, to reinforce the key leadership traits that result in winning the right way and the behaviors behind The Not So Subtle Art of Caring. The practice began as a recap of what we did in our business during the prior week, but quickly morphed into a discussion less about what we did than how we did it, which is, I believe, as or more important. The letter, unimaginatively called *The Week*, used a story about a happening or observation from the prior week to make a point. These lessons from unlikely places, if we are open to them, help make us better businesspeople, spouses, parents, friends and members of a community. My goal each week has always been for just one person to take something away from these short notes. As a result, over time, the whole of us would begin to think differently. When that happened, we won more, which, after all, is really the point of why we wake up each day.

Many of those letters are assembled here, arranged under chapter headings which highlight the required behaviors for the next generation of caring leaders. Each chapter also includes a brief introduction to each topic with some how-to's and a contrast to the old, doesn't work anymore way of doing things. My goal is to help you win.

Business, after all, is a game in which score is kept. The Not So Subtle Art of Caring isn't about softness, or a celebration of shyness. Remember, even Jesus flipped over a few tables. It's about winning. But it's about making a conscious choice to win the right way, by first and foremost, choosing to care about others. This book is meant to act as a manual, of a kind, for a new generation of leaders, intent on finding an alternative to the traditional, self-centered, Baby Boomer management techniques of the last century. There is a better way. I've seen it. I've proved it. And I'd like to tell you a story about it ...

P.K.

Introduction

(What is) The Not So Subtle Art of Caring?

"If I have seen farther than others, it is by standing on the shoulders of others."
Isaac Newton
1643-1727
English Physicist

This is NOT just another same old, same old book about Servant Leadership. It's a book about stewardship – about winning *while* wholeheartedly looking after others. It's a book about The Not So Subtle Art of Caring.

In 1970, Robert K. Greenleaf published *The Servant Leader*, coining the term. Undoubtedly, Greenleaf did not invent the philosophy, for passages dating as far back as 4th century India and China refer to servant-based leadership goals. Throughout following written history, many other practitioners of subservient leader styles can readily be found. Jesus Christ, often pointed to as the example/model for many contemporary thought leaders on the subject, is quoted in the Gospel of Mark as saying, "Yet it shall not be so among you; But whoever desires to become great among you shall be your servant." (Holy Bible

(ESV) Mark 10:43)

Since Greenleaf's groundbreaking work, a host of new writers have added to the compendium on the topic of Servant Leadership. Folks like Ken Blanchard, James Autry, Larry Spears, John Maxwell, Jim Hunter, Margaret Wheatley, Simon Sinek, Ken Melrose, Herman Hesse, and Kent Keith have all written in favor of Servant Leadership. Among all of these boosters of the servant style – though reasonably varied in their approach to the topic – is, at their core, one seemingly bedrock principle; that the leader exists to serve those they lead.

While there is no agreed upon definition of the term, the most commonly cited definition of servant leadership is Greenleaf's: "The servant leader is servant first ... It begins with the natural feeling that one wants to serve, to serve *first*. Then conscious choice brings one to aspire to lead." (Greenleaf, 1977) Most later definitions have stayed generally true to Greenleaf's. For example, some 45 years after the standard, a leading scholar in the field, Peter G. Northouse, wrote that servant leadership is "a paradoxical approach to leadership that challenges our traditional beliefs about leadership and influence. Servant leadership emphasizes that leaders should be attentive to the needs of others, empower them and help them develop their full human capacities." (Northouse, 2013).

Like the lack of agreement in regard to a definition for the philosophy, there exists no agreed upon list of attributes that fairly nor exhaustively describe the servant leader individually. Robert Greenleaf offered 10. Other authors and scholars, like James McNerney, Kathleen Patterson and Robert Russell along with Gregory Stone have put forth their own lists of generally one half-dozen or more items. It can be said with great confidence that common to any list of traits defining the servant are terms rooted in altruism and giving. Generally shared among any lists are words like empowerment, vision, and service. Generally absent, with few exceptions are active verbs and/or power words. When considering the sea of descriptors as a whole, the leadership style is generally, on par, positioned as softer and kinder. Rarely is a focus on winning or delivering results mentioned as a key priority of the servant leader.

As a result, unfortunately, it is often mistaken for a too soft to be effective form of leadership. In his book, *The Leader's Guide to Radical Management*, author Steve Denning describes Servant Leadership as "boring", saying "It smells of the Jimmy Carter school of leadership. Solid. Beautiful. Moral. Yes, but it will have difficulty getting anyone's pulse beating faster or taking us into the future." Then he adds, "As formulated by Greenleaf, being a servant leader is about serving people and is *relatively passive* [emphasis his]." (Denning, S., 2010) Others have gone as far as to call Servant Leadership a bad idea, based entirely on their (incorrect) perception of a "paternalistic" philosophy, and accuse proponents of the philosophy of merely "switching from critical parent to nurturing parent." (McCrimmon, 2010) In a sea of literature taking aim at Servant Leadership, the most common criticism is that it is not tough enough to actually work; that it's an inmates in charge of the asylum theory that will fail in practice.

In my own experience, when asked to share my own leadership style, I have typically and generally described myself as a servant. In doing so, I have commonly, particularly in face-to-face encounters, detected negative facial and body language feedback. See, those who hire for C-Suite and board roles in the US of A remain nearly 100% convinced that the extroverted, hard-charging, take-no-prisoners, my-way-or-the-highway, table-pounding, voice-raising, intimidating micro-managers that often fail to make it 18 months in role are their best bet, despite study after study to the contrary. But is it any wonder? Because the Servant Leadership community has failed to provide an agreed-upon definition for the genre, folks are left to conjure up their own. Worse, many within the Servant

Leader industry itself are directly responsible for the image of the style as being too laid back to be taken seriously. A recent presentation by The Francis A. Schaeffer Institute of Church Leadership Development contained this gem, "Servant leaders are not weak. They are meek." (Krejcir, 2000)

When the Servant Leadership industry has, in the 51 years since 1970, done such an awful job convincing anyone that servants actually care about delivering results, we will be left to our own devices to quickly follow up our admissions of guilt with qualifiers that put the mind of our interrogators at ease. So, we tell them such things as, "The nearest description that would make sense is that I'm a servant leader. I deliver extraordinary business results by putting people first. With the teams I have led, I have been able, to accomplish breathtaking things, by connecting the objectives of the business to the behaviors of individual associates and ensuring that each person completely understands two things (1) that care for their physical, emotional, and economic safety is non-negotiable and (2) that their lives will immediately improve when we accomplish our goals." Or something to that effect. The reason I **need** to do this is because the prevailing opinion of Servant Leadership in the world is that it is a passive, feeble, nice all the time management style for introverts who are not tough enough to actually lead. Servant Leadership clearly, as Steve Denning points out, "has some inherent limitations as a catchall phrase." This is NOT a baby and bathwater situation however.

Servant Leadership simply has a PR problem. Servant Leadership practiced correctly, the way that the oft quoted Jesus Christ practiced it, the way that Martin Luther King Jr. practiced it, and the way that my father practiced it works. It delivers results. The way I have practiced Servant Leadership emulating the folks listed above and a handful of others like Tony Kaskocsak, Fr. Casmir Maduakor, and Larry Mason, works. It works because I practice what I call *The Not So Subtle*

Art of Caring.

Out of the gate, you can think about The Not So Subtle Art of Caring in three ways:

First, as its name suggests, it is NOT subtle, nor are those who practice it. Its leaders, while potentially introverts and those who intentionally do not seek the limelight as well as those who on the humble, braggart scale from 0 to Boor, rate about 4-5, are NOT shrinking violets. Not So Subtle leaders are not push-overs. Among qualities typical to the Not So Subtle leader, expect to see a leader who

- Believes
- Loves the One they're Looking At
- Is Wholehearted
- Tells it Like it Happened
- Persists Courageously
- Makes Others Big
- Wins the Right Way
- Talks to Others, Not About Others
- Stirs it Up
- Knows Why They are Here
- Makes a Lot of Mistakes … Once
- Has Fun … Achieving Something

These among other not terribly subtle attributes are not the characteristics of a shy, retiring individual who is scared to come to the front, or to take the stage, the reins or the mic when required. The leader actively participates in the team she leads and in the attainment of results. Throughout the following pages, each of the traits listed above will be covered in greater detail.

But even now, it should be clear that Servant Leadership is *not* the polar opposite to autocratic, authoritarian, command and control management. I have isolated on that style of leadership not because it is the flip side to a coin, or simply because it is such an easy target (which it is), but for two clear reasons. Number one, autocratic, domineering command and control management remains the prevailing style of leadership in most corporations. This is because boards continue to hire to the formula. A recent analysis by The Sutton Trust showed that extroverted, type A managers were still 25% more likely to be hired for top jobs than their counterparts. (Rentfrow, 2016) This is despite the fact that study after study finds that these Type-A extroverts do not do as well in these positions than their more introverted counterparts. (Oliver, 2016) Second, I focus on this prolific type A management style because it is awful. In the pages ahead, I will describe just how awful. It hurts people, and it should be stomped out as a means of leading other breathing things. There is a better way, and I will show it to you.

Finally, with no offense at all meant to Mattel, nor any misogyny thank you, I will, here and there, for fun, use Ken Doll and Pantsuit Barbie as a means of personifying those who practice the autocratic, table-pounding style of management – first because I don't believe this is a management style that should be taken seriously, and also because Ken and Barbie are easier than typing things like "authoritarian, type A command and control, soul-crushing management" each time I want to refer to these people.

But the point I want to stress more than any other is this: Caring leadership is not an alternative for individuals hesitant about leadership who see it as an opportunity to quietly and meekly "lead from behind" as a former US president was fond of saying. That's following. Leaders, including caring, steward leaders go to the front. It is what leaders do, and the front is where they hang out. If being in front isn't for you, it could be that leadership isn't your bag. Leaders lead. Leaders are not subtle. They are assertive. Their teams have a clear vision and clear goals which they confidently and courageously pursue and talk about loudly and constantly. They walk around with their heads up. They deal with confrontation. They look out for each other, protect each other and fight for each other. They have fun and celebrate loudly when things go well. You'll note a general lack of subtlety demonstrated by caring leaders who make winning their principal goal in life. Make no mistake, though. A lack of subtlety and humility are not mutually exclusive. It is entirely possible for one to lack subtlety and be an effective leader and servant of others, without becoming a lampshade on the head, Ken Doll boor. They win and they artfully make a point of making a point of it.

See, leadership done well is an art. So is non-subtly caring for others. It is a craft that is honed over time with practice, with trial, and error. One learns to play a musical instrument by putting fingers to keys. To paint by putting brush to canvas. To sculpt by putting chisel to stone. To lead by putting heart to other human beings. All are arts. Women/Men are rarely born with high performing abilities in any of these areas. Knowledge and wisdom can be gained from reading, attending coursework and from observing others. But skills are not learned without doing, without practicing the art. As the great sales mind David Sandler said, "You can't teach a kid to ride a bike at a seminar." To become great at anything, time must be invested. Learning to lead others happens when one actually leads others. But time is not the only determinant of success of the learning leader. The level of acceptance of a leader by those they lead is directly proportional to the level of care they provide.

Finally, true leaders care deeply for those they have the privilege to lead. They earn the loyalty and absolute acceptance of those they lead by placing their physical, emotional and economic safety above all else. The attributes of the caring leader described above are not possible to achieve passively, or from leading from behind. Caring for others is not soft. Concerning oneself with the greater good is not easy. Loving and caring for others in pursuit of a greater good is hard work. Putting the needs of others before your own while pursuing the goals of the business is not for the faint of heart. There is a reason that most traditional managers are self-centered; it's far easier.

It takes almost zero talent to look out for yourself. It takes no skill to treat everyone exactly the same or to react in precisely the same way (poorly) when things go wrong. It takes no imagination to run a business 90 days at a time, to micromanage every significant decision or to lead by intimidation or fear. But these are the same people that US boards continue to hire; despite the fact that a recent Edelman Trust Barometer study reported by Forbes showed that a sickening 63% of American workers report that they don't trust their CEOs. (Comaford, 2017) The answer is found in caring leaders that deliver results. In leaders that practice The Not So Subtle Art of Caring.

To be clear at the onset, I am not arguing against the Servant Leader movement. I am one. I am, though, arguing *for* a form of leadership rooted in service to others where leaders *assertively* and *artfully* focus on winning and what is right *while* caring for others. If I am protesting against anything it is against a misinterpretation of the philosophy, and those so-called Servant Leaders who choose the people before profit route, and who take the whole humility angle to Ghandi-esque extremes; these leaders lose sight of why they are there. They neither drive for results nor show the assertiveness to fight for their people when the time comes to do so; I don't see the point in that.

I am, principally, arguing against authoritarian management anytime, anywhere, anyhow. Those who demonstrate self-centeredness and incivility ever, and who deliver results through micro-management, fear and intimidation are pure-D jerks who have no place managing other human beings, EVER under any circumstances.

Finally, I want to make it clear that what I'm sharing with

you is not a theory. It's not the result of an academic project. I'm not providing poll results. You won't find a single chart, graph or (perish the thought) Excel spreadsheet anywhere within the cover of this book. That's because what I'm sharing with you happened in real life. Over 30 years of success in real roles in some of the most well-known brands on the planet have proven that The Not So Subtle Art of Caring is a better way to lead people to deliver results. Note that I didn't say, "I think" this way of leading people is more effective or that "surveys show" this way of leading people is more effective or "clinical observations of 936 workers indicate that" this way of leading people is more effective. Nope. I said that more than 30 years of actually leading thousands of real, breathing human beings to create hundreds of millions of dollars in value after replacing, in every circumstance, an authoritarian leader proves in real life that this actually works.

The definition of the caring leader is:

"A Caring Leader works with those closest to the work to develop and execute plans, that once achieved, result in balanced improvement in the lives of the owners, associates and customers of the business"

(For a non-profit, just change business to organization, then change owners, associates and customers to stakeholders, volunteers, and beneficiaries)

In the pages that follow, we'll explore the attributes and behaviors that characterize the caring leader and The Not So Subtle Art of Caring.

In Chapter 1, we'll begin with The Rules, a set of guiding principles for the caring steward. Those you have the privilege to lead expect guidelines. They want structure, order and consistency. They want to know what you stand for and that you will do what you say. Exactly what rules you choose is a less important consideration than the act of declaring a set of principles then maintaining faithful adherence to them.

In Chapter 2, you'll be introduced to the fundamental objective of the caring leader, to make others big. The seeming paradox of The Not So Subtle Art of Caring is revealed: that by making ourselves really, really small, others can get really, really big. In doing so, the path to winning is revealed.

Chapter 3 identifies the true source of charisma and helps explain why the old-school command and control micromanagers of the last century are completely ill equipped to lead. Eleven more key traits of the caring leader are revealed.

Leaders without teams to follow them are just folks out for walks all alone. In Chapter 4, the traits and behaviors of caring, winning teams are fully detailed.

Chapter 5 details the final transformative quality of those that practice The Not So Subtle Art of Caring – Stewardship – acting as a caretaker for that which is entrusted to us as leaders. I'll also show that traditional views on permanence and possession block managers from fully achieving their potential as true, caring leaders.

Finally, Chapter 6 includes 12 selected stories that reinforce other key learnings crucial to the practice of The Not So Subtle Art of Caring, followed by a short Afterword on grace, which is arguably, the most important leadership attribute of all.

Throughout the book, I will provide you with some real-life examples of how the art takes shape. In some 85 real letters to real people about what really matters, you'll get a glimpse into how, through storytelling, businesses can be transformed into organizations where people care deeply – both for one another and the goals they set for themselves. You'll see how love takes hold. And how dynasties are built.

You'll notice that the letters often begin with I and me language which is atypical to my leadership style. That is merely because the letters were always based on something I would observe in the week and use as a basis for the stories I'd share. But the letters were for the us that was our team.

My goal always, with these letters was for one person to take something away from them, to help our team progress along a continuum of caring. Sometimes that person was me. For you see, in a lot of weeks, I wrote these letters as much for myself as for others. Remember, leaders need reminders to stay on track too.

That's what this book is about, after all. A reminder to all of us, as leaders, that there is a better, more caring way to lead other human beings to accomplish extraordinary things. My hope, as you read this book, is that you too choose to embrace a more caring style of leadership and that you find this book to be a help in enabling you to do so. People like Linda Hoptry, Marty Connor, Michelle Dukeman, Todd Tyler, David Evans, Richie Schlatter and too many more to list inspired and encouraged me to write this book. They are all living proof of what happens when love collides with a desire to do great work. My desire is that there are Lindas and Davids and Todds among all of you; that you become better individuals, leaders, and team members after reading this. But most of all, that you perfect the art of caring. Not just because caring leads to enhanced results in all aspects of life, but simply because the world could benefit from a little bit more of it.

Chapter 1

The Rules

"True conviction is believing something to be right even after it becomes disadvantageous to you."
Gabrielle Zevin
1977-
American Author and Screenwriter

Rules matter. Now, for those of you wondering why a book largely about winning by caring for others comes right out of the gate with a chapter about rules, stay with me. Here I'm talking about rules in the sense of guiding principles. If you intend to lead people you should have some. There's an old yarn (and old yarns get to be old yarns because they are true yarns) that says, "If you don't stand for something, you'll fall for anything." Guiding principles are that something.

Guiding principles tell others what you are about, what you will and won't put up with. They tell others where the sidelines are ... and where the goalposts are. People want to know where the boundaries are – because as a rule, humans tend to avoid pain. People likewise want to know where the end lines are too – because they, more importantly, like to be recognized. In between, people want to know what you care about, what makes you happy, what makes you mad, what makes you real. A list of guiding principles tells them these things and more. For people looking to be led, this is critical information. Without it, you can start walking ahead, but don't be surprised when you turn around and no one is behind you.

People won't willingly follow you until they trust you. Citing recent Gallup research, Cheryl Beth Kucher, writing for, CEO Think Tank points out, "The ability to trust a leader is essential to cultivate followers." (Kucher, 2014) The Not So Subtle Art of Caring begins with building that trust. That starts by telling them what you stand for. It starts by proving to them that you have principles, and that you live a life guided by a set of rules – a set of rules they can fairly expect will consistently govern their life with you in the organization you have the privilege to lead.

My list of rules, there are 12 in all, grew out of a handful of things I would tell my children as I put them to sleep at night, when I was lucky enough to do so. Many were originally written in a way that kids could grasp and relate to. I decided to keep those in their original form. I figured if they could get it, anyone could. As the years went on, I added a few, dropped one or two, added a couple more, then stopped at 12. As you will see, I've resisted the urge, solely out of superstition, to move to 13, though I have a good enough reason to want to. But whatever the number, The Rules, as they are known, have almost entirely to do with how we conduct our lives, and very little to do with what we do in our lives. Because they are, in fact, guiding principles. They are meant to tell others what I stand for – what they can expect from me, and what I, in turn, expect from them.

Having The Rules has enabled those I have led to learn, without asking, what sort of leader I will be. They are also a yardstick to judge *my* future actions against. Note the emphasis on my. I've been careful to point out that The Rules are mine, intended for me, and that I don't impose them on others. I've always been amazed though, how many actually start following them. Maybe I shouldn't be so surprised. People will both engage in reciprocal behavior (put another way, they will give what they get) and they will follow rules if they see their leaders first following them. It has first and foremost to do with setting an example, with standing for something.

Most of what's wrong with American management today is the fact that by and large, these folks don't stand for anything, except their own financial well-being. They have signs behind their desk that read, "World's best Boss" or "Rule #1: Make the Boss Look Good." Their guiding principle is: "I look out for me." Working for these people is soul-robbing. Forbes contributing author Glenn Llopsis describes the workplaces dominated by these traditional managers as buildings, "Where one must often check their best and most authentic selves at the door as they walk in each morning and learn to conform to the company way of doing things." He goes on to caution that, "In this kind of organization, you can be whatever you want to be – as long as the company already has a slot for it. Individuality? Forget it." (Llopsis, 2013) Having your own guiding principles in an organization run by one of these ogres will be all well and good until one of your rules conflicts with their Rule #1. Then you will have a choice to make: compromise or else. I spent a lot of my life choosing to work for people like this ... until I decided not to. The best piece of advice you might get from this book is this: if you are working with or for one of these "World's Best Boss" types, **leave**; then establish and live by your own set of rules somewhere else. I promise you, that you will never look back. I did, and I've never been sorry.

This generation of worker is craving leadership. They want rules and boundaries. They want to follow people they can believe in. Helping them believe begins with unsubtly telling them what you believe in – what you stand for, what your rules are. The more they know that you believe in something the more they will believe in you.

Worry more as you get started about having rules than about exactly what your rules are. What matters most to people is that you have principles and that you consistently follow them. Better to have fewer, simpler rules religiously followed than a great many, meticulously word smithed principles casually adhered to. Simply start by telling people what you believe in, what matters to you.

As you might imagine, over the course of hundreds of weeks, I've had a chance, more than once to touch on a rule topic or two over time. Following are a handful of my favorites. I've added some updated and expanded commentary to each in an effort to provide not only context, but, more importantly both a practical understanding for how each topic connects up with a care-centered leadership style, and ways each clearly contrasts with the increasingly out-of-date and out-of-touch management style of the last millennium. Enjoy.

* * *

In each business I've led, I've always introduced The Rules as guidelines, not mandates. To me, it's always been more important to tell people what The Rules mean, not just what The Rules are. Here's an example from the last business I was responsible for.

January 25, 2019

Last week, I made reference to my "Rules." So, I've decided to share them with all of you now.

I'll preface things by telling you that I didn't compile these principles for the purpose of imposing them on others. If there is a point for the week, that's it.

Remember, life is a choice. We cannot make others do anything, my rules included. "The Rules" aren't commandments. They are personal guideposts that mark my way along what is, for me, a life better lived. Like each Friday's installment of *The Week*, my words are not mandates. They simply represent what I believe to be the right thing to do – things I try hard to live by (and don't always live up to). I don't have it all figured out. I don't do the right thing all the time. I try hard though and have a set of rules to help. And when I don't, I expect all of you to call me on it.

That the rules are written down at all happened as I started sharing them with my children; that's why many of them are written in plain, simple vernacular, like that of a child. Many of the rules are not original to me; they are things I learned from my father and others, or via lessons learned from unlikely places. Nor are most of the rules at all original; they express concepts that are as old as human interaction. Finally, the rules are not comprehensive; I know I've overlooked things, and that the list may continue to grow.

As of today, though, the list numbers 12 rules. They follow.

And so, whether it's these or some other set of principles, use guideposts to mark your way.

And win.

The Rules

1. Believe
2. Love the One You're Looking At
3. Be Wholehearted
4. Tell it Like it Happened
5. Persist Courageously
6. Make Others Big
7. Win the Right Way
8. Talk To Each Other, Not About Each Other

9. Stir it Up
10. Know Why You Are Here
11. Make a Lot of Mistakes ... Once
12. Have Fun ... Achieving Something

Here's what they mean:

Believe – Winning is rooted in a simultaneous belief in both something greater than ourselves and in the fact that we can achieve what we desire.

Love the One You're Looking At – This is self-explanatory. Treat others the way you want to be treated.

Be Wholehearted – Accomplishing anything of value is easier when we bring our entire heart to the task.

Tell it Like it Happened – The truth matters. Period.

Persist Courageously – Those who most often win are those who persevere, who refuse to give up, and who display the courage to try in the first place.

Make Others Big – The truth of winning is that we achieve more when it becomes less about us. What we accomplish is directly proportional to our care for others.

Win the Right Way – The way we win is more important than winning. No victory is worth salt if achieved the wrong way.

Talk To Each Other, Not About Each Other – Winning leaders communicate, a lot. They know they will more often win when they discuss issues they have directly with others. Gossip is a cancer and has no place on winning teams.

Stir it Up – Doing nothing will result in nothing. Achieving anything important requires that we change the status quo. Leaving perfect ingredients on a table will never result in a perfect cake.

Know Why You Are Here – If you don't know where you're going, any road will take you there. Achieving anything requires purpose with aligned effort.

Make a Lot of Mistakes ... Once – Anyone who has ever achieved anything important has failed often. But winners almost never make the same mistake twice.

Have Fun ... Achieving Something – Life should be enjoyed. Effort should not be drudgery. But fun with no material end is a waste of time.

* * *

Rule #1 is Believe. It's pretty self-evident. I put it in a way that is very easy to understand: if you don't buy it, you cannot sell it. Besides, if you do not care enough to believe in what you are doing or in the possibility of achieving what you're charged to do, you may be in the wrong line of work. It won't take long for others to notice. And when they do, their willingness to follow you will evaporate. Leadership guru Simon Sinek says, "Unless you give motivated people something to believe in, something bigger than their job to work toward, they will motivate themselves to find a new job and you'll be stuck with whoever's left." In the art of caring, a must have is belief – in yourself, in those following you, in what you are trying to accomplish **and in something bigger than you**. The final point is not a religious one. It's a where you stack up in the scope of things one. If you are the biggest thing in your universe, you are destined for a life of loneliness, heartache, and loss.

People don't follow people who believe they are without equal; it's a turn-off. Narcissism is a malignancy. On the other hand, people are inspired by those who believe – in them, in the work of the collective team, and in something bigger than themselves. People seek hope. They fight for what they believe in. And they love an underdog. Achieving anything starts with believing it can be done. Likewise, leading anyone must begin with believing in them, and telling them that, often. I wrote about belief one Christmas more than 10 years ago.

The (Christmas) Week 2009

Saturday is Christmas.

As Annie and I prepare to leave our Akron home, I can't help but reminisce about the Christmases we spent, together, there. Among others, I've recalled the year of Thomas the Train and the hours Will and I spent building ever longer and more complex layouts of his track. As I considered Thomas, my thoughts naturally turned to his distant relative, The Little Engine that Could.

I say "naturally" as it is one of my favorite stories ... because it contains what is, to me, one of the most important life lessons ever told.

It's a lesson about believing.

That little engine climbed the hill because it believed it could.

We all ought to be more like the little engine. We all ought to believe.

That's the point for the week.

On my list of rules for life, Rule #1 is, for more than one reason, to Believe.

Life is, to me, a self-fulfilling prophecy. I've learned that whether you think you are a winner, or think you are a loser, you're right. If we believe we can, we more often will. It's truly that simple.

Our objectives for 2011 are significant, headlined by a 15%+ increase in G3 MRT sales and a more than $10M increase in EBIT.

Achieving these sorts of numbers must begin with believing we can.

I know well that it's going to be hard. I know there are things beyond our control that will make it harder still. I know there are folks who think we can't. I know there are some who will refuse to help – just like in the story.

But we have a choice ... just like the little engine did.

To believe, or not to.

You see, every day of our life is a choice ...

Between happiness and sadness. Between a smile and a frown. Between cooperation and conflict. Between passing the buck or the buck stops here. Between helping someone or walking right by. Between thinking we can or thinking we can't.

Doing anything important in life begins with a choice – to think, to believe, that we can.

That's my Christmas wish for you. To be more like the little engine that could.

Believe.

And when you choose to believe ... when you choose to disregard all the reasons why you can't ... repeat in your hearts after me ...

I think I can, I think I can, I think I can.

And you will.

Win.

* * *

Rule #2 is to Love the One You're Looking At. It's another bedtime rule. If you try "Love thy neighbor as thyself" with 3-year-olds and 6-year-olds, I can all but promise you that they will not be picking up what you are putting down. They may say, "I understand, Daddy." But inside, they are thinking, "What is this old person talking about?"

So, I taught my kids to love the person they were looking at. It was simple and non-negotiable. If you're looking at them, love them. Kids get that.

It was also easy for 35, 45, and 55-year-olds to grasp. If you are looking at them, love them. Not just care for them. Not just like them a lot. Not just be nice to them. Love them.

It's one of those easy to say, hard to do things. Especially in traditional cultures where the micro-managers had a 100-year head start, sowing strife, division, suspicion, and internal competition. But once, two, then four then eight, then sixteen, then thirty-two people start to see that life becomes factorially better when love, not hate is the common denominator, then the business begins to turn rapidly. Once achieved, the results can be phenomenal. With it, you can achieve almost anything. Without it, though, you will fail. Any endeavor between two or more human beings is not sustainable without love.

People will, however, very readily choose love over the traditional emotionless micromanagement of the autocratic authority figure. Always. People want to be loved, respected, and cared for. Each one of us is born with a natural calling to be included, to be nurtured, to be part of the pack – to be loved. It's a fact.

There is no need to soft peddle it. It's love. It takes a stronger leader to enforce love than the absence of it. It's your job to unashamedly talk about love, a lot. Love is not a common concept in American business. So, it will feel strange at first. Even a bit uncomfortable. But persist. There is no human emotion stronger than love or more capable of delivering a dynastic winning team than love. Tell people you love them. It starts with you.

Be open with your team about what you are trying to achieve. Measure your progress. Accept no detractors or behavior that impedes your progress. Soon, the behavior will be self-policing and self-sustaining. But it starts with you; model the behavior and talk about it constantly. The simplest and easiest thing you can do though is to tell people, collectively and individually, that you love them, and mean it.

It begins by creating a culture of mutual respect. Arriving at a place where associates truly love one another must be founded on respect for one another. But respect is only the first stop; it's not a synonym. It's foundational to love, not a substitute for it.

If my 30+ years of repeated success creating cultures built on love after taking over for tyrants isn't enough to convince you, listen to others. Robin Benincasa, writing for the Association of Talent Development says, "If you want to have extreme performance from your teams, you need to have mutual respect." (Benincasa, 2019) Earlier, in an article written for Benedictine University's Center for Values Driven Leadership, Amber Johnson tells the story of Lt. Colonel Joe Ricciardi standing in front of a battalion of 1,000 soldiers charged with clearing improvised explosive devices (IEDs) in Afghanistan and giving them one simple message, "You need to love one another." Johnson reports that Ricciardi shared with her that at first "I got a few funny stares, I saw a few smirks, but after reinforcing the concept, I realized that they got it." As Johnson put it, "If love can enable the toughest soldiers to excel in the most extreme environments of stress, its success in the IED-free workplace is guaranteed." (Johnson, 2014)

What are you doing to create an environment where love can thrive on your team? Do you talk about love? What can you start doing tomorrow to demonstrate to your team that you truly love them? Here's a thought ... just write them a love letter.

A letter I wrote this past Christmas, helped make a point about love.

December 26, 2020

This week, I was reminded of the old holiday tale about exactly why Christmas trees aren't perfect. The gist of it is like this: Christmas trees end up becoming all misshapen and generally imperfect in the giving to others. In giving shelter to deer. In providing nesting material to birds. And so on. The story changes our thinking about perfection and love. If there is a moral to the story, it goes something like this: Just because something is not perfect does not make it any less worthy of love.

And that's the point for the week.

I'm good with that. No one who walks through the door of this place is or ever will be perfect. Nothing we ever do will ever be judged as perfect. And that's OK. Because perfection shouldn't be the goal.

Perfection shouldn't be the goal because it's an impossible standard. Perfection shouldn't be the goal because we can't write down what it looks like. Perfection shouldn't be the goal because it takes far too long to achieve and is universally regarded as the enemy of progress. But maybe above all, perfection can't be the goal because it is alienating and gets in the way of love.

We live in a world that immediately rejects that which doesn't meet the standard – for appearance, for hipness, for groupthink, for lack of likes or followers, as somehow undeserving of anything but disdain. Forget love, we are being conditioned to not even "like" things that don't fit the conventional wisdom or popular culture. It's gotten so bad that we now worry about being cancelled ourselves, if we don't join the cancel culture in throwing over that which we dislike, disagree with, have a distaste for, are afraid of, or don't like the looks of.

But that's not the way that the world should work.

Just because something isn't perfect doesn't make it any less worthy of love. Just because something is disagreeable to us doesn't make it any less worthy of love. Just because someone doesn't share our views doesn't make them any less worthy of love. Just because someone believes in a different thing or God than us doesn't make them any less worthy of love.

One of my rules for life is to simply Love the One You're Looking At. It doesn't have strings attached or qualifiers. It doesn't depend on anything. It's not conditional. It firmly rejects the notion that anyone is less worthy of love. It's simple. If you are looking at them, love them.

When it happens, everything in life is better. Here, at home, and in our communities. More gets done. Less time is wasted on things that don't matter, and in one year won't even be remembered. Greater bonds of trust are formed. And the force and speed with which things are accomplished begins to multiply each time hate is given over for love. Eventually, with nothing left to divide them, these teams become invincible, unstoppable forces not only for their own good, but for the greater good.

Because they chose to love the imperfect that is all of us. Because they chose to love the one they were looking at.

So, abide by Rule #2.

And win.

* * *

Be wholehearted. The third rule. Most of what we accomplish as leaders – of families, or of businesses, or of community organizations – we accomplish by setting examples, by becoming positive role models for others. Others will follow us and emulate our behavior regardless of the example we set – good or bad. The Not So Subtle Art of Caring begins with the realization that those we lead look to us for direction and that whatever degree of heart we bring to our role, they will display the same.

Great leaders, those who truly care, understand this intrinsically. Some so much so that they become heroes to others. I have mine. My father, a Catholic priest named Casmir, a salesman's salesman from Dayton, Ohio named Kaskocsak, former Goodyear CEO Bob Keegan and a man named Martin Luther King, Jr.. Among the many things they taught me about life and caring for others, they taught me this: to bring my whole heart to things.

Great caring leaders bring their whole heart to things, to all things. They believe that anything worth doing is worth bringing one's entire heart to. It's part of why caring leadership is not easy – regardless of what the prevailing wisdom dictates. Caring leadership requires maximum investment, of one's whole heart. As Randy Noe, author of *Leading Well*, puts it, "Being a wholehearted leader is courageous. It's showing up and daring greatly." (Noe, 2014)

When you show up for work each day, are you bringing your whole heart to the deal? If not, what's stopping you? Figure it out and remove the impediment. Do nothing you cannot bring your whole heart to.

Thinking, one day, about growing up pushing a broom in my father's shop reminded me of a King quote, which led me to write about wholeheartedness.

August 14, 2020

Several times this week, as you might imagine, I've had a chance to share a bit about my background with others here. The story includes my first job working in my father's truck dealership – pushing a broom. Almost always, the thought of a push broom brings to mind one of my favorite quotes. It's from Martin Luther King, Jr., from a speech he made to a graduating class in Kingston, Jamaica, nearly two years after his Lincoln Memorial address.

If you are called to be a street sweeper, sweep streets even as Michelangelo painted, or Beethoven composed music, or Shakespeare wrote poetry. Sweep streets so well that all the hosts of Heaven and earth will pause to say, 'Here lived a great street sweeper who did his job well.'

It's an admonishment about bringing your whole heart to things. Because anything worth doing is worth bringing our whole heart to.

That's the point for the week.

From time to time, I'll make reference to a list of rules for life that are, for me, guiding principles – things I try hard to do well by and to teach my children.

One of those rules is simply, to "Be wholehearted."

Reverend King's street sweeper quote is about just that.

In whatever we do, here at work, at home or around town – whether we want to be doing it or not – we'll win more when we do it with our whole heart.

In any given week, each of us will walk through many doors – to one of our facilities, to a customer, to our homes, and to places in communities. The quality of the work we perform, the strength of the relationships we develop, and the amount of good we do will be directly proportional to the degree of heart we bring to them.

In whatever we do, we should treat it as our life's work – because, in reality, it is.

When we do, as the King quote suggests, people will notice. It's how we move ahead, as individuals and as teams. By the example we set, others will be inspired to follow, and likewise influence those around them, to do the same. It is then that the full power of wholeheartedness is realized – as one by one, whole hearts are brought to bear on the goals of the enterprise, beating loudly, together and bringing dreams that once seemed entirely impossible well within our grasp.

So, bring your whole heart.
And win.

* * *

One of the rules that resulted from talks with my kids was Rule #4: Tell it Like it Happened. It's simply a way of saying, "tell the truth," in a way that a child could better comprehend. Telling the truth, like winning the right way, is a simple, non-negotiable matter of integrity. There's no such thing as a little lie. Any deviation from the truth is a deviation from the rule. People follow people they can trust. Jim Kouzes and Barry Posner, authors of *The Leadership Challenge,* have surveyed over 100,000 workers over the course of 30 years to gain an understanding of the most important qualities in a leader. What they've found is that "for over three decades, there are only four qualities that have always received more than 60 percent of the votes … for the majority of people to follow someone willingly, they want a leader who they believe is":

- Honest
- Competent
- Inspiring
- Forward-looking

(Kouzes, 2017)

First, and foremost, people want leaders who are honest. To ever be anything less than 100% truthful with people who have entrusted their livelihoods to us, risks destroying trust that may have taken months or longer to build. Without trust, there exists no currency of trade between us and those we have the privilege to lead. The Not So Subtle Art of Caring for other human beings demands that we be honest always in all things.

How would the people in your life rate you on the Tells it Like it Happened scale? If you're unsure, ask them. If you have work to do, get on it. Tell them it's a priority, and make it one.

More than a decade ago, I used a story of my son dropping his mom's cell phone in the tub to make the point.

October 29, 2010

A few days ago, my son, Will, who is six, came bounding down the steps in a state of panic and upset. After confirming he had no open wounds, Annie and I asked him what was the matter.

It turns out that Will, who enjoys downloading and playing apps on his mom's iPhone, had, in an attempt to multi-task, submerged the phone in water. He had come down to come clean about the incident.

I was proud of him.

While it may seem strange to be proud of someone who had just ruined a few hundred dollars-worth of cell phone, I was – because he was following the rules.

One of the "rules" I have for life is to "Tell it like it happened."

Will could have dried the phone off and put it back where he found it then denied any guilt later. Or, he could have hidden it. Worse, he could have made up some dog ate my homework story. Instead, he told it like it happened.

He knows worse things happen when you don't tell the truth.

That's the point for the week.

Every day, life presents us opportunities to choose between the truth and something else. When we choose something else, fixing what happened becomes harder. Any trouble we create is magnified. We have to remember what we said. Worst of all, we erode the most important bond that exists between ourselves and others – trust.

Bad things happen in life. As humans, we make mistakes.

What's most important in any situation isn't what happened but what we do as a result.

Fixing any problem occurs faster and with better result when we have complete and correct information about it. Telling it like it happened better ensures we do.

We can handle the truth. There is almost no situation that we can't overcome together – when we have all the facts we need to in order to fix it.

When we deal honestly with each other we win more. We waste less time focused on what doesn't matter. Small problems stay that way. Vital trust remains intact.

So, tell it like it happened.

And win.

* * *

Rule #5 is about courage. One of my favorite bosses and teachers, a man named Larry Mason, taught me about schoolyard bullies and the courage to deal with them.

We all had, or knew, a bully. That person who made terrorizing those they perceived as weaker than them their life's work. They'd take people's lunch money. They'd lie in wait for their quarry, the smarter and most fearful of whom would find new routes to and from school to avoid daily beatings and shakedowns. Inevitably, in the heroic morality tales which are our own lives, we'd learn that bullies don't care for direct confrontation, and they certainly don't care for being punched in the throat.

Schoolyard bullies, when applied to business, are no different. They are the people and things we know need confronting and fixing, but we keep giving them our lunch money or taking the long way to school to avoid dealing with them. They are our worst customers. Our most awful vendors. Our most disruptive associates. A ridiculously unbalanced comp plan. A trade show that has become a boondoggle. You know the drill. It's any of 100 things that you know has leverage over you but that you've failed to act on.

I keep a little plastic bronco close to my desk as a reminder to me that these problem horses need breaking and that true, caring leaders have the courage to do so.

Common among the traditional management set is a general inability to deal with conflict. Walden University researchers, Gene and Patricia Fusch report that "conflict is perceived as being on the increase in the workplace." (Fusch, 2015) Current leaders are either unable or unwilling to deal with crisis. But according to research by Paluku Kazimoto, when leaders kick the can on dealing with conflict, negative outcomes follow, along with damage to the manager's own credibility. (Kazimoto, 2013) Caring leaders, though, step up to these issues.

One of the common misperceptions about caring leaders is that they are weak. It's false. Bad leaders of any stripe are weak. Caring leaders though are more apt to have the courage to confront bullies, because they understand the toll that they have on their people and their business. So, they act. Caring leaders don't shy away from trouble; they confront it head on.

If you have bullies negatively impacting your operation, stop giving them your lunch money. Stop taking the long way to school. Find the courage to deal with awful situations and people. Care enough to stop paying off your schoolyard bullies. And when you do, make it known. There was a reason that one could buy and send postcards made from photos of prominent hangings in the 1800s. These postcards of the hanging were meant more to discourage future bad behavior than anything else. So, when you confront a bully, send a postcard from the hanging.

February 11, 2011

While home this weekend, I caught up on some Tivo'd episodes of some shows I missed while on the road. One of them is *Modern Family*.

In virtually every episode of the hit series, one of the main characters does battle with a broken step. In many cases he trips, both going up and coming down. In others, he remembers the defective tread just in time to wildly contort his path around it. In still others, he makes temporary repairs that never quite hold.

Rather than fix the step, our protagonist simply manages the situation – but only when he remembers to do it. On TV, this sort of thing is funny. We'd miss the broken step routine if it were corrected. But in real life, managing problems rather than fixing them isn't the laugh riot it is in make-believe.

When we manage a problem, it's still a problem.

And that's the point for the week.

None among us is immune to problems. We all have them – here, at home, and in our communities.

You'll hear me refer to them as schoolyard bullies. Like the fictional step, it's a fitting metaphor. Our problems are like bullies. We have three basic choices in dealing with them. We can avoid them, say by taking another way to school. We can postpone our beating, by giving away our lunch money a little at a time. Or, we can fix them, by confronting the issue head-on and putting an end to it. When we fix problems, they go away.

Trying to manage a problem doesn't fix anything. It only hides it for a little while and only if we remember to manage it. Often, unattended issues get bigger. Folks get hurt – and not just physically. We waste time and money on the bad cost of temporary solutions. Worst of all, we send a message that fixing what's broken is not important.

The better way – the winning way – is found in fixing what's broken, not walking around it, paying it off, or pretending it isn't an issue.

When we courageously deal with our broken steps – our schoolyard bullies – we'll save time, money, and aggravation. We won't have to keep track of what's broken and isn't because what's broken gets fixed. We'll better protect those we care about. We'll let others know by our actions that fixing what's broken matters, that they matter, and that there is nothing we can't overcome - together.

Don't manage problems. Fix them.

Confront your schoolyard bullies.

And win.

* * *

Rule #6 reminds us to Make Others Big. In many respects, it simply boils down to just being kind to others. On a trip to Europe with my wife in 2012, a literal reading of an arrivals/departures board inspired me to remind my team that there is nothing soft about being nice. The world is full of jerks. Unfortunately, the American management playbook for the last century and a quarter has been to hire tall, dark and handsome extroverts who are committed to managing through fear and intimidation. The playbook states that kindness and care for others are soft skills to be eschewed for toughness and an ability to hold others' feet firmly to a flame (literally if required). So rough treatment and rudeness have become the standard M.O. for the preponderance of Baby Boomer and GenX managers.

According to Harvard professors, Christine Porath and Christine Pearson, in studies of workers over 14 years, 98% of respondents reported experiencing uncivil behavior from their managers, and more than half report being treated rudely at least once a week. (Porath, 2013) People don't willingly follow these sorts of men and women. According to Porath and Pearson,

78% of their respondents who had been on the receiving end of incivility said their commitment to the organization declined, while 48% intentionally decreased their work effort. Where these people stay in the employ of these old-school ogres, they do so out of fear, a sense of obligation, or a belief that they have nowhere else to go. But consistently, they long for something different, something better, something, well, nicer.

One of the easiest things in the world to do today is to act in an uncivil way. Being nice is hard. That old saying about nice guys finishing last only matters if you're playing by the mean people's rules. What are you doing to demand niceness among your team? Remember, leaders set the tone. When you demand civility, you're likely to get it.

May 6, 2012

This week, Annie and I flew to France to help host our Innovation-level trip in Monaco. As we prepared to embark from New York, I consulted the flight board to confirm our departure gate. Our flight appeared at the top of one of the panels, directly below the column heading reading, "Destination." Top-down, the board read, "Destination Nice." Although our travel would ultimately take us to Nice, (pronounced, "Neece"), France, I couldn't help but smile. An entirely English reading of the board produced what, to me, is a more admirable, albeit figurative, point on the map. Being nice is a better place to be.

That's the point for the week.

In my office is a painted, wooden sign that reads, "Be Nice or Leave." It serves as an effective guidepost along a preferred route of interpersonal travel.

When we take care in any interaction, at work, at home, or in our communities, to maintain a commitment to kindness and civility, we will accomplish more. We'll do so for no other reason than we'll eliminate the distractions brought about by, and time wasted dealing with, unkindness.

It's more than just flies and honey. While it is true that those who are treated well tend to cooperate more often and do so more quickly, kindness is fundamentally about trust, respect, and a high regard for the dignity of others. People yearn to matter. Kindness tells them they do. As a result, they approach any endeavor with greater self-confidence, zeal, and fortitude.

Niceness and toughness are not mutually exclusive. Behaving poorly and deriding others are not prerequisites to effective leadership. Quite the contrary, these traits eat away at the bonds that tie teams together, ultimately resulting in the failure of link after link until the entire group goes down to defeat, all because someone mistook being nice for being soft.

Like most else in life, it's a choice. When we choose kindness, we choose the better road, along which teams reach their complete potential and whose destination is bathed in the light of the upturned and shining faces of those who have been told they are valued – often without ever saying a word.

Be nice.

And win.

* * *

Al Davis, late owner of the Oakland Raiders, was famous for encouraging his team to, "Just win, baby." This unqualified demand led to a reputation for teams that would win at any cost. True winners don't win that way. True winners win the right way. Rule #7, is about just that. It's an encouragement to forgo winning if the cost is too great. Today's corporations are chock-full of Al Davis types – those who would win regardless of the cost. As a result, they have organizations full of people who follow them only when and because they have to. Find a leader being followed by individuals who want to be following them, and I will show you a leader who wins the right way.

Dr. John Izzo, author of the book, *Stepping Up* says simply, "the difference between a good leader and a great leader is the bravery to do the right thing." (Izzo, 2012)

Integrity matters. It matters in little things and it matters in big things. Those we have the privilege to lead don't distinguish between the two. If we fail the test in small matters, it can be assumed that we will fail in big things too. To me, integrity is a simple function of doing good. Victories won the wrong way are not acts of good, they are acts of fraud. The people who preside over them are frauds too. People follow people with integrity, people who care enough about those they lead to not do things the wrong way – ever. The art of caring extends to caring about doing things the right way, every time.

Would you follow you in the integrity department? What are you doing and saying to your team to ensure they know that integrity is a non-negotiable aspect of working on your team?

I used the example of doing a job right to make the point that integrity matters even in the way we do our work.

October 2, 2020

This week I asked Rich Schlatter and the Indy Shop team to please help get their place ready for some visitors. I wasn't any more specific than that. From there, Rich took over. At that point, he had full control, and as such, free will with which to choose how to execute the task at hand. He could mail it in. He could half-patoot it and stuff things under, behind and on top of things. Or, he could do it the exact right way, despite the requirement of time, cost or leadership capital. He and his crew chose the only correct option. They did it right, and, as a result, their place looked phenomenal. See, in real life, the one where truth matters, there are only two ways to do things: the right way or the wrong way.

And that's the point for the week.

Every day of our lives, usually more than once, whether at work or at home or in our communities, we will be faced with the opportunity to choose between doing things the right way or the wrong way. Oftentimes no one will be looking, and sometimes it won't impact anyone but ourselves. But it's probably in those moments when it matters most; because if we develop a habit of disappointing ourselves, we will surely develop a habit of disappointing anyone.

Victory is almost never found down these paths of wrong choices. And even when it is, these wins are often short-lived, bittersweet, and unsustainable.

Doing the right, good thing often costs more. But it is always worth it. It is worth it in the trust it builds among our customers and those we have the privilege to work with and to lead. It is worth it in the time we don't waste apologizing for or making up for the mistakes that inevitably result from doing things the wrong way. It is worth it in making sure that everyone goes home safe every day. It is worth it in creating a workplace that people are proud to come to every day. It is worth it in creating a destination that customers value and can't wait to return to again and again. And, maybe most importantly, it is worth it in protecting the value of our good name.

When each of us more often makes a decision to do the right thing, something amazing will start to happen: this business will launch skyward, of its own propulsion, to heights none of us ever imagined. And when that happens, we won't ever look back, because we won't want to, because we will have learned that not only is there is a right, better way to do things, but because it feels better to do things the right way too.

So be like Rich. Do things the right way.

And win.

* * *

Nothing will destroy a team more quickly than politics and intramural rivalry. You might wonder, then, why these things are a hallmark of American business. Despite the mounting pressures brought by international competition, forex challenges, labor uncompetitiveness and a host of other headwinds, US businesses persist by and large in doing nothing to eliminate internal competition, politics, and gamesmanship from their halls. Though these tactics have been the stock and trade of the traditional authoritarian management set, one might have imagined that the poor performance of these businesses would have led to changes by now. Though the reasons why these behaviors have been able to persist nearly unabated for decades is a matter of debate, one fact is certain: that internal competition, gossip, and strife will precipitate and accelerate the decay and decline of any organization.

In an article written for Management Study Guide by Prachi Juneja of the Institute of Management Technology, the author cites a litany of negative consequences associated with workplace politics, among them: decreases in overall productivity, affected concentration, spoiled ambience, changes in the attitude of employees, demotivated employees, increased stress, and wrong information.

Imagine a football team whereupon each time the quarterback handed the ball to the running back, the tight end turned around and creamed the guy. How effective would that team be at putting the ball in the end zone? Not at all. But these behaviors persist in most traditionally managed American businesses. Why? Because internal competition has become institutionalized in American business. And "some tension" is viewed as "healthy" by today's HR leaders who have given up trying to build actually healthy teams. The better path, the not so subtle path, is to care for others. It is a path built on kindness and mutual respect. It is a path that does not tolerate teammates that speak ill of each other, let alone compete with one another.

If you have hopped on the "healthy tension" train, I recommend that you hop right back off. It's a ride to hell that will tear your team apart. Actually, think about it. You are going to somehow improve cohesion by promoting tension amongst your team. It's preposterous.

Rule #8 is to Talk to each other, not about each other. I wrote about it in September of 2020 to reinforce the fact that there is no place for acrimony on winning teams.

Before we get to the letter, note as well that this rule is also about communication. Winning, caring leaders talk to their teams, a lot. As you have no doubt seen, *The Week* will very often focus on a topic that happens to be one of the 12 rules. See, repetition and reinforcement are keys to effective leadership. One of the biggest mistakes made by many would-be leaders is that they believe that having said or done something once, they can check the box, imagining themselves on the deck of some aircraft carrier somewhere declaring "mission accomplished." Unfortunately, life doesn't work that way. To effectively make a point, things need to be repeated a minimum of three times. Some say seven. I often say, repeat it until you are sick of hearing yourself talk.

The "rule of three" is rooted in research conducted in the late 1800s, by Hermann Ebbinghaus, a German psychologist. Ebbinghuas studied how many repetitions were needed for his test subjects to memorize a list of nonsensical syllables. He determined that three was the optimal number, so that became the rule of thumb. My children have picked up on my habit of triple repetition and, now, will often, after my second utterance of any point, chant in unison, "wait for it, wait for it, here comes number three."

Are you speaking until you are sick of the sound of your own voice? If not, keep talking.

The Rules

September 19, 2020

On Monday of this week, I was out of the office to attend a funeral. Then, today, Supreme Court Justice, Ruth Bader Ginsburg passed away. For many reasons, some you'd easily fathom, I don't care for funerals. I do not like them in large part because I have almost no tolerance for the veritable outpouring of disingenuous comments in regard to the deceased. I was treated to it all day Monday, and now again from every judicial and political panel expert on television. People, who, in the life of the dead, had nothing but ugly things to say about the individual, suddenly became great fans of the fallen, extolling their many, seemingly countless, virtues. Typically, these same behavioral differences would have applied during the lives of the deceased, depending on whether the person was talking to the departed, or about them. To me, there should not be a distinction. What one says about someone should be the same as what they say to them.

And that's the point for the week.

On the list of rules that I have for life is one that reminds me to talk to people, not about them. It's much easier to say than to do. To be sure, I fail to follow my own good advice sometimes. Minimally, how we talk about people must match how we talk to them. Any variance from the above is certain to destroy trust, the foundational basis for all human relationships, a high functioning team included. Without trust, the prospect for teams to achieve anything meaningful is nigh on impossible.

The point is not to ensure that every conversation or interaction between people is pleasant. That would be folly. There will inevitably be occasions when these meetings involve difficult subject matter, direct dialogue, and hurt feelings. To avoid them, or worse, to have them in the court of public opinion, will only erode trust. But when we have these critical, albeit tough, conversations directly, relationships are

49

strengthened, obstacles to progress are removed, and barriers to competitive inroads widen – all because we choose to confront issues constructively, together.

Back-channel gossip, internal competition, intramural scheming, and other under-handed chicanery have no place on winning teams. These are the tools of the weak, the insecure, and the dishonest. Any such behavior will prevent us from achieving anything, let alone the transformation which will result in better lives for every individual who works here. But when each of us commits to the rest of us and the success of this team by making a promise to talk to each other not about each other, the heights we can attain will be limited only by our imaginations and the effort we are willing to expend.

So, talk to each other, not about each other.

And win.

* * *

Napoleon Bonaparte said, "Men who have changed the world never achieved their success by winning the chief citizens to their side, but always by stirring the masses. The first method is that of a schemer and leads only to mediocre results; the other method is the path of genius and changes the face of the world." The ninth rule is "Stir it Up." Stir it up is both about a refusal to accept the status quo and an appeal to the heart of each individual follower. It's also about mixing people together and leading them in such a way as to derive the greatest possible contribution from the combination of them. Teams are multiplicative, not additive. To extract the total value from teams of people they must be stirred together and stirred up.

Great, caring leaders stir up every single associate to take action; put another way, they motivate everyone to engage in the work of the team. This is a rare talent. In a recent HBR article reporting on twin Gallup research projects, the research found that great managers comprised only about 10% of US bosses today and that one of the five skills common to this elite group of leaders was an ability to appeal singularly to every associate. (Beck, 2014) Great leaders have an ability to stir the hearts of those they lead.

Are you stirring things up on your team? Ask yourself each morning, what can I do today to create a stir?

One of the earliest letters I ever wrote was on the subject of stirring it up, which later became Rule #9.

August 27, 2004

One night a week, I volunteer as an overnight attendant at the Shrine of the Immaculate Conception shelter. The work isn't hard. Those of us who volunteer serve dinner, clean up, provide drinks until lights out, then sleep alongside the men until morning when we stack things up and go on about our way, usually to our jobs. Each week, I have a chance to visit with a man I know only as Michael. He's middle aged, a bit older than me – but much wiser.

Recently, he looked at me and said simply, and curtly, "stir it up." I wasn't certain at first if he was referring to the boring scene at the shelter, my similarly boring life as a GPC executive, or just life generally. But as I began to think more about his words, simple as they were, it occurred to me that they were meant for all of us; and they are worth living by.

See, nothing of any great significance has ever occurred in the history of human existence without some amount of disruption to the status quo, without some stirring up of things ... and people.

And that's the point for the week.

Progress comes at the expense of the current order of things. Letters are mixed up to make words which form ideas which are the fuel that drives collections of people forward to states that would be unrecognizable to those two or three generations before.

In every instance, people meet others they have never seen before and without aid of the stir of progress they never would. The state of human knowledge, love and kindness are catapulted forward. The ideas, hopes, and dreams of many are shared, mixed, and stirred. Time and distance are compressed. And barriers crumble to the ground.

Without the stir, teams would stand still, stuck in place while others sprint past them. Without the stir, there would be no winning. With the stir comes progress. The faster the stir, the faster things go.

Best of all, with prolonged stirring each part begins, more and more, to lose itself to the whole, until the prior parts are no longer recognized individually. Soon, only the team exists, as one thing, moving forward with tremendous force, and exacting fluidity, a thing of one mind and being, able to overcome any adversity or setback. All because of the stir.

So, stir it up.

And win.

* * *

Rule #10 is about purpose. It's a charge to know our role in life – to be cognizant of and entirely focused on that which we are trying to accomplish. But it's partially about avoiding distractions, too, about keeping our eye on the proverbial ball. According to Daniel Goleman, Co-Director of Rutgers University's Consortium for Research on Emotional intelligence in Organizations, "A primary task of leadership is to direct attention. To do so, leaders must learn to focus their own attention." (Goleman, 2013) In one letter, I used a story about my observations of a croquet match to make a point about maintaining focus on the ultimate goal. People want to follow leaders who can maintain a train of thought, who are consistent, and who are not distracted by petty squabbles, particularly of an intramural, political sort. The Not So Subtle Art of Caring includes the capacity to maintain vigilance to the cause and line of sight to the goal – a goal that will lead to improved lives for the people they have the privilege to lead.

Are you maintaining focus on your goal? Or do you allow petty distractions to divert your attention from what matters? Practice not allowing things that should not command your time to stay off your screen. Just play through.

May 11, 2012

This week, I watched a group of folks playing croquet. It's a game that isn't played much anymore, so the contest caught my attention. For those unfamiliar with croquet, it is an old English game that requires players to strike wooden balls, roughly the size of a grapefruit, with wooden mallets through a course of metal hoops, called wickets. The first player to successfully run the course of hoops is declared the winner.

During the course of play, one may strike an opposing player's ball with his or her own ball, whereupon they may place their ball alongside the struck ball – then, with a foot on top of his or her own ball, knock the opposing player's ball into a place of disadvantage. As I watched the sometimes humorous proceedings, I was struck by the fact that the players who engaged in the typically emotional, somewhat vengeful, ball-striking strategy tended not to prevail. Those who minded their own affairs, adhering always to their game plan, won most often.

That's the point for the week.

Croquet presents a fitting metaphor for life. The shortest distance between us and winning is a straight line.

When we deviate from our intended path to engage in activity unassociated with reaching our goal, we waste time, energy and other precious resources. Meanwhile, those who maintain discipline and focus place distance between themselves and the also-rans as they move forward, without interruption, their eyes firmly on the prize.

In almost any endeavor, we'll find our attention lured by the siren call of meaningless challenges, predatory competition, and ill-advised shortcuts. When baited to avert our eyes from the desired destination, we'll find ourselves presented with a very simple choice: pressing forward or taking the bait.

By choosing the better way, and laboring ever onward, we'll enjoy the last laugh, eating the fruits of victory while those whose goats were gotten duke it out over that which ultimately means nothing.

Know why you are here. Stick to your own game.

And win.

* * *

To traditional, command and control, management types, any mistake is to be avoided. When mistakes occur in their world, they are almost always followed by some form of discipline, lecture, or loss of stature. Now why in the world, in the care and development of other human beings, would anyone turn the greatest opportunity to learn something into a negative? Because they are self-centered and backward thinking, that's why. True, caring leaders celebrate mistakes.

Mistakes, and unforced errors should be encouraged. If your team is not making mistakes, they are likely not moving fast enough, trying hard enough, or pushing hard enough against the status quo. Mistakes are the natural outcome of these things – of lifting up rocks we've never lifted before or pulling levers we've never pulled before. Mistakes offer teaching moments. In The Not So Subtle Art of Caring, mistakes should be cheered –

once. Rule #11 reminds us to do just that.

Failures are inevitable on the path from a less than desirable Point A to a more desirable Point B. Until something new is tried, the outcome, no matter how much preparation and speculation occurs, is unknown. When a lever is pulled and something bad happens, make a note to not pull that lever again. But never punish the lever puller, unless it is your goal to squash creativity, honesty, and risk. Organizations that encourage risk taking and mistakes are healthier, faster growing organizations. Likewise, leaders that encourage mistakes are more likely to be followed and respected. Amanda Hagley, writing for Verb, suggests that organizations that foster openness and honesty in regard to mistakes and setbacks actually build greater trust within their organizations. (Hagley, 2019) But these organizations must maintain vigilance to be certain that the same mistakes are made only exactly once. Failure should be encouraged. But multiple examples of the same failures cannot be tolerated. For almost any rational person, this is a more than fair arrangement.

Do you encourage failure on your team? I'm reminded of the story of Alan Mullaly, who in turning Ford around, started having his direct reports publicly share their scorecards (which had never been done at Ford). The first time one of his people shared a sea of red, he started clapping. He knew that without pushing, there's no red and without red, there's no knowledge of what needs fixing. So ask yourself, am I celebrating the red?

I wrote about this using an old country story about a mule to make the point of making mistakes, once.

October 7, 2011

I was reminded this week of an old country saying. It goes like this: There's no education in a second kick from a mule. It's just a more-clever way of saying that we don't learn much from repeated occurrences of the same mistake.

That's the point for the week.

There is little to be gained by making the same mistake twice.

Not only do we learn nothing, but we ensure further heartache and jeopardize our standing with others as well.

When kicked by a mule, it's wise to change one's position relative to the animal. When we fail to move, the likelihood of repeated kicking remains. Meanwhile, the possibility of any understanding, let alone sympathy, from onlookers slips away with every occurrence.

Making mistakes is an inevitable outcome along any path of progress. Mistakes are accretive to goal attainment. We learn things from their first happening. We develop character that strengthens our resolve amidst future failures. Teams are brought closer together by adversity. I love mistakes. Mistakes should be celebrated – once.

But repeated instances of the same mistake delay forward movement. It's a circumstance that resembles marching in place. Energy is expended to no good end. Teams are torn apart in the process. Our personal development and advancement are stifled. Respect for us and our capabilities wanes.

Any mistake is the effect of some cause. The trick is very simply to understand what led us to our low point, then seek higher ground with the resolve to never again engage in the behavior that failed us in the first place.

When we do, we'll excel. We'll earn the respect and admiration of those whose opinions should matter to us. Most importantly, we'll achieve more of the limitless possibility that is the central feature of our humanity.

Make the same mistakes once.

And win.

* * *

Rule #12 reminds us to Have Fun, Achieving Something. In one iteration, the rule read, "Have Fun, Making Money." But I was reminded by a non-profit group that the rule was a bit lost on them, so I changed it up a tad. The gist is the same. Work should not be drudgery. Nor though, should work be fun for the sake of fun. Your workplace should be one where people can have fun while accomplishing something.

I was once told that I did not take things seriously enough. Meanwhile, my team and I were clobbering our objective. I shared the encounter with a workmate and true friend of mine by the name of Todd Pickens, another of those names I mention when people ask me "what" I am proud of. Todd laughed, and reminded me that, "We are selling tires here, not running up and down the halls with human organs in Igloo coolers." He was right. We kept the fun quotient right where it was. And we kept on destroying our numbers, in large part because Todd was there and in large part because we had fun (which often went hand in hand).

Study after study has proven that workplaces that have more fun, accomplish more. A recent report from St. Edwards University looking at some 2,500 employees found that 81% believe a fun working environment would improve productivity. 55% of the sample said they'd actually take less pay to have more fun at work! (Breeze, 2004) In the Journal of Applied Communication Research, Owen Hanley Lynch writes, "Organizational humor has been linked with successful leadership, with increases in profit and work compliance, with a successful business culture, with message and goal clarity in managerial presentations, with improvement in group problem solving" (Lynch, 2009) The message is simple: work should be something people enjoy.

But remember, the rule is to have fun *accomplishing something*. It's also wise to make sure that you don't violate the associate handbook. Things like "Pajama Fridays" are a bad idea. It's hard to connect the dots between pajamas and accomplishing something, and you'll probably violate the dress code. The modern rehabilitators of the notion of fun in the workplace, the gang at Pike Place Fish Market in Seattle had fun by throwing fish customers had chosen. They had fun accomplishing something. The more they threw fish, the more fun they had, and the more customers arrived to have their fish thrown. They had fun accomplishing something.

What are you doing to make work fun? Note that I didn't ask, what are you doing to have fun at work. There's a vast difference. What can you start doing today to make work more enjoyable, more fulfilling while also accomplishing your goals?

Paradoxically, it was the loss of an associate one September that provided a perfect opportunity to remind our team about Rule #12.

September 11, 2009

Many of us will long remember 9/9 as the day John McAfee passed away.

Those of us who knew John McAfee will each remember him differently.

But collectively and individually, we will not forget him.

John was, after all, unforgettable.

For me it is John's humor that I will remember (and miss) the most.

I cannot recall an encounter with John – however short or however serious the subject matter – that did not conclude with me laughing.

Just seeing John on most occasions was enough to make me smile.

John was fun. And he brought out the fun in those around him.

But John didn't fail to take things seriously.

He seemed to innately understand Rule #12 and he lived it. He had fun accomplishing things. John woke up each day intent on enjoying life. He understood that work was not only more enjoyable when he brought his sense of humor to it, but he knew that people get more accomplished when they are having fun.

And that's the point for the week.

In the many beautiful, wonderful choices that life provides us each day, one is almost always between a smile and a frown. Between making work fun and making it a living hell. Between accomplishing something or contributing nothing. Between the old way of life here or the something better we are building together.

Be like Johnny Mac.

Choose to have fun, accomplishing something.

And win.

* * *

One week, in referencing The Rules, I opined about a potential, alternate rule, Release Joy, that I have, from time to time, considered adding to the list. Regardless of its alternate status, Release Joy should be a guiding principle for those intent on winning and leading others. People want to follow individuals who exude something that could best and most succinctly be described as joy. Joy is like happy kicked up a notch, or five. Joy is contagious. Joy is attractive. In The Not So Subtle Art of Caring, Joy is that certain something that every best leader you can remember had in spades – because they understood the value of it. And you recognized the way that just being around them made you feel.

Joy is unbridled glee simply in return for having another day just to put your feet on the floor.

Joy is rare. Joy is missing from most American management teams today, mostly because there isn't much to be joyful about, but also because most tall, dark and handsome managers believe that spreading joy, or any positive emotion is a show of weakness. This old-school thinking misses a valuable opportunity to leverage a priceless trait. According to Harvard researcher, Paul Zak, joy is highly correlated to trust in the workplace. This "means that joy can be considered a "sufficient statistic" that reveals how effectively your company's culture engages employees." (Zak, 2017) For those who have figured out the value in it, Joy is like rocket fuel. With joy, B level talent will run circles around joyless A players seven days a week and twice on Sundays, because joy is evidence of care. And those who care more often win more often.

Do something tomorrow to spread joy where you work. It does not have to be something big, or a production even. Just release a little joy and watch what happens …

I wrote about joy a couple of years ago when a plaque on my daughter's dresser reminded me to.

February 8, 2019

On my daughter Charlotte's dresser is a small pewter plaque from a local Akron artist. On the plaque are only two words, "Release Joy." Charlotte, who we call "Chuck," has never needed additional encouragement in this regard. Whether from creating an entire multi-generational family from unopened soup cans and a Sharpee marker to bringing lavishly decorated cakes home for special occasions of her own invention, Charlotte naturally wrings every bit of life and happiness out of every waking moment. Charlotte releases joy.

Recently, I shared with all of you the list of "Rules" that I have for my life. I have more than once considered adding "Release Joy" to the list. It is probably only that I don't want 13 rules that I haven't added Release Joy. And adding two rules swells the list to 14, which isn't as neat and tidy as 12. So, I've been content to leave the list alone, leaving Release Joy to suffer the fate of poor alternate, waiting for another rule to fall off the list. But Release Joy is truly as important as any of the other 12. That's because, personal happiness matters.

And that's the point for the week.

Performing a task with or without joy will make the difference between a job well done or not. The presence of joy will affect the quality of human relationships; when it is absent, relationships suffer. Having joy in our hearts for each day we are given makes good news feel even better and bad news sting a little less.

Joy, like any emotion, is automatically and freely shared. It can light up a room. Ignite passion in others. Heal a hurt. Elevate. Propel. Calm. Inspire.

When each one of us here spends more time releasing joy, (which is almost never found in things, by the way) and less time looking for reasons to be sad, angry or disappointed, we will accomplish more together. We will keep each other safer. We will teach each other more things. We will reach the heights we have dreamed of together. We will win, together.

And when we do, we will be happier, for we have sought the better part, the joyful part. A life better lived, where people we have the privilege to interact with smile more, laugh more, help each other more, watch out for each other more, lift each other up more, and win more.

So, be like Charlotte. Release joy.

And win.

* * *

So, those are The Rules. Again, they are more truly guiding principles. I just like "The Rules" better than "The Guiding Principles." It sounds better, more definitive, more absolute. Because having guiding principles or rules or whatever you want to call them should be absolutely defining – of you, and of the culture you want to build as a leader. When I say defining, I mean whatever rules you say you have, you better commit to living by. They better define you. You can talk and talk and talk all day about, "These are my principles." But if your actions don't match up, forget it, you'll just be a person out for a walk all by yourself.

If you only choose to have one rule, make it some version of "Treat each other the way you want to be treated" or "Love one another." It's not complicated. Most of the cultural problems in American business today can be traced back to people treating other people poorly. If you address that one issue with one rule, you'll be well on your way.

But have rules. Have principles. People want and expect to have boundaries. Create them. Set the example of living by them.

And win.

Now that we've established the rules, or more accurately that leaders dedicated to the care of others have rules that govern their lives and relationships, let's turn our attention to the foundational characteristic of caring leaders – Making Others Big.

Chapter 2

Make Others Big

"It's that wonderful old-fashioned idea that others come first, and you come second. This was the whole ethic by which I was brought up. Others matter more than you do, so 'don't fuss dear; get on with it."
Audrey Hepburn
1929-1993
British Actress, Humanitarian

One of my heroes is John the Baptist. It's because, for JTB, as he's known around my house, it wasn't about him. In fact, on more than one occasion, John was quoted making this abundantly clear to those who had inquired whether it was, in fact, about him. "I am not," he said. He said other things, of course. But the most important three words he ever uttered were those – "I am not." See, the leaders of the Jewish faith at the time were very aware of the prophecies. So, when John appeared on the scene, they were quite interested in this new celebrity. John was a big deal. He drew large crowds wherever he went. So, these cats wanted to know if he was "the one," if he was Elijah, if he was the prophet. John was clear about who he was. "I am not," was his simple reply. For leaders interested in perfecting The Not So Subtle Art of Caring, these words matter. These words are a declaration that, "It's not about me." Which is to say, "It is about others."

True leaders make it about others. Their #1 goal in life is to make others really, really big. They understand innately that their success is facilitated by the success of those they have the privilege to lead, not vice versa. JTB understood this. He could have gotten all wrapped up in the pub. He could have made it all about himself. But, he knew that his success was contingent upon preparing the way for another. True leaders, those invested in The Not So Subtle Art of Caring, create organizations that put others first. Making it about others takes many forms. But first and foremost, it is about putting the needs of others before your own. It is about ensuring that those you have the privilege to lead have everything they need to be successful. It's about ensuring that they understand exactly what they are being asked to do; why they are being asked to do it; how to do it; and, most importantly, that their lives will improve when they do it.

Apart from senior management, most in a business care little about things like record earnings, or giant year over year sales increases – unless things like record earnings in the business lead to record earnings in their households. The frame of reference for the average associate anywhere is a house payment, two car payments, tuition, food, clothing and maybe an occasional vacation or night out with a sitter. Typically, their level of concern for the success or failure of the business begins and ends there. Unless it becomes about them. Unless the success of the business is connected to their personal success. Worse, personal appeals by traditional managers to win one for the Gipper, to do all they can for him or her because they, "need this one," are generally viewed as insulting. Consider the scenario. Someone clearly economically advantaged to 100% of his audience is begging that same group of people, most of whom will gain not one iota for their trouble, to extend themselves for the purpose of furthering the economic advantage of someone who is already significantly advantaged. Not likely. But when it becomes about others, when the needs of those being led are put first, when they recognize a direct correlation between the success of the organization and their personal well-being, something tremendous happens. People become fully invested in the work of the business. They automatically take care of customers, because taking care of customers leads to organizational success which leads to their personal success. Leaders who care get this. Leaders who put others first understand this automatically and their compensation programs reflect it.

Putting others first also includes being fully present in their lives. That means making the person in front of you the most important person to you in that moment. At a point in my life, I had eschewed the wristwatch for the clock on my phone. In order to tell the time, I would periodically glance at my phone. But I had begun to receive feedback that I was not giving people my full attention. I eventually pin-pointed the issue to my time-checking practice. People were mistaking that behavior for me checking emails or otherwise paying attention to matters other than what was on their mind. Trying to explain that I was simply checking the time would have made no never mind. To them, I was otherwise occupied; I was not fully present. Leaders intent on caring for others, on putting others first, are fully present.

Too, putting others first means spending time with the people closest to the customer and closest to the work. In helping teams, I often create a visual aid by placing the thumb and forefinger of each hand together, forming a triangle. I describe the traditional business hierarchy with leadership at the top of the triangle and customers and rank-and-file associates at the bottom. One of the great problems in American business, today, I suggest, is that those at the top of the triangle, those who create the bulk of the policies and programs for the business, spend almost no time at the bottom of the triangle. They then wonder why the programs and policies they've created are soundly rejected by the marketplace and even by their own rank-and-file people. The answer is simple. It's because they spend no time with the people who know best what to do – the customer, and the people closest to them. They fail to put others first, believing that they and others at the very top of the triangle know best. What these CEOs say without saying it is, "I am." When truly, winning is found in the words, "I am not." Jon Picoult of Watermark Consulting, in fact, found a correlation between CEO success and time spent "in the trenches," citing the behavior of winning CEOs like Jeff Bezos of Amazon and Costco's Jim Sinegal (Picoult, 2017)

Finally, making it about others can take the form of any of 1,000 acts of kindness or other expressions of care for those you have the privilege to lead. These simple, and often no-cost efforts are, in fact, priceless. People being led simply want to be valued. Sometimes, it's as easy as greeting people by name and with a simple, "hello" when you walk down the hall or through the shop. I handwrite birthday cards. Survey after survey has proved that workers place monetary recognition well down lists of other forms of kindness and attention. For example, Victor Lipman, writing for Psychology Today, cited one such study of 1,200 US based employees, reporting that "83% of respondents said recognition for contributions was more fulfilling than any rewards or gifts, and that "88% found praise from managers very or extremely motivating." (Lipman, 2013) Often, a handshake, literal pat on the back, or look in the eye while expressing thanks goes miles with associates seeking to create a meaningful bond with a leader who makes it clear that it is not about them. In The Not So Subtle Art of Caring, small things can make an extraordinary difference. The trouble with many of today's traditional managers is that they know these things to be true (because someone told them, or they read them in an in-flight magazine), but they leave the execution to others. So, their organizations end up with orchestrated kindness; things like The Chairman's Award, staged photo ops on the factory floor, or the CEO in mom jeans one day of the year raking leaves at the Y camp. But people see through these things; they are worse than expending no effort at all. Because manufactured kindness is like anything artificial, it's no substitute for the real thing.

I like to ask people to think about those who have most positively impacted their lives. I ask them to think specifically about why those individuals made such an impact on them. In almost every case, it's because that person made them feel big.

Now think about your own leadership journey. What are you doing to make others big? Better yet, what are you doing to make yourself really, really small? What are you doing to say, without saying a word. "I am not?"

Over the years, I've spent many Fridays writing about making others big. Following are some that others told me meant the most to them. You may find a few ideas that might help you along your way.

* * *

Fundamentally, making it about others is about caring. Caring doesn't require much in the way of context or instruction. It's self-explanatory. But as easy as it is to isolate on, displaying care for others requires great courage. Treating others poorly is easy; anyone can beat on another human being. Treating others with care is hard; it requires great personal investment. Caring for others is, likewise, an art, perfected over time, with trial and error, good days and bad. We're the producer, director and the actor. The only role we're permitted to play is our own authentic self; the only lines we get to speak are the truth – not some made up, made for TV, sounds good in the moment saccharine.

And it's 100% binary. Either you care or you don't. Part of the motivation for me to put this project together in the first place was a belief that care as a leadership trait was distinctly absent among the command and control, authoritarian management set. These are the "charismatic" Type-A extroverts whom American boards continue to roll the dice on despite disaster after disaster. Just how bad is it? The Center for Creative Leadership reports that now 50% of leaders and managers are "estimated to be ineffective, incompetent, or a mis-hire." And that 38% of new CEOs fail in their first 18 months on the job. (Leslie, 2015) Thankfully, there is an emerging group of workers who are asking for something different, something better – leadership that cares, people who actually give something of themselves for the good of others.

There is no positive outcome that will occur from apathy. From empathy, yes. But from a conscious decision to stop caring? Nope. Remember, when someone arrives with what seems like a small deal to you, it could be the biggest thing in their life at that moment. So, ask yourself, what am I doing to create a culture of empathy and care? Or am I encouraging apathy?

It was seeing a best-seller that actually encouraged readers to stop caring that motivated me to motivate my team to think about things differently some five years ago and which was the impetus for The Not So Subtle Art of Caring.

September 16, 2016

On a flight back home this week, I couldn't help but notice that airport booksellers' shelves had just been hit with a new release which apparently encourages readers to stop giving a f*ck. According to the author, the path to self-actualization and inner peace is best found when one simply stops caring. As I stood in front of a new display of the orange and black bible for a new age, I couldn't help but think, almost aloud, that such apathy is the root of much of what is wrong in the world today. As if on cue, a traveler brushed against a nearby display, knocking part of it to the ground, then hurrying on her way, not to be bothered. It became abundantly clear to me in that instant that if there is an art to anything, it is to actually giving something of yourself for the good of others.

And that's the point for the week.

It takes almost no effort not to care. The apathy that is the hallmark of most C-suites today requires zero investment. On the other hand, to carry others, to put their needs before your own, or to work for the greater good instead of self-gain, all require things like sacrifice, pain, personal risk, and even loss. But those who care enough to work in the service of others understand that they are playing a longer game, one where happiness and success have different goal posts.

Those who serve others put the success of those they lead ahead of their own because they derive joy from caring for others. In their hearts they believe that when others win, they win. For those who awake each day with a servant heart it isn't about them. It's about others. It's about giving a f*ck about the greater good.

Like all else in life, it's a choice. A choice between apathy or concern. Between putting our needs first or those of someone else. Between caring or not. Between picking up a fallen display or walking on our way.

When we choose to care, others notice. Bonds of trust form. Care is reciprocated. Wagons get circled when threats appear. Effort multiplies. People look out for each other. All because one leader made a choice to care a little less about himself or herself.

So, practice the not so subtle art of actually caring.

And win.

* * *

Like JTB, step one in making it about others is recognizing that it isn't about you, that you are not the center of anyone's universe, that there will never be a room in which you are the most important person, that there should never be a table at which you should be the head, and that our ability to care is inversely proportional to our own sense of self-importance.

Leadership expert, John Maxwell, in his book, *Everyone Communicates, Few Connect*, wrote that, "When we learn to turn our focus from ourselves to others, the whole world opens up to us." (Maxwell, 2010) While it would seem that Maxwell is speaking in hyperbole he's not. He's simply communicating the necessity of a wholesale change in the way we think about the world and what we value; shifting from a focus on our own accomplishments to those of others.

In interviews, as you'd expect, I'm generally asked to name my top two or three accomplishments. I often name people. I generally get pushback, "No. Please give us something more concrete, something serious, a business goal you've achieved, or the like." I stick to my guns, telling the inquirer that I am giving them something concrete, something serious – an achieved business goal that I am extremely proud of; a human being that was able to accomplish more than they ever dreamed possible. All because of a leader who made a choice to make it about others. I highly recommend the practice. Part of not being subtle is having the courage to be unabashedly proud of what you're proudest of.

Who are you proudest of? Are there names you could rattle off in an interview of people's lives you have helped make markedly better? Even if it's your own children that's OK. But the THINGS you're proudest of in life should not be things.

Sometimes it takes a story of a guy with 10 kids to remind us of that.

January 28, 2011

While at our recent Commercial Sales Conference in Nashville, I had an opportunity to spend some time with Derl Curry. For those who don't know him, Derl is a District Sales Manager in Region 2. More importantly, Derl is a father ... of 10.

Derl and his wife, Carlene, raised four children then adopted six more.

For most, such a commitment would be enough. Not for the Currys, who have additionally founded a non-profit organization dedicated to the promotion of local adoption called One Child's Voice (onechildsvoice.com).

One need talk to Derl for only thirty-five seconds or so to realize that for Derl, it's not about him. It's about doing for others.

When less of our life is about us, we'll get more out of it.

That's the point for the week.

It's the great paradox of life. We get more when we give more. This apparent contradiction is central to who we are as human beings. We complete ourselves by giving more of ourselves away.

When we step out of the center of our own universe to make room for others, strange, wonderful things happen. Our world instantly seems bigger. There's suddenly more of us to go around. We quickly realize that what we once wasted time longing for was in front of us all along.

What's more, human kindness is infectious and contagious. That which we do for others is almost always paid forward and returned many times over. One act of goodness on our part spreads quickly, touching the lives of many, ultimately coming back to us in ways we could never have imagined.

Best of all, a focus on others will enable the formation of relationships that endure for a lifetime, withstanding anything this world can throw at them. The strength of the bonds we forge with others – here, at home, or in our community – won't ever be enhanced because of the numbers we post, the size of our paycheck, or the awards we win, but by the degree to which we show others, in word and deed, that our world revolves around them.

When it ceases to be about us, we'll win more … if for no other reason than we'll find more hands on the rope. Like Derl Curry, who has 12 more little hands pulling away – all because it isn't about him.

Be like Derl. Make it about others.

And win.

* * *

This is fundamentally a book about service to others. I learned most of what I know about leading others from my dad. He was a servant leader before there was a name for it. My father, a truck dealer, woke up each day intent on making the lives of the people entrusted to his care better. It is mostly from him that I learned The Not So Subtle Art of Caring. It is, I think, beyond argument that individuals, if given a preference, would choose to follow those who serve them, those who place their needs above their own. In fact, a 2018 study by Udemy found that a whopping 50% of workers had quit a job because of a bad boss. (Udemy Research, 2018)

Workers want a leader who cares about them. In a study of nearly 1,000 workers by Robert Liden and others published in the Academy of Management Journal, "When managers create a culture where employees know the boss puts employees' needs over his or her own, measurable improvements in customer satisfaction, higher job performance by employees, and lower turnover are the result." (Liden, 2013)

The starting point, and the point that I and Liden are making, is that it's a choice: to put others before yourself, or not. Understanding the right way to lead people is not difficult; that's not what trips most people up. It's in making the choice to actually lead the right way that most can't cut it. But that's all it is – a simple choice.

Throughout my life in business, I have sought to make the right choice, to be "that" leader, to emulate my dad, and another handful of heroes, one of whom is Martin Luther King, Jr. who inspired a story one Friday to make a point about the value of serving others.

August 28, 2020

I woke up today thinking about the words of Martin Luther King, Jr. See, today, August 28, is the anniversary of MLK's "Dream" speech, delivered 57 years ago from the steps of the Lincoln Memorial in Washington, D.C. Almost five years later, King gave the last sermon he'd ever preach – at Ebenezer Baptist Church, in Atlanta. The sermon was titled, "The Drum Major Instinct" and included these words:

"If you want to be great, wonderful.
But recognize that he who is greatest among you
shall be your servant...
everybody can be great,
because everybody can serve."

To me, what King was saying was simple. Greatness has nothing to do with wealth, status, or words on a business card; it is solely a function of service to others.

And that's the point for the week.

Greatness is not assumed or claimed. One cannot say by themselves, "Look at me, I am great." Greatness has nothing to do with title or trappings. Being rich, or the Vice President or Chief of something doesn't make one great. Greatness isn't a function of education. Having a master's degree or PhD in anything has exactly zero to do with being great in life.

All of those things guarantee only that anyone who follows you will do so because they have to – even those with the same last name as you.

True greatness is derived from service.

Serving others means providing them whatever they need to grow, and to achieve their fullest potential. Sometimes that means having tough conversations, to make them aware of the fact that they've let you down – but doing so without destroying their dignity. Most of all, it means purposefully putting oneself in a place subordinate to those we have the privilege to lead – whether at home, at work, or in our communities.

Those regarded as great will be willingly followed anywhere, without demand or threat. Those regarded as great can expect others to behave the same when they are gone as when they are three feet away. Those regarded as great will be made aware when something goes wrong, instead of having to find messes hidden by anonymous culprits. Those regarded as great will be watched out for by those they lead. Best of all, those regarded as great will win more often, because those behind them understand that when the servant they follow wins, their lives will get better too.

Tyrants can win through intimidation for a while to be sure. Jerks can use fear to achieve results for a time. The worst of all can promise retaliation to push teams to a finish line. But this false greatness is temporary. It never lasts. Because such awful behavior is always exposed, the oppressed are always liberated, and light always overcomes the dark.

Anyone can be great. Likewise, anyone can be a jerk. It's a choice. All that is necessary is a loving heart and a dedication to the service of others. When brought to anything, a servant heart will fuel progress, then pace, then winning. And ultimately greatness, and impressions on the lives of those we touch that will last forever.

So, serve others. Be great.

And win.

* * *

A rather obvious step in making others big is simply being nice to people. For any of us, a description of the best (fill in the blank) we ever had, including our best boss or chief executive will almost assuredly include some simile of nice. Kindness to others is a prerequisite to caring for others. It's also a prerequisite for effectively leading others. Most traditional managers believe that kindness, or niceness is a sign of weakness. They believe that niceness leads to the inmates running the asylum. In their minds, kindness erodes authority; it's the old give 'em an inch thing. But why is it then, that the best anything in our personal histories includes niceness?

It's because kindness matters. Amy Cuddy, Harvard Business School researcher, and her partners, showed that leaders who project kindness are more effective than those who lead with toughness. (Cuddy, 2013) It's because, as has been said before, people want to be valued. And nothing tells someone they matter like a simple act of kindness. People will work for a man with a whip, for as long as the man with the whip can reach them. But people will work for a man they love no matter where that man is standing.

Being kind is like caring. It's binary. You either are or you aren't. It's not a part time thing. It's a full-time commitment. And it's hard. Author Katherine Henson wrote, "Having a soft heart in a cruel world is courage, not weakness." The reason most micromanagers are cruel is because it's a piece of cake. The purpose of this book, though, isn't to teach you how to be kind. At this point in your life, that should be self-explanatory.

The purpose of this book is to teach you that being kind is a better way to lead other human beings.

What are you doing to make kindness a non-negotiable aspect of your operation? Because it should be.

The importance of kindness cannot be overstated. So, I've included two stories on the topic, each with a slightly different take.

Seeing a kiosk for a little company I love in an airport one Friday in 2019 reminded me to make a point about simply being good to others.

Then, a story about a man buying my lunch helped make a point about little, random acts of kindness.

October 4, 2019

This week, as I made my way through the Denver airport, I walked past a kiosk for a little company I love. The company is called, *Be Good to People*. It was started 11 years ago by Kris Wittenberg, a promotional products executive after she had an awful experience with another human being. She wondered aloud, "Why can't people just be good to each other?" Then she put it on a t-shirt, "Be Good to People."

And that's the point for the week.

Treating others poorly, taking advantage of others, being mean to others, profiting unfairly from others, or relishing in the humiliation of others – all of these things, and more, are easy to do. They take no courage. No guts. No fortitude. They are signs of great weakness of character.

But showing kindness to others consistently – being good to others – requires effort and often self-sacrifice. It requires honesty and integrity. It requires conscience and an ability to put oneself in the place of others.

But when you commit, like Kris Wittenberg, to being good to others, something mancentifical happens. It becomes contagious. And the be-gooders start to organ reject the bad parts within the organization that now stick out, like proverbial sore thumbs.

People who care for one another keep each other safe. They teach each other things. They help each other achieve goals and dreams. They help prevent falls and failures; they don't celebrate them. They console after mistakes; they don't try to capitalize on them.

These are the people we want and need to lead this company forward. I care less about how many mistakes someone had made than how kind they are to other human beings.

Because kindness is the rocket fuel of organizational growth. Individual interests, profiteering, falsehoods, and the celebration of others' failures are cancers that will destroy us.

But when all of us wakes up each day intent on doing good, on being kind to others, the payoff will be astounding. The bonds we create will be unbreakable and the growth we can achieve will be unmeasurable.

So, be good to people.

And win.

P.S. You can find great things from Kris and her team at www.begoodtopeople.com

* * *

September 5, 2009

This weekend while shopping with my family I encountered a store that specializes in hot sauces.

I went in looking for Crystal Hot Sauce.

Here's why.

Seven years ago, Annie, the girls (Will wasn't born), and I were having lunch at a favorite restaurant in Destin, FL. I asked the waiter what sort of hot sauce they had. He rattled off three or four kinds one being Crystal. I asked for Crystal. After ordering dessert, Annie took the girls to the ladies' room. Even as dessert was brought to the table (Key Lime pie, my favorite) I continued to eat Captain's Wafers covered in Crystal. After asking for the check, the waiter replied, "It's been taken care of." "What do you mean, it's been taken care of?" I asked. "It's been taken care of," he said again. "Why?" I asked, "Everything was perfect." He smiled and said for a third time, "It's been taken care of." As we were preparing to leave, a man stepped over to our table. He had been sitting at a table nearby. He said, "Hello, I'm Al Baumer. I own Crystal Hot Sauce. I bought your lunch." I thanked him and assured him that his act of kindness wasn't necessary. He told me that hearing me ask for his hot sauce over others got his attention, but when I kept eating it even after my pie had arrived, he knew I was a true fan and had to buy my lunch.

Seven years later, I will buy no other hot sauce than Crystal.

All because of one random act of kindness from Al Baumer.

Here's the point for the week.

People remember and are intensely affected by little things.

Your relationships with your family, your customers, those you work with and those in your community will be more positively impacted by small courtesies than by a string of material accomplishments or expensive gifts.

Small acts of kindness require little effort on our part. But the effect of them can last years.

They are the cement that strengthens relationships.

They are the currency that is exchanged for intense loyalty.

They are the fuel of smiles that can last for days and come back each time they are remembered.

And they cost almost nothing.

Be like Al Baumer. Engage in simple acts of kindness.

And win.

* * *

True, caring leaders recognize the profound impact that praise can have on the lives of those they have the privilege to lead. They know that catching people doing things right and recognizing their contributions to the forward progress of the organization are priceless gifts to the recipient – especially when the praise is specific, made in close proximity to the completion of the good deed, and delivered in-person or written by hand. All human beings simply want to be recognized when we do something good. In fact, in their 2018 People Management Study of more than 4,000 US workers, The Predictive Index found that 76% of respondents said that, "Recognizes me when I do good work" was a key trait of great managers (The Predictive Index, 2018). And, by the way, simple progress is good enough to recognize.

Reward good. Don't wait around for great to tell people that you value them. Any time the ball is moved further down the field than it was an hour ago or a day ago it's progress, and that's good. Remember also that the output does not need to be perfect, it simply needs to represent progress, and that's good. Recognize and reward good every time you see it and as closely in the moment as possible. And be specific. Don't just say, "Hey, good job." Or "I really appreciate that." Saying things like, "Nice job" are barely better than saying nothing at all. Say things like, "Hey Paul, when you take the time to provide that level of detail, it leads to a better quality of output with less time spent by me having to do it myself. So, thank you." Simple, timely and specific praise goes a very long way.

Watching a father fail to praise his son at a little league baseball game was a perfect reminder for the rest of us to always do so.

May 27, 2011

My son Will, who is seven, plays Super Pee-Wee baseball on a church league team here in Fort Smith.

During warm-ups prior to his last game, I had a chance to observe a father of a player from the opposing team giving his son, who was unfortunately not bestowed with a wealth of raw diamond talent, a little work out prior to the game. The man employed a disturbing method of encouragement that included tossing the ball off the boy's chest, screaming at his son, calling him names, and more than once communicating with his nose not more than an inch from his son's face.

It was sad. The boy wanted nothing more than to please his father. He tried with all he had in him to throw the right way or to get his glove in front of a thrown ball. One or two out of ten times he'd get it right; eight or nine, he didn't. But rather than applauding and praising his son on the few occasions he got it right, the father chose instead to tear into him whenever he didn't.

The father failed to grasp the fact that his son would be more likely to display correct behavior when he understood – because he was praised when he demonstrated it – what correct behavior looked like. See, positive outcomes are more often achieved when positive outcomes are praised.

That's the point for the week.

Screaming at or belittling someone for not doing what they don't know how to do is like tilting at a windmill. It's a waste of time. Worse, it drives wedges in the middle of human relationships that once driven deep enough, create absolute barriers to love and progress. That is, after a time, even positive messages aren't heard by the hearer because they've been over conditioned to expect the worst.

To get the most from any human being, whether a seven year old on a pee-wee ball club or a thirty-seven year old on a commercial tire team requires that we show them what positive outcomes look like – through instruction and our own example – then laud and reward them when they display it themselves.

When we do so, over time, the correct result will occur more often and with less effort and intervention on our part. Learning and love take hold. Those we are leading and instructing will feed on their own positive outcomes and will seek on their own to more often deliver them. What's more, they'll develop a loyalty and affinity for their instructor that results in life-time bonds and a willingness to do almost anything to help those who helped them. Too, they'll pay it forward by praising and encouraging those they have the privilege to lead and raise whenever they catch them doing something right.

Every human behavior will land somewhere on a scale between dead wrong and perfect. By positively responding any time that the result ends up somewhere on the plus side of awful, we'll achieve positive outcomes more often, we'll develop encouragers out of others, and, best of all, we'll create attachments to others that will weather any toil, storm or strife propelling the entire team to levels of achievement that all the beatings in the world could never, ever produce.

So, heap on the praise.

And win.

* * *

Caring leadership is about ensuring that those we lead have whatever they need to be successful. Sometimes this includes difficult conversations to let them know when they've let us down. This is the hard edge to caring leadership. The common misperception about caring leaders is that they are push-overs. And that they tolerate mediocrity, because they are "nice." Nothing could be further from the truth. The Not So Subtle Art of Caring requires, in the pursuit of excellence, ensuring that associates are held accountable to deliver results, and that they are made aware when they fail to do so. But one of the most critical parts of making others big is NOT tearing them down when they fall short. Caring leaders always protect the dignity of other human beings.

The significant difference between these more enlightened leaders and their "my way or the highway" counterparts is one word – respect. Caring leaders are careful to have constructive, respectful conversations with people when things go wrong, in private. They don't raise their voices, throw things, or destroy the self-esteem of other human beings. They don't ever engage in public humiliation. When discipline has to be meted out it is done with discernment and control. The caring leader, the practitioner of The Not So Subtle Art of Caring shows mercy when appropriate. No wonder caring respectful leaders are preferred to their traditional authoritarian counterparts. In a study of a whopping 20,000 workers globally, Harvard researcher Christine Porath found that one leadership trait among all others was responsible for garnering associate engagement and commitment – R-E-S, P-E-C-T. (Porath, 2015)

Remember, respect is earned in large part along a path of ensuring that even the tough conversations occur when they need to, but that they happen the right way, every time. People want to be told when they can do better, and how. Because people want to be better versions of themselves. They simply want to be respected when those conversations occur. It's not hard. It's a simple Golden Rule thing. Just ask yourself, how would I want to be treated in this situation; then act accordingly.

April 20, 2011

This week, my family and I went out for dinner at a local restaurant. The establishment was well recommended. That reputation was seemingly confirmed by the capacity crowd and

20-minute wait we encountered upon our arrival. Unfortunately, our experience failed to match our expectations. Almost nothing was good about our meal. The five of us unanimously agreed that we would not be back.

However, when asked by our server if everything was OK, we took the easy way out. We replied that all was fine. As we drove away, it occurred to me that I had just violated what is, for me, a principle of serving others: when someone lets you down, you owe it to them to let them know, respectfully.

That's the point for the week.

People won't fix what they don't know is broken.

In every interaction among human beings, each party will come to the event with expectations for the outcome. It is crucial that we tell others when these are not met – so that they can avoid missing the mark in the future. Unless we have these crucial conversations, nothing changes. Nothing gets better.

Our principal calling in life is to leave this world – including the lives that we touch along our way – better than we found it. As leaders, our primary role in any relationship with others is to help enable them to become more, and achieve more, than they ever could have without us. When we tell others, by our words or deeds, that sub-par performance is just fine, we tell them, whether we mean to or not, that they should keep doing what they are doing. And silence is as good as affirmation. When things go poorly and we say nothing, we may as well have shouted that all was perfect. Because that's the impression we give.

Simply rubber stamping a "Meets Expectations" rating on any human interaction that doesn't warrant it does no one any favors. In almost every case it's a simple distaste for confrontation or fear of hurting someone's feelings that keeps us from doing the right thing. But while easier in the short term, everyone involved suffers in the long term as opportunity areas remain, worsening over time. These issues, known but not discussed, stand in the way of productive human relationships, slowly eroding trust with each passing day. Individuals never reach their true potential, all because that which keeps them from doing so is never disclosed to them. The paradoxical truth of the matter is this: we sometimes hurt people more by trying not to.

Certainly, self-awareness must count for something in the equation. Individuals should be able to identify, on their own, many things that hold them back, by using end results, body language, and off-hand remarks as inputs to the process. But folks cannot be expected to get it right entirely on their own. Achieving an improved state of personal development is a two-way street upon which both the leader and the led must travel. While having these conversations is crucial, how we have them is just as important. These conversations can and must take place in a manner that preserves the dignity of those on the receiving end, always. Better to not have the discussion than to have it in a way that is disrespectful to the other human being. Helping an associate identify opportunity areas in a respectful manner is not only possible, it is the stuff of building trust-filled relationships that will endure anything and enable organizations to achieve goals they never dreamed were possible.

I never cease to be amazed at the number of instances where constructive feedback is followed by a sense of gratitude, relief, and exclamation that goes like this, "Thank you. No one has ever told me that before." These conversations aren't fun, but they are critical. They are first steps along a path to a far better place, and a road whose only toll is courage and a commitment to respecting those we have the privilege to lead.

Tell others when they fall short, with respect.

And win.

* * *

Leaders who win more often, encourage others more often. The Not So Subtle Art of Caring requires that we encourage others, that we build them up, that we make it about them. The encouragement of others is a selfless act of service. Managers preoccupied with themselves and their own personal success make horrible encouragers because it's entirely about them. They may at times cheerlead the team; but it's only ever on their own behalf. Because the team winning results in a personal gain for them. People see right through these antics. They find them demotivating.

The true servant, though, is focused on making others big. The true servant understands that his or her bigness is a function of the bigness of those they lead. In a great article by Christopher D. Lee, he said it beautifully, "Great leaders make others the focus of their efforts and, specifically, by helping others feel positive, empowered, worthy, appreciated, and supported. Great leaders encourage the heart above all else." (Lee, 2019) Find a winning team, you'll likely find an encourager.

What specific steps do you take each day to encourage your team both individually and as a group? Are you certain to provide encouragement in both good times and bad? How do you promote encouraging behavior in others? One of the most important roles you play as a leader is an encourager of the hearts of others; it's a 24/7/365 proposition. It's your job to be your team's biggest fan – and you can't ever take a day off.

I found a 24/7/365 encourager under an oak tree in South Carolina, and wrote a story to my team about him.

July 10, 2010

For the last 34 years, for just about every night, Gregg Russell has been singing under a giant Oak tree in Harbor Town on Hilton Head Island, South Carolina – just him, a stool and a guitar. Oh, and a throng of children who pack the little benches that surround the simple stage.

Some of you may have seen him.

Many children bring signs for Gregg – sort of like those you'd see at sporting events. Gregg reads every single one. Some are elaborate, with clever rhymes and colorful drawings. Some are basic. Remarkably, Gregg makes every sign-bearer feel like theirs is a work of art.

The highlight of the show is the time when kids in the crowd are given a chance to sing. Some are promising young performers. Others are, well, not. But, as with the signs, Gregg Russell makes each child feel special – like a star.

See, Gregg Russell isn't so much a folk singer as he is an encourager of children.

Grown adults remember seeing Gregg Russell as kids and recall watching him from those benches. That's because we humans are more apt to remember those who encourage us.

That's the point for the week.

Think about those bosses, teachers, coaches, or counselors that you've never forgotten. The people who you'd follow anywhere. The people who made you feel you could be or do whatever you dreamed of.

Chances are these people are encouragers.

Encouragers know a few things to be true. When we encourage others, they want to win more. They want to keep trying more. They want to dig deeper more. They want to do the right things the right way more. They want to win more.

With encouragement, people believe they are valued – that they and what they are doing matter.

With encouragement, people believe they can achieve anything they set their mind to do.

When people WANT to win and BELIEVE they can, they become a nearly unstoppable force. They win ... all because someone told them they could.

Encourage others.

And win.

* * *

True, caring leaders place great value on each associate as a human being. They do not take people or their contributions for granted – ever. According to Aine Cain, wring for Business Insider, "If you value your employees as human beings, then you're already a huge step above many managers." (Cain, 2019) The caring leader recognizes the great value in something as small as enthusiastically greeting those they come in contact with each day. It's because they fundamentally value other people. They greet others because a simple "hello" is a way to say, "I value you." They know this because they feel valued when others take the time to greet them.

It is a Golden Rule thing. By treating others the way we want to be treated, the entire equation changes. Suddenly, we start spending time in places we never did, speaking to people we've never even met, and recognizing the contribution of employees and teams we didn't even know existed. Even the quality of our decision making improves when we stop taking others for granted because we more often consider the impact on others of things we're about to do. Love breaks out, and trust starts blossoming everywhere.

As a result, almost just as quickly as making the change, our business lurches forward, with speed and force. All because we chose to stop taking anything or anyone for granted.

See, it's a simple choice, like almost everything else in life. How many people, will you come in contact with during the course of a single day? Imagine if you made it a point to enthusiastically show each of them that you fundamentally value them as human beings … Think how different your world could be.

A story about the wonder dogs enabled me to perfectly make the point.

April 29, 2012

Each time I return home, I receive a raucous greeting by the wonder dogs: Redd, Rosie, and Bella. It doesn't matter whether I've been gone for ten minutes or ten days, it's the same story every time, as it has been for each of them since day-one. I open the door, whereupon the three of them come charging forth in a pack, nuzzling and jumping, tongues full out, with their tails wagging a mile-a-minute. Each and every time, it's as if they haven't seen me for a year.

As I considered things further one day this week, it occurred to me that dogs don't learn to take others for granted. The value they place on their owner never changes. As a result, the returning owner is made to feel special every time they open the door. It's a simple equation: the more individuals are valued, the more they will be appreciated.

That's the point for the week.

The degree to which we make others feel valued is inversely proportional to the degree to which we take them for granted.

People fundamentally want to feel that they matter and that what they do is important.

When we take care, each day, to let others know, by our words and actions, that we appreciate them and what they do, we will accomplish more. When folks know that they matter they'll bring more energy to the work they do. They'll display greater confidence to take on that which is hard. They'll stick with things longer and pull harder on the rope.

More importantly, through simple acts of kindness and recognition, we build trust and loyalty that drive others to do almost anything for us – because they want to, not because they have to.

Best of all, appreciating others takes very little time and costs almost nothing. But what we get in return is of extraordinary value: relationships with other human beings that endure through time and trial and that deliver us all to a destination far better than today.

Show others they matter. Wag your tail more.

And win.

* * *

Leaders committed to The Not So Subtle Art of Caring are likewise committed to the notion that the input of others matters. They seek out the opinion of others and rarely seek to impose their own. They know, either innately, or from experience, that when they make it about others by putting those people's ideas first, they win more often. Traditional managers believe they were born with (or are expected to have) every right idea. Not only would this be impossibly exhausting, it would be incredibly annoying to others. No one likes a know-it-all. No one likes the guy or gal who believes they need to be the smartest person in the room. People don't want to be around people like this, let alone work for them. According to leadership expert, Gordon Tredgold, CEO of Leadership Principles, "There is nothing worse than working for a know-it-all boss." (Tredgold, 2018)

So why traditional tall, dark, and handsome managers feel the need to behave like autocrats when the results are disastrous is a mystery. It's the leadership equivalent, one of many, of putting one's hand on a hot stove. The better way is self-evident. Make it about others. Ask them for their input. You will be amazed not only at the improved quality of the output, but maybe, more importantly, at the degree to which people will believe in and fight for the programs, plans and policies they had a hand in creating. They will also grouse less. I tell people often that folks tend to complain less about the taste of soup that they helped make.

But more than anything, people simply want to feel valued. They want to feel big. Simply think about it logically. The bigger your people become, the greater the possibilities for your organization. Making them smaller, as is the game of the autocrat, has the opposite effect. So why play the diminishment game? Ask yourself, what am I doing to make my people really, really big? What steps are you taking, or can you take starting tomorrow, to include those closest to the work in the decisions that matter to your organization?

I used a story about Henry Ford to help make this point in a letter one Friday not so long ago.

June 13, 2019

I was reminded this week of a famous quote by Henry Ford, founder of the Ford Motor Company. He said, "They can have any color they want, as long as it's black." As humorous as this seems today, Ford was dead serious at the time. See, it was Ford's notion that by limiting his customers' choice of color to one, he would dramatically improve efficiency in his plant. The operative word in the prior sentence was, "Ford's." This was Henry's idea. It was not a matter of committee, nor consensus. Henry was fond of running things based on his own ideas. What Henry failed to realize over time, however, was that his infatuation with his own ideas was limiting customer choice and causing them to go elsewhere. Worse, it was discouraging creativity among his own associates, creating morale issues, and encouraging them to leave. See, when you fall in love with your own ideas, to the exclusion of all else, bad things happen.

And that's the point for the week.

Unfortunately, the lessons of American business are not passed down from one generation to another. Like children who refuse to heed the lessons of their parents, we often choose not to pay attention to the lessons of the past. So, the lesson of Henry Ford is lost on many.

And so, owing to human nature, many are driven by the

economy of me, instead of the economy of we. In love with their own ideas, they fail to see that a combination of their notions and those of others will often deliver an even better outcome. Had Henry Ford listened to those around him and added greater color selection earlier, no doubt he would have had an even more successful auto company.

The same is true here. You all have probably noticed by now, that in the context of our business, I don't often use me language or I language. That's because it's not about me, it's about us. Today, you all will receive a t-shirt with the word TEAM on it. Team doesn't have time for the drama of me and I.

It is important that we operate under an economy of we. That the ideas of many are considered. That many participate in the solutions to the problems before us. That many hands help create the platforms upon which this company will launch itself into the future.

When that happens, we will move forward faster. We will make better decisions. We will win more often. And the people who work here will be far more engaged. Certainly, those who are intent on having only their ideas considered may be unhappy. But that's OK. There isn't room here for lime-lighters. There is, however, abundant opportunity for team players, those who are eager to work with others to come up with creative solutions to compete with those outside of our building to create a tremendous organization – one that makes the lives of those who work here better, and delights our customers every single day.

Don't be like Henry.

And win.

* * *

In order to make others big, you must be fully present in their lives. Leadership, particularly leadership practiced in The Not

So Subtle Art of Caring, is not a part-time job. Leading people is not something that can be done while multi-tasking. It does not matter whether you are a certified next-level thinker, it is not possible to divide your attention between someone you are leading and some other distraction. It's a lesson I learned the hard way. But when the human beings whose care has been entrusted to you know that you are clearly and fully present, you tell them, without saying a word, that they are the most important thing on the planet to you at that moment. And when they know that, there is almost nothing they won't do for you in return. In a survey of 2,000 employees, Bain & Co found that among 33 leadership traits – including creating compelling objectives, and being receptive to input – the ability to be mindfully present is the most essential of all (Horwitch, 2016) It's a simple Golden Rule thing. People treat others the way they want to be treated. Or, as I'm fond of offering as very specific advice, people give what they get. When a leader is fully present in the lives of those they lead, those they lead will be fully present in the life of the leader.

Being present includes listening intently to others when they are speaking, with both ears and both eyes. When someone is speaking it is because they want to be heard. So, when that is happening, as a caring leader, pay attention, listen, and acknowledge what they are saying. Then play it back to them so they know with 100% certainty that you heard them. Be present and listen. One of the leaders I most admire on the planet is Martin Pedersen of the JP Group in Denmark. Martin invests a considerable amount of time in being fully present in the lives of his associates. He moves around his operation, greeting people one on one, making certain that they know they are the most important thing in the world to him. He even bought a working train to emphasize the point. Team meetings are held in a working train that moves around the campus; it tells people that at that moment they have one particular focus, and that when he is with them on the train his one focus is being fully present with them, paying attention to them and listening to them.

Short of buying a train, what can you do, starting today, to be more present in the lives of those you lead? Remember, it's a simple choice. It's binary. Either you're present or you're not. So, starting today, just choose to be more present – listen intently more, look people squarely in the eye more.

A story about being more present with my son, Will, was the catalyst for a letter reminding my team of this important lesson.

August 29, 2009

This past weekend was Will's turn for his getaway with dad.

Since he's just five, his trip is a local affair versus his sisters' more exotic weekend jaunts.

So, we went to Cleveland for a Tribe game.

As we walked through the concourse, I noticed that when Will (who is soft-spoken like his father) would say something I'd have to stop, crouch down to his level and ask him to repeat himself so as to hear him.

When I didn't stop and come to his level, I only half heard him. No doubt my responses gave me away. I am sure he noticed.

As we sat in the stands, I thought about our stop-start trip to our seats and was reminded of an important lesson – one in fact that I often forget.

Communication between Will and myself was optimized when I was fully present and paying complete attention to him.

Here's the point for the week.

Getting the most from your relationships with your family, your customers and your co-workers happens only when you give them your complete attention – when you are fully present.

When you are elsewhere – mentally or physically – your ability to relate to others is impaired just as if you take your eyes off the road while driving. The crashes that result while slightly less violent are no less damaging.

When you are fully present, people notice. More is done more quickly. Less is missed or forgotten. Relationships are made stronger. More tires are sold.

I have joked with Annie for years that unless she has made eye contact, there is no guarantee that I've heard her. See, I've been known to "unh hunh" from behind the book I'm reading or even a Blackberry as she tells me something important. As a result, I forget things and disappoint her and others.

But, when I put the book down and give her, my kids or you my undivided attention something just short of magic happens.

Eyes connect and light up. Faces brighten and smile. And something in my heart tells me I did the right thing.

The book or email still gets read. We still get to our seats. Just a little later.

The more present you are in any relationship, the more that will come back to you. Whether at home, here, or in your communities, when you give more of yourself, when you are fully present in interactions with other human beings, when you show that you truly care, those on the receiving end of that presence will respond in kind. See, in the economy of human relationships, people give approximately what they get. It's likely been true since the dawn of time.

So, as you engage in any interaction, even as the leader of a group, ask yourself, "am I being completely present in the life or lives of whoever I have the privilege to be serving at the moment?" If the answer is yes, keep on. If the answer is no, use the gift of choice to do something different. Choose to be present – and not only because you get something in return for it, but because of what it will mean to the person in front of you, who, because of you will dream bigger, jump higher, or persist longer, only because someone took a greater interest in them and what mattered to them.

So, be present.
And win.

* * *

A simple part of making it about others is recognizing that people are different. A one size fits all approach to leading people almost never works. It's the stock and trade of the old-school command and control, authoritarian crowd, but it's another in a long list of reasons why the traditional management styles of the last century's managers are increasingly failing to work on now three new generations of worker. According to Robert Bacal of Bacal & Associates, "When you try to lead by treating very different people exactly the same, you deny their uniqueness, which often alienates them."

People want to be recognized for their own uniqueness and the uniqueness of their contributions. They want to work for people who take the time to understand them, what makes them tick, what matters to them and motivates them. The more you cater to someone as an individual, the bigger you are going to make them feel. Leaders who care enough to invest the time to first learn about the differences that exist across their team(s) then work to lead their associates accordingly can accomplish truly amazing things. But by treating everyone the same, a manager will suboptimize across the entire group.

I'm often amazed by leaders that can learn truly intricate differences between one piece of equipment and another and then handle them accordingly but who attempt to treat people exactly the same. When we realize that people are as different and as complex as any piece of machinery, we can do amazing things – because people, by combining individual talents can achieve truly amazing things. It's about multiplication, and it's a choice.

So simply ask yourself, what can I do to learn about the

differences in my people then treat them accordingly? Take notes. Keep a journal of what works and doesn't with each individual. Wherever possible, simply ask them; they will tell you.

A story about differences between my two daughters helped me further the point.

August 6, 2009

This past weekend I took my daughter Charlotte to St. Louis to Busch Stadium for a Cardinal game.

A few years ago, not really knowing what she was signing up for, Chuck agreed that every year we'd visit a different Major League Baseball park until we had seen them all together. She's now starting to do the math and knows that she'll be a mom before we're done.

Earlier this year, I had taken Caroline, my twelve-year-old daughter to St. Louis for the Women's NCAA Final Four – her annual getaway with dad.

As Charlotte and I toured St. Louis this weekend I was struck by the fact that several things Caroline enjoyed during her trip weren't Chuck's cup of tea and vice versa.

There are also staple traditions to each girl's weekend that are different and have nothing to do with the three years that separate them.

They are just different.

I knew that. But this weekend made it clear in a way that was unmistakable.

Making sure that their weekends were special to them required that I treat them differently.

Here's the point for the week.

People are different.

Treating everyone the same rarely results in success of any kind.

Getting the most from your relationships with your children, your customers, or the associates you work with happens when you understand what makes them different from others then serve their needs accordingly.

When you do, you'll not only learn more about the people around you and yourself, you'll also do and see different things.

Like finally having breakfast at Uncle Bill's Pancake House.

Treat people differently.

And win.

* * *

Part of making it about others includes leaving your desk and getting out among them. As Eric Geiger of Facts & Trends put it, "It takes a love for the people and the work, coupled with a discipline to throw oneself into the work, for leaders to leave their offices." (Geiger, 2018) It has been said about me that I am equally at home in a board room or a service bay. To me, there is almost no greater compliment. During my 15 months with Goodyear's Commercial Tire and Service Center business, I visited more than 70 of our locations, from Massachusetts to California and Washington State to Florida. In many instances, I would use the occasion of new service truck deliveries to drive to a location, stopping at others along the way.

After a time, our associates stopped being surprised when I showed up, because it became a part of who I was to them. Both building and maintaining a level of comfort and credibility with front-line associates requires spending time with front-line associates. And from time, I don't mean the occasional visit, or photo opportunity, I mean real, quality time. Change your clothes. Fly commercial, or better yet, drive. But get out with the folks. Not only will you learn a great deal, but your believability with those whose care has been entrusted to you will skyrocket.

I used the occasion of checking the box on my 50th state visit to make this point not very long ago.

September 26, 2019

This week, on my way home, I stopped in Fargo, North Dakota. ND was the last of the 50 states I had yet to visit. By spending a night in Fargo, I could check the box. All 50, done.

I'm not sure why this was so important to me. Except that it was a goal, something I said I would do. And now, in finishing it, I had kept my word. But more than that, in finishing it, in seeing all 50 states, I saw things, I learned things, I became a better leader. See, you can't manage what you've never seen before.

And that's the point for the week.

In my career, I've had the privilege to lead organizations I could touch end to end in an hour. I've also led groups of over 8,500 people that would require a week or more to get around. But in every case, I have done just that. I have gotten around.

And in doing so, I've met people and learned things, seen things and uncovered opportunities that I never would have had I sat behind a comfy desk at HQ.

My desk here isn't particularly comfy. That's on purpose – for a lot of reasons. But among them is this: a reminder that nothing truly important happens behind it. Instead, what matters happens closest to our customers, closest to where our work gets done.

Most of the states I've seen have been in visiting customers or front-line associates. I'm a better leader because of it.

Keeping my word, well, that's a big deal. But it pales in comparison to all that I've seen, all that I've learned, all the hands that I've shaken, all of the eyes I've looked into and all of the lives that were made a little better because people forgot for a moment who was in charge and thought instead about the incredible possibility of a tomorrow when all of us work together toward one common goal.

So, get out in the world. Get close to the work.

And win.

* * *

Sometimes the others we have to make it about are people we don't particularly care for. That's no excuse. Leaders who care don't get to pick and choose who they get to care about. Also, in the game of example setting, they don't get the luxury of showing their teams that it's OK to reserve kindness only for those people you like. Nothing will destroy a leader's credibility faster than playing favorites.

In the 2018 sample of their highly regarded "People Management Study," the team at Predictive Index found that the #2 (of 10) trait in describing a bad boss is "Plays favorites," cited by 57% of their over 5,000 respondents. (The Predictive Index, 2018) True caring leaders don't play favorites. In The Not So Subtle Art of Caring, no bets are off; there is no cancel culture. Tolerance means tolerance of all points of view, not just those we agree with, and not just of those who look like us, think like us, vote like us, or believe in the same god as us. In The Not So Subtle Art of Caring, everyone gets cared for.

There is no faster way to destroy your team or your own credibility than by letting your personal politics or values guide the complexion of your team or by allowing your team to vote good people off the island. Take stock of how you behave toward people. Do your personal beliefs spill over into what you say and do? If so, stop it. Does a cancel culture exist in your shop? If so, stomp it out.

To make this point, I used a story about a sports figure whose commitment to being a tremendous human being often made him a very polarizing figure.

January 13, 2012

Sunday night, the Denver Broncos achieved an improbable win over the favored Pittsburgh Steelers. At the center of the discussion of the dramatic victory was Bronco quarterback, Tim Tebow. What I've been struck most by during the week has been the polarized opinions of him, opinions that started brewing during the regular NFL season. People seem to love him or hate him; there's not a lot of in-between.

As I further considered his detractors and their comments, the dislike for Tim Tebow seemed not particularly surprising. Human nature often leads us to be resentful of someone else's success in their profession or in the field of humanity, for reasons either real or imagined. We suffer jealousy, envy, anger and other figurative diseases of the heart. Left untreated, these disorders, like their physical counterparts, limit our own achievement or worse. There is, however, a way out ... hidden where we least expect to find it. Paradoxically, the cure to our resentment of others, our disease of the heart, can be found by celebrating their success.

That's the point for the week.

When we seek to build ourselves up by tearing another down, we lose. The winners go on winning, undeterred by our antics. Meanwhile, we stand in place – expending precious energy and other resources on our dreams of reversing another's ascension instead of focusing on our own forward progress. Our candle will never burn brighter by blowing another's out. We will never stand taller because we chop another down. These are incontrovertible truths.

The better way is to first celebrate the achievements of others. When we do, we'll get something in the bargain too. By extending well wishes to others we'll get some on ourselves; we'll feel better and happier in the process. Best of all, we open our heart to the possibility that something better is available to us too. As we do, we'll begin to copy and follow the example of those who achieve whether consciously or not.

As a result, we'll learn, grow and become better. We'll gravitate to more and more others who represent the best in ourselves. We'll diminish, then erase that which impedes our advancement – at work, at home and in our communities. The notion of a learning organization doesn't begin and end at Goodyear; nor is it limited to that which enriches our minds. What we learn by heart is as or more important.

As with any improvement, it won't just happen. It requires work. It's hard. But then, nothing good comes easy. Like the behavior changes needed to improve the health of our beating heart, these things require commitment, repetition, and the fortitude to get back up when we fail. But the end result is worth it.

We and the teams we lead will achieve more – if for no other reason than we'll more often focus on what's possible then endeavor with all our hearts to attain it.

Celebrate the success of others ... then emulate it.

Be like Tim.

And win.

* * *

This chapter provided a guide to making others big. It showed how leaders who care can accomplish extraordinary things by putting others first. You were introduced to the paradox that says we achieve big things ultimately by making ourselves really, really small so that others can get really, really big. Making it about others is foundational to The Not So Subtle Art of Caring. Until we make it *about* others, accomplishing anything *with* others is not possible.

Next, we will take a closer look at the character of the caring leader by defining *The Charisma of Caring*. We'll answer,

"Who is this person?" We'll also come up with a truer notion of charisma than the one US boards and hiring managers have been unsuccessfully using for decades, and we'll outline some of the problems with long-held beliefs around exactly what defines charisma in American business, and why those who US boards think have what it takes keep flaming out. We will then identify 11 additional attributes that comprise caring leadership and that will help those wishing to practice The Not So Subtle Art of Caring home in on the traits and behaviors necessary to win with today's worker.

Chapter 3

The Charisma of Caring

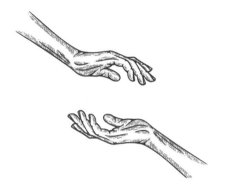

"Charisma without character is postponed calamity."
Peter Ajisafe
1962-
Nigerian Businessman & Author

One can tell a great deal about another person simply by the way they act. If a picture is worth a thousand words, behavior is worth a thousand more.

As I share in a later story, my father had an expression we would use any time I or one of my three brothers would make a promise to him regarding our future behavior. He'd simply look down at us and say, "My hearing isn't very good, but my eyesight is 20/20." It was his way of saying talk is cheap, that what one *says* in life matters very little; it's what one *does* that counts. Obviously, more than 40 some odd years later, I've never forgotten it. I even use it on my own kids in those now less rare, "I've become my father" moments.

How one behaves is a clue to who they are as a person, especially when they believe no one is watching. What I'm referring to is the character of the individual.

Both of my parents, Kenneth F. and Phyllis L. Kane, were exceedingly good judges of character and fast ones too. Either of them, after spending a matter of minutes with someone, could read them like a book. And they were almost never wrong. So, it didn't come as a surprise when I realized I had the same gift. At times, I've wished that I could turn it off, especially having met someone I had great hopes for. In those cases, I'd prefer not to know what's coming. But the trouble is behaviors are like flashing lights, radar beacons, or cartoon thought bubbles. Once they are sent out, they are very hard to ignore.

Cues to someone's character tell us a great deal about what makes them tick. They tell us things about their sincerity, about what's important to them, and about how they treat other people. And once those things are known, it becomes very easy to predict how they are going to fit in your shop and perform on the job. Like leopards and their spots, these things are easy to see, and they don't change. At that point, it's a simple matter of comparing what we see in them against what we know makes someone effective as a true, caring leader. They either display the qualities of a great leader, or they don't.

As leadership expert, and author of Breakthrough Leadership, Thomas Griffin has said, "I have said it before, and I'll say it again: great leaders share common traits that separate them from the pack." (Griffin, 2020) Throughout this book, and more than once in regard to a few of them, I have highlighted and expanded upon 10 non-negotiable rules-based traits for the caring leader. They are:

1. Belief
2. Love
3. Honesty
4. Making Others Big
5. Wholeheartedness
6. Being Present (which includes listening)

7. Persevering with Courage
8. Effectively Communicating
9. Talking to people, not about them
10. Having Fun / Spreading Joy

I say these are non-negotiable for two reasons. First, as a leader, you cannot bargain with yourself over your character. It is never OK to justify a decision to do the wrong thing based on whataboutism, some form of an eye for an eye, or some vigilante justice or cancel culture scheme concocted to make you feel better about a purposeful breakdown of your own moral code. Second, these traits are non-negotiable, because all 10 are necessary. As Griffin says, "Character can then be described as the sum of all the qualities that define an individual." (Griffin, 2020) Building character takes every ingredient. It's not possible to pick something else and trade it out for one of these 10, telling yourself. "I'm good, I have ten, I'll come back for that one later." Nope. Nor are you good with a majority. Seven of 10 won't cut it. Get these 10 down. Get your caring self in order. Practice them every day. Tell your team what you are working on. Ask them to help you, and to hold you accountable. But go 10 for 10.

Remember, my definition of the caring leader is:

"A Caring Leader works with those closest to the work to develop and execute plans, that once achieved, result in balanced improvement in the lives of the owners, associates and customers of the business"

(and for a non-profit, just change business to organization, then change owners, associates and customers to stakeholders, volunteers, and beneficiaries.)

I've included 11 more traits of caring leaders below. These are traits I've written about a lot and believe strongly in. These are traits that I know are predictive of success in caring leaders and which make practicing The Not So Subtle Art of Caring possible. You'll notice that almost none of the 21 traits are original to me or to the other 47 authors who cite their importance. These are leadership attributes you have, undoubtedly, seen before. Most have been in existence since the first caveman carved a wheel out of a rock and put a price tag on it.

If anything, my choosing these 11 specific attributes and declaring them causative of success in *a caring leader*, that's different. But my goal was not to break new ground, or to say, "hey look at me, I cracked the code." My goal was simply to share with you what has worked in my life, in my business, in my home, and in my community, for over 30 years. Between my own and the experience of others, history is on your side. You can use what has worked in my life and what any others say works in theirs to make you a better, more caring leader.

What you should be seeing develop here is the concept of a different sort of leader. One who deeply cares for others AND drives for results every single day. Remember the ampersand. And remember that every day means every day.

These are not things you needed to be born knowing how to do. These are things you can learn and improve on through practice and repetition. Trust me when I tell you that I don't live up to these attributes (or my rules) every day. But I try. And the people around me know I try. And they help and support me as I do. But because I know who I want to be and what attributes are important to me, I more often get it right than wrong; and because of that, I win way more than I lose. And when I do lose, well, it ain't no big deal, because I can fix it. What is a big deal though are the lives of the people around me, and that's why these 11 things do matter. They are:

1. Being Grateful
2. Doing the Right Thing

3. Being Civil
4. Being Authentic
5. Being Consistent
6. Leading by Example
7. Making the Most of Every Day
8. Stepping Out of Line
9. Admitting Fault
10. Resolving Issues Now
11. Being knowledgeable about what you do

Over the years, I've written more than one story and letter about each one of these things. On the pages that follow, I've included one for each of the 11 attributes. I've also added a more detailed discussion for every one of them as well.

For now, please recognize that these traits are not ethereal. These are traits that after being around someone for a matter of several minutes almost anyone can have a sense of. In hiring, they are traits you can ask about directly, or ask for examples of if you are unsure. They are traits that are easy to ask references for instances of. Like the non-negotiable 10, they are traits that are simple to tell your team you are working on, and to ask for their help with. Best of all, none of them are complicated. All of them, though, will be important to those you lead; and all of them will help you deliver results in whatever enterprise you are leading. I promise you that.

You'll notice that my list does not include anything about height, good looks, perceived charisma, gregariousness, or athleticism. That's because these things have nothing to do with leadership success. Zero. Boards of directors believe they do. That's why they continue to hire to a formula. One that continues to disappoint. One that results in over half of CEOs, hired to their spec, flaming out in less than 18 months. But there is no actual connection between any of these mostly physical characteristics and leadership. None. There may be a correlation between these characteristics and success as a Hollister model, but for a leader of human beings not so much. It's largely because these people with high perceived charisma are train wrecks. And the data confirms it. Research by House et al in 1991 looked at the personality traits of individuals with high personalized charisma. What they found wasn't good. They described these individuals as having, "A high need for power (that is) coupled with low activity inhibition, high authoritarianism, an external locus of control, low self-esteem, high narcissism, and high Machiavellianism." (House, 1991) These are not the sort of people that should be entrusted to lead other human beings ever.

As if that's not enough, here's what else you should know about charisma. Charisma is not the same as attractiveness. Attractiveness is related to physical appearance. Charisma is a quality, rooted in personality traits and interpersonal skills, that affect the degree to which others willingly follow another human being. Gregariousness is not charisma, no more than shyness represents an absence of charisma. The world is replete with loud boors that could not buy a follower, just as it is with introverted leaders whose followers would willingly walk over hot lava for them. Unfortunately, the conventional wisdom has been hardwired all wrong. Ask almost anyone to describe a charismatic leader and you will get something akin to "talk, dark, handsome, life of the party." Additionally, words like bold, colorful, confident and flair have been typically used to describe charismatic managers. It's why C-Suites all across the country are full of people that fit the bill. But it is also why the stays for these folks tend to be short lived, disastrous, or both. It's because highly charismatic people, as traditionally defined, tend to be less effective. A recent study published in the Harvard Business Review showed that for leaders with charisma scores beyond the 60th percentile, "which is just above the average score relative to the general population of working adults, perceived effectiveness started to decline." (Vergauwe, 2017) Even the words researchers are starting to use to describe what actually makes someone charismatic are changing. In contrast to the more superficial descriptors used historically, in describing a new definition of charisma for transformational leaders, Y Scouts now offers up words like maturity, humility, compassion, substance, and listening (with no mention of a lampshade on the head). (Y Scouts, 2020)

So, for true, caring leaders with self-effacing charm, concern for others, and a true sense of self, there's hope; the tide is changing. So, the new generation of authentic, caring leaders should not change a thing about themselves. Being inauthentic ever is a mistake. Hiring managers and those you lead can spot a phony a mile away. Pretending to be a highly personalized charismatic jerk just because you believe it will help you get a job is a mistake. Be careful what you wish for. Because even if you were to succeed, today's worker will quickly remind you that character is what they actually want in a leader. Because true charisma comes from character and true character from caring.

As they should. In hiring or promotion decisions, when weighing both character and charisma as predictors of future success, character should win every time. Because character matters. Because character is substantive. Because character is derived of attributes that are actually causative to positive outcomes. Because those with more character than charisma make better leaders and drive better outcomes. In fact, a now two-decade old research project from the *Journal of Leadership and Organizational Studies* was clear about the absolute connection between superior leadership and character, **not** charisma, when they said, "The quest for leadership excellence is based more on character than charisma." and "a virtuous character is the building block of leadership excellence." (Shankar, 2003)

Speaking of hiring, when asked whether I prioritize talent

over character or vice versa, I don't blink, pause, or equivocate. I immediately reply, "character, followed by attitude, with talent somewhere down the list." As a leader, you can teach absent skills to almost anyone, but there is almost nothing you can do to repair faulty character, or a broken attitude for that matter. Leaders that hire for skill believing they can somehow recalibrate someone's flawed moral compass will not only inflict incalculable damage on the business but will destroy whatever trust they have developed among the current workforce who will view this act by their leader as a lapse in judgement, integrity or both. According to Peter Schultz, writing for TriSoft, "It is much easier to train a person of good character to do a job well then to try to develop character in a very adept and experienced employee but who lacks essential human values." (Schultz, 2019) So, hire for character, every time. You won't ever regret it.

Character is formed of several handfuls of attributes that likewise define the true, caring leader, the leader who practices The Not So Subtle Art of Caring. In this chapter, as promised, on the pages that follow, I'll discuss 11 new attributes, each in detail, with some practical insights for you as a leader. Remember, on your journey, dedicate yourself to getting better each day. Find a mentor/hero. And ask your people for help. Those you lead will love it when you ask them, and they will love helping you even more – because they love you; and they want to see you succeed.

* * *

Great, Caring leaders, those who practice The Not So Subtle Art of Caring are grateful.

They show up each day with gratitude in their hearts, thankful for another day to lead and for the people they have the privilege to serve.

People need to know that they are valued and appreciated.

Humans simply want to believe that what they do matters. And they want to do it for people they believe actually care and are grateful for what they do. There's no way to fake it. Either you care, or you don't; either you are grateful, or you aren't. People can spot a fraud a mile away. And throwing money at the problem won't fix it either. People don't want to be showered with cash. They want to be showered with thanks – when they deserve it. Gratitude is free. But remember it has to be real.

Any behavior must be genuine. The point isn't to change your interaction so dramatically that people wonder what happened to the real you. Your actions must be authentic. The object is to show people that you are truly thankful for them and the contributions they make to your success and the success of the organization. It isn't hard. A handwritten note. A handshake or a literal pat on the back. Public recognition for a job well done. Words of praise and encouragement vs. a dressing down when things don't go so well.

These simple acts of kindness, done with genuine feeling, convey to others that they matter, that they are valued, and that you wouldn't want to go through a fight with anyone but them. Best of all, while they don't cost a dime, to those on the receiving end, they are near priceless.

Associates who feel valued, who believe their supervisor is truly grateful for them and the work they do will become intensely loyal to that leader. It's just what they do. Gratitude begets engagement. By showing gratitude to your associates, you are telling them what they do matters, that it makes a difference. Gratitude also leads to increased resilience. Because gratitude increases trust between leaders and their associates, they are more likely to weather downturns intact; when things get hard, because workers know that their leader values them and what they do, they will fight harder and longer. Finally, according to research by Robert A. Emmons Ph.D. at the University of California at Davis, who conducted a significant study on the effects of gratitude, there is a significant causative correlation between gratitude and achievement of goals. Which is, after all, why we're here in the first place.

Mostly, it all starts with waking up each day with a sense of gratitude in your heart – for what you have, for another day, for those who love you, for the continued care and protection of whatever greater power you believe in. Without the ability to hop out of bed each day with a grateful heart, your ability to express genuine thankfulness to others, and even to receive it, will be severely limited. So simply ask yourself, how much gratitude is in my heart?

A story about "Gratitude Week" spurred me to write on the topic a couple years ago.

November 21, 2018

Earlier this week, amongst all the emails I receive, was a particular message reminding me that it was "Gratitude Week." "That's nice," I thought, "an entire week now devoted to thankfulness instead of the one day we used to have." But then, I started to think more about it. It seemed a bit like the out of touch CEO who announces that, "Tuesdays are customer day!" as if every day shouldn't be about the customer. And for me, that's what I took away from a reminder about "Gratitude Week" – that every week should be gratitude week, every day should be gratitude day.

And that's the point for the week.

Even as we have one day set aside each year as a wonderful reminder of all we have to be thankful for – which for me includes you and this company, and all that you have accomplished in the short time I have been here – every day of our lives should be a day during which we express gratitude for every great thing in our lives. We should choose to wake up each day with a grateful heart. We should be thankful for our good days and our bad days – because we are enriched by both.

Being grateful is not a once a year proposition. It is an every minute of every day thing.

Around here, it means accepting feedback as a gift. It means being grateful for new responsibilities and challenges. It means celebrating both failures and successes as opportunities to learn and grow. It means being absolutely grateful for every person around you and the gifts they bring to this organization. See, when others know that you truly appreciate them, they will stand by you through almost anything. They will fight for you, watch out for you, and take care of you. They will overlook your faults or even help you work on them. But most importantly they will love you because that's what you'll find in the depths of gratitude.

And when we have more of that around here, we will win more often, if only for the fact that more of us will be grateful for the opportunity to be here, come what may, accepting and taking on any challenge that is thrown at us. Because almost nothing can overcome the incredible force of will that comes from a group of individuals who record both ups and downs with a spirit of gratitude, and spend every minute of every day being thankful for each other

There is not a day that I am not grateful for all of you – for the way you welcomed me, for the way you are fighting for what we are trying to accomplish, for the way you are taking care of each other, and for just being yourselves. I can't wait to see what we're going to build together here. And even if we don't know exactly what that looks like today, there is one thing I do know for sure: the more of us that walk through the door here each day with gratitude in our hearts, the more we're going to achieve.

So be grateful every day.

And win.

* * *

In Chapter 1, I spoke about The Rules, mostly in the context of guiding principles. Now, I want to speak about rules in terms of doing the right thing, following a moral code, and simply obeying the law or the policies one is expected to follow.

Great leaders play by the rules. They win the right way, period.

For great, caring leaders, challenging the status quo does not extend to rule breaking. That's simply Pantsuit Barbie speak for, "I don't like the rules and I'm not going to play by them."

Great leaders play by the rules. They win the right way, period.

Those who practice The Not So Subtle Art of Caring set the example for others to follow. And they play by the rules. There is no easier way to destroy personal credibility and to encourage an open borders approach to associate handbook adherence than for the leader of the team to check out on rule following or to establish a do as I say approach to policy.

Great leaders play by the rules. They win the right way, period.

What would others say about you? Would they say you play by the rules? Every time?

I used a Malcolm Gladwell story about the poster children for rule-breaking to reinforce this tenet with my team.

February 18, 2012

Earlier this month, I finished the latest book by Malcolm Gladwell, "What the Dog Saw and Other Stories" – a sort of "best-of" collection of Gladwell essays which have appeared in the pages of the "New Yorker" magazine. One essay dealt with Enron, the gargantuan Houston energy trading firm that has become synonymous with corporate fraud and deceit.

Gladwell's assertion is that Enron's fascination with "talent" was a root cause of its fall from grace.

As I thought about it, it seemed that it was quite a lot simpler than all that.

To me, what happened at Enron occurred due to an obsession with winning without regard for how winning was achieved. Enron's executives created a win at all cost culture that its associates were only too happy to embrace – all the way down the abyss. In the ultimate irony, Enron lost because it focused singularly on winning.

Winning the wrong way isn't winning. Ever.

That's the point for the week

For some five months now, I've been sharing my view of the world with you each Friday in *The Week*. *The Week* is rooted in a fundamental belief that what we do is less important than how we do it. It's based on one of my oft referenced rules for life – Win ... the right way.

We talk a lot about winning around here. We should. After all, business is a game where score is kept. But true winning comes from doing so in a way that we can be proud of.

When how we win becomes as or more important than winning itself, teams are transformed. Trust blossoms. Teammates learn that they can rely on each other to do the right thing in any circumstance.

By committing to winning the right way, we'll be free to focus more on what matters. We'll spend less time and money cleaning up messes. We'll never have to waste thought and energy looking over our shoulders, worried that what we did might catch up with us. We'll avoid the inevitable charade of blame-shifting and back-stabbing that results when things do – and they always will – find us.

Here, at home, and in our cities and towns, life will provide ample opportunity to choose between winning the right way or winning the wrong way. It is in those moments that true winners are revealed.

Anyone can win the wrong way. It's easy. Anyone can complete a crossword by looking at the answers. Anyone can produce EBIT by slashing cost. Anyone can win a race by pushing an opponent off the track. Anyone can accumulate more by taking what doesn't belong to them.

Often no one will be looking. Many times, the corner we could cut will seem insignificant. In a lot of cases, it might seem that no one will get hurt. These times make winning the wrong way even easier.

It is, by definition, though, hardest to do the right thing when it's easiest to do the wrong one. Winning the right way is significantly harder than winning in any way. But it is the harder row that illuminates the true victors. They're easy to recognize. They are the ones that other winners flock around.

When we choose to play by the rules, we create environments that attract other winners. Associates, suppliers, and customers that value integrity seek to be part of teams that value it too. When they find it, they seldom leave. Together, they form a nearly unstoppable force, propelled by trust and held together by bonds that last a lifetime.

Like all else in life, it's a choice.

Choose the correct way, the harder way ...

And win ... the right way.

* * *

If you want to be a great, caring leader you'd better be civil. Remember, more than anything else, employees simply want to be respected. A recent study of more than 20,000 workers, world-wide, conducted with Harvard researcher, Christine Porath, found that "Being treated with respect was more important to employees than recognition and appreciation, communicating an inspiring vision, providing useful feedback,

or even opportunities for learning, growth and development."
Civility is the key to respect. And it's the one thing most
managers screw up most often. As you'd expect I'd say, it's a
choice. Whether you speak respectfully to another human being
or not is 100% your call. Most traditional authoritarian manager
types fail miserably.

So, the good news is, the field is wide open. Of course, the
bad news is that it's hard. But as with many of the other traits, it
doesn't have to be soooooo hard. Get a coach. Keep an incivility
journal; write down the times you were a jerk, and send apology
notes later. Or start by telling your team what you are trying to
accomplish. Ask them to call you out when you let them down.
Create a fine system, or an anonymous comment box, ask your
team when they are gathered as a group for an applause-o-
meter response to show if you are making progress. Until you
start and until you ask for feedback, change won't occur. But I
can promise you this. If you genuinely ask for help, people will
give it to you.

The key is recognizing it's an issue, resolving to do something
about it, then taking steps to do just that. As Porath says, "Small
acts can have big returns. Your civility will cascade throughout
your organization with benefits to you – and your organization."

A story about angry air travelers was a perfect way to address
the topic of civility.

See if you recognize this dude. If you do, ask yourself the
same thing that I ask myself. If I recognize this guy and know
how awful it looks, then why would I ever allow myself to lose
my marbles ever again?

February 25, 2011

Monday I was subjected to another day-long, delay-ridden
odyssey with my favorite air carrier.

The weather had turned bad in Cleveland Sunday evening,

making travel to the airport by car then away from it by plane more stressful than it is to begin with. While waiting to learn the fate of my scheduled 7:10 am departure, a fellow of 50 something and a lady of 80 some odd – who I learned was his aunt – huffed into the gate area around 7:25. The woman was in a wheelchair. The fellow, a tad out of shape, was still struggling to fasten his belt (removed in security) while managing his several other belongings. They'd have been late had the flight been on-time; so both were agitated. To make matters worse, his aunt proceeded to ask where her bag was, to which her nephew replied, "I thought you had it." Quickly deducing that he had just won a free trip all the way back to security, the man, already in a huff, let loose with a string of profanity that seemed to hurt his poor aunt more than had he slapped her.

I thought to myself that he seemed old enough to know better than to behave like that … in public, even. It immediately seemed odd to me that I'd have thought about it that way. It occurred to me that, truth be told, his behavior would have been unacceptable regardless of his age, regardless of location. Civility isn't just for people old enough to know better or for when circumstance demands it. Civility is for everyone, in every situation.

That's the point for the week.

The speech we use matters.

When we use words and tone that build people up rather than tear them down, we are telling them by our actions that we respect and value them. We tell them that they are needed. We tell them that integrity matters. We tell them that how they treat others is as important as anything they'll do in a day. In short, we'll be telling them how to win.

When we choose to profane, deride and otherwise verbally abuse folks, no matter if we're joking and no matter if there's no one else around, we make withdrawals from the emotional checking accounts we have with them by the handful. We create barriers between ourselves and others that don't need to be there. We create the perception that the situation is worse than it really is, adding anxiety to already tense moments. We cause others to disengage from the discussion, at times when their input would be most valuable.

When we use profanity in place of actual words, it suggests to others that we're not bright enough to know the right words to use – no matter how intelligent we actually may be. It shapes others perception of us and our abilities. It affects whether we're asked back, moved up, or brought along.

Quite simply, it's just not attractive. Accordingly, then, it pushes people away; people whose opinions matter, or should, like those we depend on to help us, those we want to look up to us, and those we hope would look out for us. When we create distance between ourselves and others we accomplish less – at work, at home, and in our communities.

It doesn't matter what sort of business we're in. Nor does it matter who is or is not around. Certainly, it matters not where we're standing at the time. People are people in every circumstance, and for most, given a choice between a barrage of curse words and a shower of kindness, they'll choose the shower every time.

By conducting ourselves with civility and encouraging the hearts of those around us, we'll create armies of folks who choose to do the right thing, who would move mountains for us, and who'll remember us for the kind of people we were and how we showed them by our example that they could achieve more than they ever might have without us.

Be civil.

And win.

* * *

True caring leaders, those who practice The Not So Subtle Art of Caring, are authentic. They are genuine, self-aware and transparent. They are true to themselves and their current point of personal development, for better or for worse. They don't pretend, ever, to be someone they are not. If they are working on something, they are honest about it. If they are a certain way and don't plan to change, they are open about that too. They in effect say, "Hi, my name is Phillip Kane, this is what I believe, this is what you can expect from me and this is what I expect from you. Oh, and by the way, I have some strange personality quirks, let me tell you about them. This is what I'm working on right now and may need your help with."

True caring leaders understand that the road to pretending to be someone or something you are not is fraught with peril. First, it's hard, really, really hard. Second, people are smart; they can normally see through an act a mile away. Third, like any lie, you always have to remember what you said; and that can get really, really complicated. Finally, you may not like who you masquerade to be.

Being authentic is a hallmark of a great leader. Being authentic has its own charisma. Authentic is the dude in boots and jeans when everyone else is in slacks and Ferragamo's and he's not one bit bothered by it. But put him in slacks and watch him squirm. Because it's inauthentic. It's like wearing a Halloween costume when it's not Halloween. People gravitate to authentic because they want to be real too. They want it to be safe to be themselves. They want it to be OK to stop pretending to be whoever the corporate standard says they need to be.

See, the benefit of authenticity is diversity. It's the range of ideas, and perspectives, and points of view, and dress, and experiences, and hopes, and dreams, and ideas, and fears that come when encouraging people to be real happens. And it starts with a leader that shows up and shows his or her authentic self.

In all of this though, sauce for the goose must be sauce for the gander. If you expect transparency from your team, you must be transparent. If you expect ethical conduct from them, you must conduct yourself accordingly. If your authentic gig means 510 Levi's and Chuck Taylors, get ready to revise the dress code, or as Hubspot says, "Being an authentic leader means leading by example. It's demonstrating through your actions that you practice the same values and behaviors you expect from your team." (Forsey, 2019)

I've included two letters about being real: one of my shortest letters ever, about a visit by our ownership team to our business and another about Bubba Watson's improbable Master's win – both helped me make the point about authenticity and being ourselves.

September 14, 2018

Recently, members of our ownership team and our Board of Directors were here for a Management Meeting. As we prepared for the meeting, Todd and I made sure to include materials that showed how we thought about the business personally. We also spoke beforehand about the importance of speaking in terms that were real to us – about being ourselves. See, it's not uncommon when company comes, that we somehow change our behavior. We try to be someone we aren't. And in the end, a few things happen: we come off as less than genuine; we set a standard we can never replicate; and we set ourselves up to disappoint others in the future. But when we just show up as ourselves, good people will see the good in us anyway and want to be a part of what we're doing.

And that's the point for the week.

In my first month, I've spent a lot of time just walking around, watching and listening. It's how I learn. Sitting with people won't tell me what I really need to know. Because often I'm going to see the side of them they want me to see and a process that is probably not the one they use every time. So, I walk around. And I watch. And I listen.

And when I do, I want you to be yourselves. Because when you are, others will know it. When you're not, they will know that too.

Authenticity matters. It's a core currency in the economy of trust. When others regard you as real, they will see you as someone they can rely on, learn from, and confide in. When all of us spend less time caring about what each of us thinks of each other and more time thinking about what we can do for each other, something incredible is going to happen. We'll recognize the true capability that exists in our organization and it's going to surprise us. Because then the power of multiplication will take over. Each of you times every other one of you aligned toward the common goal of growing this business – instead of your own self -image.

So just be yourself.

And win.

* * *

April 13, 2012

This week, Bubba Watson won the Master's. In the Butler Cabin, after being awarded the customary green jacket, Watson provided one of the truest, most authentic, most emotionally bare reactions to winning that tournament of any I can ever remember. But he won it the same way. He did so in a play-off, the highlight of which was an astounding recovery following a miserable tee shot which sailed into a grove of pine trees lining the fairway. While Bubba's recovery was astounding, it wasn't unusual. He was simply repeating a similar move made on the same hole about two hours earlier. The "dead-hook-off-the-pine-straw-over-and-around-mature-evergreens" shot is a staple of Bubba Watson's game. Bubba, who has never had a golf lesson in his life, was simply being Bubba, proving again that winning starts with being yourself.

That's the point for the week.

Winning is inversely proportional to the degree to which we try to be something we aren't.

Like Bubba Watson, when we bring our entire self to any enterprise, we'll accomplish more. Time, energy, or emotion spent in an attempt to be something or someone else detracts from the force of will that we can apply in any situation, whether at work, at home, or in our communities.

Among almost any management guru's list of traits most valued in leaders is authenticity. It shouldn't be surprising. In all aspects of our lives, we seek the real McCoy. We're willing to pay more for (and value more considerably) the genuine article. The knock-off is held in low esteem, even to the point of its negative-sounding name. People won't seek, let alone follow, that which isn't real.

Attempts to be something we are not will always impact performance in a negative way. Motion becomes less fluid. Strengths are employed less. Time is wasted while we mentally process the requirements of behaving in unnatural ways. Worst of all, trust is destroyed as others inevitably discover that what we've said or done is an act. The paradoxical truth of the matter is that in trying to be perfect, the result is always less so.

None of us is perfect. We aren't made to be. Hiding our deficiencies doesn't make them go away nor enhance our performance in any way. Accepting our deficiencies and leveraging what we are good at to compensate for them, on the other hand, does, in fact, enhance performance.

Along the way, by recognizing our own imperfections and achieving peace with them, we'll learn to recognize and forgive them in others. When we do, the full measure of trust can be achieved as those we rely on and those who depend on us come to a shared realization that each of us is, after all, perfect – just the way we are.

Be yourself.

And win.

* * *

Leaders who practice The Not So Subtle Art of Caring are consistent. What they tell one associate will match what they tell another. The way they act in front of one group will match the way they act in front of another. They stick with programs. They are not easily swayed by the court of popular opinion. They are steadfast. They are true. They are consistent because they care.

Being consistent is a choice, like most everything else in life. When one of the easiest things for a leader to do is to bend with the breeze of consensus, the true, caring leader stays consistent to his higher authority, to himself, to his team, and to the plan.

According to Fortune Magazine, "Consistency is one of the strongest traits among the world's greatest leaders. Consistency – whether good or bad, positive or negative – provides the business, its employees, and stakeholders with a known quantity. And more than anything, people respect and admire consistent leaders." (Kriz, 2016) The writer, Scott Kriz, even went on to say that, "Consistency is far better than rare moments of greatness." It is though even better when consistency and greatness collide.

One of my heroes is former Goodyear chief Bob Keegan. Bob was consistent. Bob expected a great deal from people, to be sure. But he was consistent in his expectations, and they never got yanked around. I've told many people that one of the things I loved most about working for Bob Keegan (apart from the fact that he recognized the value in being with customers and those closest to them) was that you never had to wonder which Bob was going to show up each day. Bob Keegan was consistent.

When a leader is consistent, associates know what to expect, they know that the boundaries are where the leader says they are. They know that rules will be equitably enforced. They know that pay plans are the pay plans and that they can budget accordingly with no negative surprises. They don't walk on eggshells or change their behavior for a moody bi-polar boss, because he isn't that way. They are more willing to dream, and take risks, because they know what to expect. You get the picture. Consistency is the gel that wards off the dysfunction that is the hallmark of traditional, highly matrixed, authoritarian organizations.

Much has been written of late in an attempt to excuse inconsistency. We're gaslighted into believing that a leader's thinking has merely evolved or that we should think again about the importance of consistency. Some would have us believe that consistency is the hobgoblin of small minds. People that attempt to justify inconsistency are simply those who (A) are proven to be unreliable or (B) are responsible for defending an individual or constituency who has proven to be unreliable. Their best efforts notwithstanding, convincing others that doing the wrong thing is actually the right thing will forever be a hard sell. Best case: these people are speaking in an echo chamber of lost souls. See, there will never be a time when consistency is neither the right thing nor a required leadership trait.

What do you do to ensure you are consistent? What pains do you take to make certain that what you say aligns with what you actually do? The best technique I've ever found was to ask my people to catch me being inconsistent. There's no harder rebuke and no greater motivation to get it right next time.

I was able to use a series of external conversations to make the point to my team one Friday about consistency.

March 22, 2019

In the last several weeks, including three times this week alone,

I have had the opportunity to speak to a number of influential customers and industry insiders about the work we are doing here. The conversations all contain a number of nearly identical threads. Many of these individuals I have spoken to before. Each of them heard from me on previous occasions about what we are trying to accomplish here. Each of them shared with me their stories of prior challenges with us, and their skepticism that we could actually pull off what we say we hope to. In some cases, these people expressed full-on doubt that we are actually committed to change.

But as the months have gone by, and all of you have consistently delivered on the promises I have made, and as each of you have consistently sought to find new and better ways to serve our customers, and as this entire associate body has consistently, day in and day out, fought for the words we wrote down on our card,* something amazing has started to happen: the skeptics are starting to become fans; the detractors are becoming promoters; the departed are buying again; and the phone is ringing off the hook with people who want to come to work here. See, consistency begets credibility and credibility begets belief.

And that's the point for the week.

My father used to tell my three brothers and me that his hearing wasn't very good, but his eyesight was 20/20. He didn't care what I told him I was going to do, he cared what I actually did. And he rarely cared that I could do it once ... he only started believing when he saw the behavior start happening consistently, over and over again.

People are funny like that. What they experience consistently shapes their belief system. For us to show up and tell our customers in the industry about all of our tremendous plans would have meant precious little. What people expected to see was a consistent difference in the way we acted, performed and dealt with them. That they see this happening is driving results in our business as more and more people get on board with what we are trying to do. And that's a testament to all of you. And I can't tell you how much I appreciate it.

But it shouldn't stop there. Consistency matters in your homes and in your communities too. The more consistent you are, the more credibility you build. The more credibility you build, the more belief you can engender. And when you have more and more people believing in you, there is almost nothing you cannot accomplish as, like air beneath wings, the power of others' conviction in you lifts you to new heights you never even dreamed of

So, be consistent ...

And win.

˙The Card refers to a 6"x3" card given to all associates each year detailing, in common vernacular, each strategic imperative for the business on one side and the values the business stands for on the other.

* * *

One of the lines in my bio that I am proudest of says that I am equally at home in a board room or a service bay. I'm mostly proud of that because it's true. But I'm also proud of that because it didn't just happen. I grew up indoctrinated with the understanding that no one understands more about the work of an organization than the people doing it. I also believe that it is an absolute impossibility to manage that which you have never seen or done before. So, I have spent a significant amount of my career where the work is done, for much of it actually doing it myself. As a result, I understand things better and I have more credibility with the people doing the work – people who know, as a result, that I would NEVER ask them to do something I would not do myself.

One of the biggest mistakes made by most authoritarian command and control types is that they have not spent a day in their lives actually doing the work of their business. To do so would be beneath them. To them, it would be to touch "the great unwashed." The problem is, their people know it, and they resent it. And because of it, when Ken Doll goes out for a walk expecting others to follow, if he's not using fear or intimidation, he's out for a stroll by himself.

Leading others by practicing The Not So Subtle Art of Caring isn't hard. It's a simple matter of treating people with respect, of treating them in ways we'd want to be treated ourselves. That's why I don't ask people to do things I wouldn't do myself and believe strongly that being a great leader is not possible for those that do.

And it's not just me. In an interview with Authority Magazine, well known cybersecurity expert, Tony Cole was asked to list six leadership lessons businesses could learn from his 30 years of military cybersecurity experience. Number three on Cole's list was "Don't ask anyone to do anything you wouldn't do or haven't already done." (Quiocho, 2018) This from a career military officer, where command and control are prevalent. An admission that one of the six most important things a leader can do is to not ask people to do things they won't do themselves.

How much time do you spend where the work of your organization actually gets done? Have you ever done the work of your organization? Do you do the things you ask others to do?

For any leader this should be pure common sense. But you have to set aside time to be where the work gets done. If you don't make it a priority, it won't be a priority.

Once, I used a story about morning safety huddles which we performed in our very safe HQ building to make the point to 2,600 people in not so safe locations.

September 23, 2010

This week, I've gotten into the routine of the 8:00 a.m. safety and stretching huddle here at the General Office. The sessions are a great way to start the day – together. Like the huddles in the field, the time includes a review of prior day incidents, important safety reminders, and even a few laughs (though some jokes are funnier than others ... sorry Razorback fans, I really was kidding).

As we stretched this morning, what struck me most wasn't the focus on safety (though it and our goal of zero incidents per day remain our #1 priority) but that this team is living out an important life lesson. Folks in the GO are not asking anyone to do something they aren't willing to do themselves.

When rules and responsibilities apply to everyone, we win more.

That's the point for the week.

Being a leader has almost nothing to do with title or position. It's about how we act and what we do, not who we are. All of us are leaders, or can be – at work, at home, and in our communities.

Folks don't follow leaders because they have to. They do so because they want to.

Doing the things that we ask others to do is central to creating an environment that causes someone to voluntarily follow another.

When we lead by example, we implicitly send the message that we are all in this together and that achieving all we hope and dream for this company will require the full engagement and effort of every one of us. A willingness to do the things we ask others to do also helps break down barriers that exist between ourselves and those around us. When we participate in the work of our teams, we realize a greater understanding of their experience – we'll identify what is working, what isn't and what we need to be successful. Best of all, we'll create stronger bonds within our team – bonds that aren't easily broken by bad days, tough markets or our competitors.

Leadership is a matter of the heart. When everyone jumps in heart first almost nothing can stop us. It begins by showing the way and walking the talk.

Do what you ask others to do.

And win.

* * *

Most of you have probably watched the Robin Williams movie, *Dead Poets Society* or have seen a t-shirt, rock, mouse pad, plaque, pair of socks, or other memento with the words "CARPE DIEM" emblazoned thereon. The Latin for "Seize the Day" has become a staple of the motivational products industry. With good reason, I suppose. It's great advice. Seize the day. Grab every one of them by the, well, you know … make the most of every day. Live each one to the fullest.

It does happen to be a trait of great, caring leaders. Even David Gurteen, author of the book, *Conversational Leadership* says of Carpe Diem that "It is a philosophy that I think we should take more seriously." (Gurteen, 2020) I agree wholeheartedly.

It's related to being present, and to being wholehearted. But it is more than that. It includes a recognition that the only thing one has control over is now – today. Yesterday is gone. Tomorrow has not yet arrived. Today is all we truly have influence over. And so, the choice we have is to make the most of today, or not. As Seneca wisely saged, "We let go the present, which we have in our power, and look forward to that which depends on chance, and so relinquish a certainty for an uncertainty."

Winners make the most of today. True, caring leaders make the most of today. They care not one tinkers damn for what happened yesterday, because no amount of effort, crying, wailing, gnashing of teeth, or beating of other human beings will ever bring it back or change one thing about it. They care not about tomorrow, because no amount of any of the above will impact it one iota. What they have each day is their waking portion of 86,400 seconds to affect. That's all.

And so, they do, to the best of their God-given ability every day. Oh, and they recognize that at any point, in any day, when things start to head south, they have a choice: they can ride it down, or they can choose to restart their day at that very moment. One of the writers who has most influenced my life is C. S. Lewis. He said, "You can't go back and change the beginning, but you can start where you are and change the ending." Those who practice The Not So Subtle Art of Caring hit the restart button. And they win more often because they do.

So Carpe Diem. I actually can't believe I'm writing that. But, if you can't do any better than the Latin dudes, why try? I told you, I'm not here to gain notoriety by inventing something new for the sake of doing it. If it works, it works. Far be it from me to change it. Seize the day. And win.

Do you wake up each day intent on making the absolute most of it? Or do you let worries about things from the past or the future, each of which you have no control over, cloud your enthusiasm? Is your team oriented to maximize production from every single day? If not, why not? And what can you do, starting tomorrow, to fix that?

A story about experiencing the dead of winter in the middle of fall helped me encourage my team to seize the day.

September 10, 2009

This week I had the chance to help host a group of customers for a winter tire launch in Florida. Yes, you read correctly – winter tires in Florida, in September!

The event was held at Eglin Air Force Base's McKinley

Climatic Laboratory. This facility of 4.6 million cubic feet has the capability of creating – indoors – virtually any weather condition across a temperature range of minus 65 degrees Fahrenheit to plus 165 degrees.

Walking into the test chamber, I felt like a character in C. S. Lewis' *Chronicles of Narnia* as I stepped from a sunny 90-degree day into a winter wonderland of snow, ice and 15 degrees.

Beyond the mere marvel of it all, what I couldn't help but notice throughout the day was how participants and hosts alike pined for the opposite of their current climatic reality. When outdoors, many bemoaned the heat and humidity. When in the chamber, a longing for the sun prevailed.

Rather than make the most of each moment, many chose to pass the time wishing they were someplace else.

When we wish our lives away, believing that the grass is always greener on some other side, we rarely achieve happiness or our full potential.

That's the point for the week.

The shade of the grass beneath our feet has more to do with how we choose to see it than where we are standing.

When we choose to positively respond to any situation and seek to find the best in it, we'll be disappointed less and win more.

The key to getting the most from any situation is wanting to be in it. Any time spent wishing we were somewhere else is time we're not fully invested in our present situation – time we miss and won't ever get back.

Wringing all we can from life requires a firm hold on every minute of it.

Make the most of every situation.

And win.

* * *

Caring leaders step out of line. Wrapped up in this one attribute are a number of what I believe to be critically important traits: things like self-confidence, assertiveness, a dislike of the status-quo, and a willingness to act when required. Stepping out of line is all of those things.

If it hasn't become abundantly clear yet, caring leaders are not subtle. They are not shrinking violets. They challenge the status quo.

In 2019, I purchased a 1972 Volkswagen Super Beetle for the sole reason that it defied convention. I wanted to do something that challenged the conventional wisdom, that defied the status quo, that caused people to say, "He did what?!"

See, leaders lead. They pioneer. They walk out front. They break out of line and run over to dot the i. They do things that are memorable. And they do it without fear. Because they do things intelligently. They don't write checks they or their people can't cash. They don't make bets they can't cover. And those who practice The Not So Subtle Art of Caring don't call shots they can't hit.

But their people follow them because they unsubtly step out from the pack. They innovate. They break the mold. They offer a sense of excitement to workers sick and tired of the same old, safe vanilla garbage.

Leaders that do so are in rare company. A survey conducted by Harvard University of over 1,000 employees across the USA found that 42% said their leaders never or almost never challenge the status quo; 32% answered with a wishy-washy, "sometimes," and just 26% said often or fairly often. Just 3% said always. (Llopsis, 2017)

Like love and hope, this is because stepping out is visible, it creates discomfort. It gets the gossip mill flowing. But remember, in even one year, those people and what they say won't matter even a little bit. So stand up, step out of line, and set an example for winning.

The key, in my recommendation, is to pick out a few challenge points, deliver on them, then pick a few more and so on. Don't try, as is said, to boil the ocean with an abundance of fantastic new ideas, or ideas that are so far-fetched that you'll never implement them. Pick some things, again a few at a time, that bend your team but don't break them, finish them, then go on to the next few. Before you know it, you will be a certified "stepper-outter."

I used the story of buying that Beetle one day to make this very point.

August 30, 2019

This week I fell in love with a girl named Veronica. It's not what you're thinking. Veronica is a 1972 Volkswagen Beetle. I've been told that my love affair is inappropriate. That men like me don't fall in love with girls of her age. Girls like her are often referred to derogatorily, in ugly sexist terms. They are even fat shamed. Veronica is a Super Beetle, and it's not conventional to love Super Beetles. The world prefers convention; but progress almost never comes from convention. And that's the point for the week.

Those who stay in line rarely stand out. At the Ohio State University, a halftime staple is "Script Ohio" a treat where the band literally forms the word Ohio in cursive. Once the O, h, i and o are formed one member from a line of seemingly identical Sousaphone players trots out to dot the i. One member in a blur of scarlet and gray stands out and becomes memorable. Staying in line, following years old prescribed rules, will ensure that your position, and your view, will never change. It's not hard, It's not challenging, and It doesn't take a lot of courage to not defy convention. Keeping things the same is as easy as standing still. But protection of the status quo is actually a prescription for moving backwards, as those who defy convention are propelled past them by new ideas and innovative ways of doing things. These rebels, who look at everything and wonder if there might be a different way to do things, distinguish themselves from others – even if they are wrong as often as they are right. These outliers win more often, if only because they break away from the pack more often, into open lanes and clear air. It takes guts to stand out. It takes courage to do something different. But the rewards can be tremendous as you enter into and profit from new market spaces alone. What you do will become more desirable and more valuable – because it stands out. The same is true, and critical, for our business. Doing things the way we always have is a sure-fire way to lose in the marketplace. It's why you hear me talk about innovation so often. Unless we are defying convention, every one of us, in everything we do, we are giving up opportunities to differentiate and distance ourselves from our competitors. Bucking the trend can feel uncomfortable. But winning feels fantastic. And winning will improve the lives of everyone who works here. And in almost all cases, doing something differently takes no more effort than doing it the same old, boring way. And you can act on your own, without supervision. Even if Todd and I are traveling, you can still create forward momentum by defying the status quo completely on your own. So, step out of line.

And win.

* * *

One of the hardest things for anyone to do, leader of people or not, is to admit when we make a mistake. But if you are looking for one of the fastest ways to cement your credibility with your team, fess up to a failure. Conversely, failing to own up to one's mistakes will result in a huge loss of currency.

But it makes sense. The highest price tag is almost always

placed on that which is the rarest, or the hardest to produce. Diamonds for example are both. It's why they are so expensive. Admitting when we are wrong isn't far behind.

Chris McCloskey, writing for the Association for Talent Development says, "Admitting when you're wrong builds trust and shows integrity. Typically, when leaders realize they made a mistake, others have noticed, too. Leaders who then fail to admit they were wrong leave employees feeling as though their leaders consider being right more important than being honest." (McCloskey, 2016)

Humans have egos. Many leaders, coincident to their positions, have gigantic egos. It makes it even harder for the typical leader than for the average Joe or Jane to admit when they screwed up. It takes a big person to admit failure and ask forgiveness. But it's what true caring leaders do.

Those who practice The Not So Subtle Art of Caring know there is no upside in extending a mistruth. They know that chances are the truth is already well known, so any attempt to hide it would be foolish anyway. They know that bad news only ripens, then rots with age. They know that harm inflicted on human relationships gets worse in time, not better as resentment and other bad feelings grow. And because the true, caring leader cares more about their relationship with others than almost all else, they will endeavor to fix what is broken, sooner rather than later.

Blemishes on human relationships are like sicknesses of the heart. Though figurative, they are no less painful, no less costly, and no less deadly. The cure is simple. To admit fault and ask for forgiveness. While easy to say, but hard to do, there is almost no other single act which can have a greater impact on the level of trust between a leader and those who follow them than a willingness to own up to one's own shortcomings. The formula is simple too. It goes like this, "I'm sorry for what I did. I know I was wrong. I know when I act like that/do things like that/say things like that it makes you feel like _____. I hope you can forgive me. I promise to work very hard with your help not to let that happen again. I want to move on if you are ready."

I used a story about comments made by the former Governor of New Jersey to make this point not too long ago.

September 6, 2019

This week Chris Christie, former governor of New Jersey, in an interview on CNN, posited that one of the reasons for the utter inability of Democrats and Republicans to get along lies in the fact that we have "lost the ability to admit that we have made a mistake." The phenomenon was on full display in the past few days. While hurricane Dorian was irrevocably changing the lives of millions of human beings, President Trump was quintupling down on an assertion that Alabama was in the initial path of the storm – after the media pounced on the claim, causing Trump to dig his heels in rather than simply admitting he made a mistake. Because in today's culture, admitting error is to somehow admit you are less of a person. But where I come from, admitting you are wrong makes you the biggest dog in the fight.

And that's the point for the week.

Every day, every one of us will mess something up. In recorded history, there may have been only one perfect human being. Accordingly, the rest of us fail daily. When it happens, as with everything else in life we have a choice: to accept responsibility for the error, or not. Denial, obfuscation, sidestepping, blame-shifting and any other ploy designed to ensure that one does not have to admit fault are all the rage today. It's simpler to get out of the way of a problem than to stand in the gap and admit guilt.

Admitting fault is hard. Disappointing others is never fun. Having to fess up to the fact that you failed to accomplish something sucks. But almost always, when we fail, others already know it. So, our "confessions" are more like "confirmations." Denial simply makes us look ridiculous. Many of you know I collect old-fashioned desk plates; One says "Silence is better than BS." Most reasonably intelligent people can spot BS a mile away. So, saying nothing is preferable than concocting some story which places you away from the scene of your very own crime.

In accepting responsibility for your faults, you earn the respect of others. You also earn the opportunity to learn, not only what didn't go well, but what actually did, so that you won't make the same mistake twice. You earn the loyalty of those who follow you, who see you take the lumps versus passing them along. And you earn trust. Because there is almost no better way to destroy it than to run from mistakes that others already know you made. And all of these things: Respect; Learning; Loyalty and Trust – are the building blocks of winning teams. And they come not from getting out of the way of our mistakes, but fully standing behind them, holding our hand up, and saying, "I did it, and I'm going to work really hard to make sure it doesn't happen again."

So, admit when you made a mistake.

And win.

* * *

I'm not a big fan of firefighters. Not the kind that you are probably imagining. In fact, I owe a personal debt of gratitude to the men and women on the thin red line. I'm talking about the fire fighters in business and other organizations that always seem to be the first on scene in a crisis – hat on, axe in one hand, hose in the other, boots to the knees. These are the men and women who relish any opportunity to save the day, to swoop in, douse the flames, then go back to their day job – only after receiving the praise and adulation of their adoring fans. I want to wretch every time I see it happen. Because it tells me that it's endemic to the culture.

Forty years ago, in 1981, Robert Hayes writing in Harvard Business Review identified the issue. He said, "American managers actually enjoy crises; they often get their greatest personal satisfaction, the most recognition, and their biggest rewards from solving crises. Crises are part of what makes work fun ... however, a crisis is evidence of failure." (Hayes, 1981) Nineteen years later, in the same publication, business writers were still identifying this dysfunctional behavior as a problem.

Roger Bohn, writing for Harvard Business Review in the year 2000, said, "firefighting is one of the most serious problems facing many managers." (Bohn, 2000) But it didn't stop then.

Now, 21 years later, it's still going on. And it's still just as harmful. And just as ridiculous. See, firefighting does nothing to get at the root cause of the blaze. The best firefighters will eventually become expert arsonists, or at best, they will resist root cause correction efforts. People who thrive on chaos don't want the chaos to end.

Those who practice The Not So Subtle Art of Caring don't fight fires, they resolve today's issues today. They don't just fix problems or put out fires. They resolve issues. They get at the cause of the blaze, today, and make sure it never happens again. And as leaders, they do NOT reward firefighting. When firefighters come looking for adulation, they get a simple thanks and a charge to go find the cause of the fire.

Problems put off until tomorrow merely get bigger. A fire merely doused today will only burn hotter next time.

As a leader, putting off the resolution of an issue, or failing to get at the root cause of a problem only tells those in your organization that there is no urgency. That doing things right doesn't matter. That short term fixes are more important than getting to the bottom of things. But when the true, caring leader stops rewarding the firefighters, or better yet finds them new homes, and when he/she starts rewarding immediate and terminal resolutions to issues, the entire attitude of the business will change, instantly. But as long as the hats, and boots, hoses and axes are still in the locker room, the place is going to think it's OK. Whichever you demand and reward is what you will get in return.

Here's a letter I wrote after a plant visit a few years ago that helped make the point.

June 9, 2012

This week, I visited our plant in Danville, Virginia.

While there, I had a chance to meet many of our people, and view, firsthand, several examples of associate engagement and continuous improvement taking place on the floor. A couple stood out, both for different reasons.

In one, a Throughput Optimization Project (TOP) in the 7, 8, and 9 Banbury area, our team was engaged in a floor to ceiling reclamation effort, cleaning, sorting, and purging in order to ready their environment for improved process and flow. The team had multiple presentation boards covered with beautiful charts, pictures and text. At one point, a leader of the effort emerged, covered in carbon black, dirt, and grease, only two round circles of flesh visible behind his safety glasses. It was clear that the work being undertaken was hard, unpleasant, and waaaaay overdue.

In the other, I met an extruder operator who cares for his machine as if he owns it. He's religious about maintenance and cleanliness. In fact, his innovative and self-invented method of caring for his tread printer caused the printer vendor to remark recently that they'd never seen such a perfectly maintained machine in all of captivity.

In thinking about the two interactions, it occurred to me

that, for many, the extruder example wouldn't garner much attention in comparison to the highly visible and heroic effort going on back in the Banburies. But by quietly staying on top of things every day, our extruder operator is preventing the need for dramatic undertakings later. When we deal with today's problems today, they never grow up to be bigger ones.

That's the point for the week.

Each day of our lives, at work, at home, and in our communities, will present us with problems in need of solving. In those moments, we'll find ourselves presented with a simple choice: between attending to that which needs fixing or leaving it for another day. Winners emerge in these moments.

Often, their actions make them harder to spot. Attention to detail, adherence to process, and measured redress to small dust ups don't stand out much. These folks don't wear big red hats or run to and fro with hoses in hand drawing attention to themselves. People don't write songs about them. They simply go about, quietly and courageously, doing the right thing.

When we deal with issues, however uncomfortable, as they come, we'll accomplish more. We will do so for no other reason than we'll spend smaller amounts of time correcting things along our way rather than wasting huge chunks of it cleaning up large messes later.

As a result, we'll make exponential reductions in waste and loss as increasing numbers of others follow our example. We'll have more of everything to reinvest in our business and our people. Best of all, we'll leave all that we touch better than we found it. All because we chose to act the very minute after we saw a problem.

Many of us learn this the hard way. I have, and still do. But the wonder of life is that each day provides a brand-new opportunity for redemption, sometimes hidden, but always there, among a handful of choices between passing the buck or stepping up to it.

Deal with today's problems today.

And win.

* * *

Two of The Predictive Index's Top 10 Traits of Great Managers have to do with knowledge. According to TPI's 2018 survey, a great manager both "is highly knowledgeable in the area he/ she manages" and "has a good grasp of the entire business." (The Predictive Index, 2018) 75% of respondents mentioned both attributes as being most prevalent among over 1,500 leaders that more than 5,000 employees had identified as great. Nowhere on the list did respondents mention anything about height, looks, athleticism, extroversion, being demanding, being hard-charging or a handful of other attributes commonly identified by recruiters and boards of directors as predictive of success.

That's because those things have nothing to do with success.

Employees don't look for those things because they know that in actuality things like being knowledgeable about what is happening in the business truly matter and truly connect up to what the team is trying to accomplish.

So, if you are trying to gain credibility with those you have the privilege to lead, if you truly want to project a caring attitude, save some money on the spray tan, and spend some time learning about your business. That's what those who practice The Not So Subtle Art of Caring do.

How much do you know about your business? Can you credibly describe what each person in your organization actually does? Could you demo your product or service? Could you make a sales call unattended? You should be able to do all of these things. Knowing the numbers on a financial statement is NOT knowing a business; it's not even the first step. Start by meeting the people in your business and learning exactly what they do.

I used a story about one of my favorite boyhood literary characters, Tom Sawyer, to make this point again not very long ago.

July 24, 2020

I was painting this week. Not as an artist would, but things. Like doors, and trim.

I don't care much for painting. Imagine one of your least favorite things to do. For me, that's painting. I suppose maybe it's the pure repetition and sameness of it, or the having to be in one place of it. Whatever it is, I don't care for it.

I can't paint anything without thinking about Tom Sawyer. I loved to read Tom Sawyer as a kid. He didn't like to paint much either. It's why I think of him when I paint. If you recall, he was able to entice every boy in town to take turns painting his aunt's fence, three coats, on a nine-foot tall, thirty-yard long fence while he sat and watched. He was able to do so, starting with Ben Rogers, because he had a sort of charisma of knowledge. It was why the town boys followed Tom in most instances; he was, or seemed, knowledgeable to them. The boys didn't follow Ben, or Jim or Huck, because they were, well, dumb as rocks mostly. They followed Tom because he seemed to know a lot about a lot of things. Beginning with the fence ... by purporting that there was high art, skill and flourish involved in fence painting, and that not just anyone could paint a fence, he was able to convince a town full of boys to do his work – and pay him to do it! Tom's charismatic knowledge could be found throughout the novel, in descriptions of Pirate Islands and Robber Caves; he was forever saying things like, "you'll see that in any book" or "it's so in all the books." Boys followed Tom because he seemed to know a great deal. People like to follow people who they believe know what they're talking about.

And that's the point for the week.

To the rest of the boys in town, Tom was a smart one. He read books. He knew things. So they followed him. People are funny like that.

It's no longer good enough to get by on looks alone, or the ability to talk a good game, or even to trade on who you know. The current generation of worker, which now comprises more than half of the workforce wants to work for people that actually know what they are talking about. And it's about time.

Arguably many of the issues that have plagued American business in recent decades – from outright mismanagement to ethics violations to the me-too movement have been brought on by incompetent leaders who have been put in positions they were never qualified to be placed into in the first place. Positions they felt entitled to. Positions everyone but them knew they didn't deserve to begin with.

But when people have knowledgeable people to follow, quite a lot changes. Foremost, far better decisions are made, because those making them are better informed. People are treated better by knowledgeable leaders who, secure in themselves, are not prone to angry, Machiavellian outbursts like their insecure, over-their-head counterparts. Best of all, people learn from those more knowledgeable than them, which is really what leadership should be about in the first place.

Plus, when knowledgeable adults are in charge, they engender trust among those they serve, trust that binds humans together into one connected force, able to withstand greater difficulties and endure more prolonged hardship. And when knowledgeable adults are in charge, growth occurs which rockets the entire business forward, screaming past competitors still led by "charismatic" half-wits stuck in the belief that fear and intimidation are the best tools to move a reluctant workforce off the dime.

Be smarter than that. Be highly knowledgeable about what

you do.

And win.

* * *

So far, we've established guidelines for the caring leader to follow. We've set the foundation from which to operate. Then we defined the true character and charisma of the individual caring leader. We proved that true charisma is quite a bit different from what most of us have been brought up to believe it to be.

With a picture of the true leader securely in mind, now for someone to lead ...

Leaders, by definition, accomplish little by themselves. What they achieve they do through and with other people ... in groups ... called teams. Chapter 4 details the character of caring teams. We'll look at 10 traits and 10 behaviors that are highly predictive of success for caring teams. Traits and behaviors that I've seen enable real people and real teams to succeed for over 30 years. Turn the page, I'll tell you a story or two about them.

Chapter 4

The Character of Caring Teams

"To build a winning team it's essential to build a culture of caring."
Jon Gordon
1971-
American Author

Winning teams have character. In thinking about the character of a team, you can begin by thinking about its culture. But we're going to go well beyond the cultural traits that define a caring team. We're going to go all the way to defining the behaviors of caring teams. What is it that caring teams do that gives them character? What sets them apart from others? These are the questions and others we will answer in this chapter – in two parts, one dedicated to traits, one dedicated to behaviors.

At the start, I'd be remiss if I did not remind you that teams are, in large part, a reflection of those who lead them. So, while we will, for the most part, be describing the character of great teams, it's impossible to do so without remembering that great teams are led by great leaders and caring teams are likewise led by caring leaders. So, the character of team and leader, for better or for worse, are inextricably linked. Show me a great caring team, and I'll show you a great caring leader. In this chapter, I'll show you how a few of them got that way.

So, what is it about winning teams that sets them apart from others? In my experience, there is no silver bullet or secret sauce. No one thing. As you will see throughout this chapter, there are a host of both traits and behaviors that facilitate team success. There is, however, one fundamental requirement for any team to have any hope of achieving any later goal or objective. Without it, teams accomplish nothing. That is the step one requirement of having the right people in the right roles willing to perform the function(s) required of them.

The emphasis is on willingness, NOT capability. Hire for attitude and desire, not aptitude. If you mix a bunch of in it for themselves, prima donna, A players, thinking raw talent will push you over the line, you will be sadly disappointed. Hire more for what's in someone's heart than what's in their head. Align what matters to you with what matters to the people you hire by matching up what's important to you with what's important to them.

And the best way to find out what's important to people? Just ask them. Ask them about work they did in their prior position. Ask them what the purpose of their role was, what the goal was, and what made them want to win. Then ask them to describe one setback and what happened. If you get a bunch of I/me language, you can end the meeting right then. Trust me. If you are sitting across from Mighty Mouse, boldly shouting, "Here I come to save the day!" as if he or she is there to save you from yourselves, you are in for a world of headaches and worse. Do not hire for talent and bold self-confidence. Confidence is NOT a leadership trait. Hire competent people who are coachable, love winning on teams, and who have a deep burning desire to be part of something bigger than they are. How will you know? Just ask.

But having such table stakes is not enough. I am ever amazed by the popularity of books from academics or those who, as I'm fond of saying, "never sold anything in their life" that promise overwhelming team success in 5 easy steps, or, perish the thought, by focusing on a single attribute. For example, if we as leaders just remember to say thank you more, we'd have it licked. There's a whole book on it. But it's never that simple. To paraphrase the great Woody Hayes, longtime football coach at the Ohio State University, "*Nothing good comes easy.*" Anything worth having requires hard work and a significant investment of time, emotion, and talent. Creating a true caring team that wins consistently is no exception.

Remember that teams are made up of people. As such, they are living breathing things. They are not its, they are theys. They have feelings, emotions, consciences, the capability to think and act, and abilities to choose and decide. It is important as a leader, that you recognize this, and approach them accordingly. You are caring for a living thing. When you change your mindset, and think about the teams you lead in this way, you will care for them differently – because you have to. Because when you know what truly drives success with teams, you'll rethink how you spend your time.

More than half of what drives team success will come from the formation of the team itself – who you pick, and where you put them. It's why I overstressed step one. The next 25% or so of your team's odds of winning will come from the behaviors and traits you teach them. That is the focus of this chapter – the 20 things that form the character of winning, caring teams. The last bit of winning, and it's not much, will come from what you as a leader actually do during the fight if you will. The active coaching, leading, communicating, directing, etc. So, the importance of getting the foundation right – having the right people exhibiting the right traits and behaviors – is critically important.

So, what do these winning, caring collections of people do? Of all the things I've watched teams do, and coached teams to do in 30+ years of leading people to win, I've picked 20 items that I think matter more than anything else. These 20 items are those that become foundational characteristics of great teams. I say foundational because these are items that leaders coach teams to exhibit early on then constantly thereafter.

These are not technical skills. In my role as a leader, I have always made certain, back to the steps above, that our organizations were staffed with grown adults who knew how to do their jobs. For example, you won't find, "Great teams are Microsoft Excel black belts." That's for two reasons: (1) An Excel spreadsheet never added one dollar of gross profit to any company ever in the recorded history of mankind and (2) If Excel skills are a technical requirement of a position, leaders should ensure that anyone who gets put in the position is conversant in Excel sufficient to perform the duties of the role.

Also, these are not individual skills per se. Individual leader traits have been covered elsewhere. These traits and behaviors apply to the collective of the team. They reflect the sum total of the behavior of every individual on the team. Put another way, the character of the team is defined by the predominant traits and behaviors of the members who comprise it. For example, if the preponderance of the team engages in unethical behavior, in describing the character of the team one would include "lack of integrity" as a descriptor. As a specific example, after repeated examples of undeniable targeting calls against its defensive players, more and more people are beginning to assign words like "dirty," "thuggish" and "bush league" to the character of a certain high-profile ACC team's defense. For a quick examination of your team's character, just watch how your people behave.

Following are the 20 traits and behaviors I value most and spend my time reinforcing and coaching around. I've broken them into their two parts – Traits and Behaviors. I have placed a star next to six that I believe should be woven into individual performance management objectives based on an assessment of the team. As individuals contribute to the team, they should be rewarded or not based on the team's progress in achieving cultural and character-based goals/objectives. If you are going to seek to drive results as a team, you need to measure and reward both results and leadership traits/behaviors equally.

Part I - The Traits of Great, Caring Teams

1. Believe
2. Know Why They Are Here ★
3. Play to Win ★
4. Stand for Something
5. Help Each Other ★
6. Watch Out for Each Other
7. Value Speed
8. Are Resilient ★
9. Can Win Without Their Leader
10. Act World Famous

Part II - The Behaviors of Great, Caring Teams

1. Act as One Team, Chase One Number
2. Cheer for Each Other, Not Against Each Other
3. Defend What is Ours
4. Communicate, Communicate, Communicate ★
5. Have Rhythm
6. Learn Continuously
7. Do the Little Things Well
8. Innovate ★
9. Do Epic Stuff
10. Celebrate

On the following pages I've included a letter for each of these traits and behaviors as an example of how I communicated about each of these things to real people on real winning teams in the past. Prior to each, I've also provided a short introduction to give some additional context to each letter as well as some ways for you to make these things actionable in your real life.

As you read through each, think about ways each trait is or isn't present and working in your life as a leader. If it's not part of who you are as a leader, ask yourself why. If it's an area you want to realize improvement in, make a plan to do so. Write it down. Without a resolution to drive change, nothing will happen.

As always, the first step is to Believe.

Chapter 4, Part I

The Traits of Great, Caring Teams

Winning, caring teams believe. Foremost, they believe they can accomplish the goals they have written down for themselves.

Every time winning teams take the field, which in business is every day, (and remember, every day means every day) they do so with a firmly held belief that they will prevail. When teams practice The Not So Subtle Art of Caring, there is zero doubt in the mind of any member of the team that the objective which has been set for the team can or will be achieved.

It is never acceptable for any member of the team to utter the words, "that's not my number" or any other such statement of disbelief. Whenever sentiments like these rear their heads, the organization needs to be self-policing to nip them in the bud.

None of this means that any leader or any member of these teams is blind to, a Polly Anna about, or purposely ignorant to hardship or other obstacles that may impact their ability to hit their goals. To the contrary, they are fully aware of these issues. However, they have worked to find alternate routes to their destination over, under, around or through these impediments and simply refuse to be kept from achieving what they set out to do.

By creating a culture of belief, an organization creates a sense of confidence in one another, and in the overall team that enables them to rise to heights they might never have imagined. According to Amy Morin, contributor to Forbes, "When people believe in themselves, their team members, and their organization as a whole, they can accomplish incredible feats." (Morin, 2017) It's because the team represents something bigger than themselves, something far stronger, and more powerful; something that says, "get the heck out of OUR way, we don't stop for anything."

Have you created a culture of belief? Does your team believe they can accomplish anything they set their minds to do? Do they know that you believe in them? Do they know that you are not the most important thing in your life? If you answered no to any of these questions, what are you waiting for?

A story about a man from tiny De Soto, Missouri who wasn't aware he was supposed to lose was a beautiful backdrop for a lesson on belief.

April 8, 2009

This week I had an opportunity to travel to Potosi, Missouri, headquarters of Purcell Tire. To get to Potosi from St. Louis, one must drive through DeSoto. DeSoto is a small whistle stop town of some 2,600 souls. Purcell Tire has a store in DeSoto. The store is situated alongside the tracks, downtown. There isn't much downtown anymore. What growth there is in DeSoto is among a string of big box plazas outside of town. It seems you have to want to go downtown.

For years, the DeSoto store was a perennial loser. Until Chuck White came along. Now DeSoto is a moneymaker. See, no one told Chuck he couldn't make money in DeSoto. Chuck never believed that he couldn't make money in DeSoto. In fact, he believed he could.

He began by changing his environment. He painted and remodeled – with minimal expense. Then he organized to win. He hired an excellent team, trained on processes, held all associates accountable, and told them they could win.

And then he did.

Here's the point for the week. Or points, maybe.

First, if anyone tells me that their territory, location or environment keeps them from making money, I won't believe it. If you can win in downtown DeSoto, you can win anywhere.

But the big point is this, one you've heard from me before ... Winning starts with believing you can.

Whether you think you are a winner or think you are a loser, you're right. I learned that from another one of my heroes, a man named Charlie Plumb.

Changes to your environment or those around you certainly help as well.

But the first step in winning is a belief that you can.

Be like Chuck. And Charlie. Believe.

And win.

* * *

Long before someone made finding your why popular, I started talking to those I had the privilege to lead about knowing why you're here. It is, in fact, one of my rules for life. Every organization has, or should have, a purpose or goal, which it employs people and capital in the pursuit of each day. It's the reason the doors are unlocked, and the lights are turned on each morning. I promise you the CEO of your company knows what it is (or should). Every other person in the company should know what it is too. The purpose is why everyone shows up every day. It's the destination. It's the place that, when arrived at, everyone's lives improve (right?). It's why you and everyone else are there. It's what drives those who practice The Not So Subtle Art of Caring.

So, for anyone, from the chief of the company to the person hired five minutes ago in Des Moines, knowing why you are there is no more complicated than knowing that number and then determining exactly how what you do fits into the delivery of that number. If the people in your organization cannot do that, you have work to do. The good news is, it's not hard. You can tell them the number, they can help you understand how what they do fits in; because no one knows what they do better than them, not a living soul.

Can everyone on your team tell you why they are there? If not, get to work.

Once accomplished, the organization will start moving forward as a bloc. It will find and form connection points you never dreamed of that strengthen over time creating a nearly unassailable force that can weather any downturn or cycle simply because everyone knows their why. This gives the organization the feeling that everyone is in it together and is on the same page. According to Dan Hoppen of Quantum Workforce, "when everyone understands how their work is contributing to the organization's main goals, bonds form as everyone works together." (Hoppen, 2018)

Winning, caring teams know why they are there.

December 3, 2010

Last weekend, while watching an impressive Razorback victory unfold, I found myself, again and as usual, energized, amazed, and encouraged by the 60 second celebrations of personal achievement known as Nike ads. As I considered the ad and the company, I found, as you might imagine, a lesson, waiting to be shared.

Nike has not always been Nike. After a decade in business, the company incorporated as *"Blue Ribbon Sports"* (I know, boring, right?) changed its name to Nike, for the Greek goddess of victory (not boring). The new name served as a reminder to all associates of the larger purpose of the organization – to win.

What Phil Knight, founder of Nike, knew implicitly was that winning begins with an understanding of and commitment to purpose. Winning is facilitated by individuals who know why they are here.

That's the point for the week.

Not coincidentally, one of the rules for life you've heard me refer to is to "Know Why You are Here."

Today, the front and rear doors of 1000 S. 21st Street in Fort Smith, Arkansas were both adorned with small vinyl letters identifying the building as the Wingfoot Field Service and Support Center.

This subtle name change, and the letters on our doors which declare it, is designed to remind everyone in Fort Smith why we are here – to support our customers and the folks who take care of them. Without our customers we wouldn't be here.

This positive change is NOT intended to be, nor should it be allowed to become, an example of symbolism over substance. If anything, it is symbolism behind substance. It's the first step in a declaration of our purpose – why we are here.

To me, winning is facilitated when every member of a team completely understands why they are here and what is required of them for this team to succeed.

What's in a name? Nothing, unless and until every associate believes in and buys into what we are trying to accomplish.

It's about the customer. It's about ensuring that every one of them would recommend us to a friend or colleague.

When that happens, we'll win – by creating a customer and associate base who wouldn't want to go anywhere else.

When each of us arrives here each day with a complete understanding for what it is we are trying to accomplish, we will create real and sustainable competitive advantage, true fuel for the growth that we all want so much for our company and ourselves.

So, know why you are here.

And win.

* * *

Great, winning, caring teams play to win.

It's part of knowing why they are there. But it is fundamental to greatness. Great teams understand that the objective in any game where score is kept is to win. Period. These teams, those that practice The Not So Subtle Art of Caring, have days of mourning when they lose. In those rare events, they hold after action reviews to determine what went wrong and they take steps to ensure it won't ever happen again. These teams do not have members who befriend their competitors. They believe their competitors are not entitled to any business. They have a deep dislike for these people and wake up each day intent on putting them out of business.

They are 100% committed to winning the right way and will never sacrifice their integrity to do so. But losing is always viewed as a failure to keep their word.

While not a given, playing to win assumes your team has a winning proposition, the systems to support winning, and as mentioned earlier, the table stakes requirement of the right people in the right roles (capabilities) to win. You must further know precisely where you will win and how – and have the metrics in place to know whether you are. Assuming you do …

The play to win attribute is more centrally a mindset within the team that fully defines your approach to the game: never giving up, never giving in, running through the tape, never playing not to lose. It is a description of the behavior of the team; of relentless pursuit of winning from gun to gun, month in and month out. As researchers from the Motivation Science Center at Columbia University put it, "Promotion-focused people see their goals as creating a path to gain or advancement and concentrate on the rewards that will accrue when they achieve them. They are eager and they play to win. You'll recognize promotion-focused people as those who are comfortable taking chances, who like to work quickly, who dream big and think creatively." (Halvorsen, 2013)

Recent generations have devalued winning in the belief that losing is damaging to the fragile psyches of young people. I don't buy it. Business is a game in which score is kept. Your competitors are entitled to exactly ZERO share. They are not your friends. Your people should be taught to take everything from them and to play to win in every instance. Have you built a wolf culture or a sheep culture? Is your team trained to win? Or to lose?

Caring, winning teams go for two. Yours should too.

December 14, 2018

Last night the Los Angeles Chargers beat my adopted Kansas City Chiefs, on the road, on a last second play to win by 1.

The point of this week's letter isn't about not giving up – although it could be. It isn't about every part of the team having to do their job (as in the Chiefs actually playing defense once in a while) – although it could be. It isn't about believing then accomplishing something that everyone said couldn't be done – although it could be. Nope. It's about what happened after the Chargers scored their final touchdown.

They went for two.

Not satisfied to kick the PAT to tie the score, and head to overtime, LA played to win. And they did. See, the Chargers understand that when you play to win, sometimes you won't, but more often you will.

And that's the point for the week.

The competition isn't expecting us to play to win. Andy Reid and the Chiefs weren't expecting the Chargers to play to win. That's why Philip Rivers found a wide-open receiver in the end zone to complete the two-point conversion and win the game. We will play to win, and we will, win.

We will play to win by doing everything better than our competitors. By ensuring that we never prioritize cost over quality. That our performance products are invented here and help people go faster than anybody in the business. That our policies are developed to make our customers' lives easier, not ours. That we aggressively seek to take business from our competitors every day. That the people who work here are safer, faster, friendlier, more creative, more accommodating, more competitive and hungrier than anyone in our industry. This is what playing to win looks like.

It looks like 80 people working hard every day to make sure that our brand forevermore stands for quality, speed and innovation. And that we never forget that – not for one second of one minute of one day. Because that's playing to win.

So, play to win.

And (we will) win.

* * *

Winning, caring teams, those that practice The Not So Subtle Art of Caring, stand for, and are known for, something. As a leader, YOU have to know what that is, then every single person in your organization needs to know what that is. Even if it is something that you are not known for yet, but want to be, that's OK. You need to be clear about what it is, then talk about it, a lot. What you are known for is what will put the swagger in the step of every person who works in your organization. It's what fuels the pride in your team. Think about Nike, mentioned earlier. Nike is known for bringing inspiration and innovation to every athlete in the world. Starbucks, for inspiring and nurturing the human spirit – one person, one cup and one neighborhood at a time. These are not cheesy three sentence mission statements that get written by the executive team and a paid facilitator at an off-site meeting at a Ritz Carlton then hung all over hell's half acre in lovely frames for no one to read while the CEO mentally checks the box on, "Yep, got a Mission Statement."

Nope. These are statements of identity. What these people want to be known for. Think of it this way. If tour team died tomorrow, what would you want written on its tombstone? Here lies your team. It stood for _____. Write it down. Hang it up. Believe in it and fight for it. (By the way if you have cheesy three sentence mission statements framed all over your building, take them down – unless everyone there knows the thing by heart. Otherwise, people make fun of those, and no leader needs that.)

In a recent stop, I helped our team determine that we needed to stand for three simple things, things that resonated with our customers and the wider industry. They were quality, speed and innovation. So, we wrote them down and said these are the things we want to stand for, then we said it over and over and over again until everyone could repeat it back to us including our customers, the trade and our suppliers. We were standing for something and it put a zip in our step.

April 19, 2019

Earlier this week another of our leaders and I took a field trip to a well-known vehicle customization house in greater LA to discuss opportunities to work together. Afterwards, I shared a brief post about our visit on Instagram. One of our followers immediately began speculating about how radical our build might get. You see, the custom shop is well known for unusual and statement builds. You think of the shop, you think "Wow." Nearly every successful enterprise has that one positive attribute that is immediately associated with them whenever their name is thought of or mentioned.

And that's the thought for the week.

You hear Nordstrom, you think extraordinary customer service. You hear Rolex, you think finest timepieces in the world. FedEx, and you think worldwide leader in overnight deliveries. Being excellent at something for a sustained period of time earned these companies their reputations.

Likewise, companies can earn reputations for incredibly negative outcomes too. Such examples aren't hard to think of either. The trick is simply to declare your intention to join the positively memorable camp and to refuse to ever accept negative infamy.

This can and should be true in all aspects of your lives, but it is absolutely true here.

We are now firmly fixated on quality, speed, and innovation. Likewise, we will rabidly defend a culture of winning and mutual respect. When these things become the outcomes sought by every person who works here for every other person who works here, every customer who buys here, every vendor who sells here, every end user who gets a part here, or every individual who interacts with us in any way, we will become known for these things – and we will more often win.

Because that's the way life works.

At Nordstrom, every associate didn't become committed to customer service because they were winning and life was good. Nope. When every associate committed to customer service, Nordstrom started winning and life got good.

I want us to be known for something positive. I want us to be known for Quality, Speed, and Innovation. I want us to be known for promoting a culture of Winning and Mutual Respect. And when every one of us commits to these things, we will.

So, do the right things to be known for the right things.

And win.

* * *

Great, caring teams help each other.

For this to ever occur, teammates must be highly connected and operate in an environment of trust and mutual respect.

These are cultural features of teams that require not only time but invitation, education, demonstration, communication, and zero negotiation expectation from the leader to effect within their organization. For the adoption of cultural features like these, people can be plotted along an axis, with say, "I trust until you give me a reason not to" on one end, and, "I will not trust you until you give me a reason to do so" on the other. As with anything else in life, a bell curve (normal distribution) will form. The leader must then, over time create conditions to enable these cultural features to thrive while stomping out impediments to their progress and removing from the building human obstacles to their complete adoption. The goal is to push the distribution of the curve to the right while chopping off the left-side tail. Only when human beings are fully connected, fully trusting and fully respecting will they fully help each other.

But once they do, the full power of multiplication will be available. Once humans start helping each other, they become intrinsically aligned. Each takes on the power of many, failure becomes rare, and the process becomes self-sustaining and factorial in its growth.

This goes well beyond teamwork. This is about The Not So Subtle Art of Caring. For most, teamwork is defined as a process of orchestrated contribution where each team member completely buys into the process then fully executes his or her part in a plan, performing their role with maximum effort. Helping one another goes beyond the bounds of mere teamwork. Teamwork represents interconnectivity; a culture of help represents interchangeability which is often spontaneous and transparent even to the leader. It happens because the leader speaks about it in terms that transcend teamwork. It steps past the organizational framework and becomes personal. People helping people, motivated more by love for one another, and a concern for each other's well-being than the achievement of a number.

But fear not, they will deliver the number, because they care too much not to. If you build a culture founded on individuals who trust and help one another, your team will deliver extraordinary results. I've lived it for 35 years. And I'm not alone. According to a study published in the journal Academy of Management, "When team members are motivated to help others, even at the expense of their own performance, their teams perform better." (Hu, 2014)

How have you encouraged your team to help each other? How can you create opportunities which require your team members to rely on one another more?

I used a story about my hero Moses to contribute to my own culture of help more than a decade ago.

October 22, 2010

At mass this Sunday, I'm sure not so coincidentally, I heard the story of Moses and the battle of Rephidem – against Amalek. So, here's the set up. The Amelekites show up and without provocation, attack Israel. Israel fights back. It is discovered that as long as Moses holds his arms in the air, his staff held high, Joshua, the leader of the Israelite army, smites the enemy. But whenever his arms would fall, so would Joshua's fortunes in the fight. As the battle rages on, we can only imagine that Moses' arms would tire, what with holding his staff above his head and all. So, Aaron and Hur are called upon to help keep Moses' tired arms aloft. And, as such, the battle was won by nightfall.

My moral of this story is that victory is always achieved through the participation of many, not one. No one can do it alone.

And that's the point for the week.

In any endeavor, we win more when we enlist the help of others. Odds always improve with numbers. With more hands on the rope, work becomes easier and is accomplished faster. Working shoulder to shoulder to accomplish great things accelerates trust and the formation of lasting human bonds.

These are truths that seem self-evident – so simple that children understand them intuitively. So, why is true teamwork so rare?

For children, asking for help comes easy. But somewhere around our 12th or 13th birthday, we are finally and fully indoctrinated into adult-thinking which seems to suggest that asking for help is a show of weakness. It isn't. Asking for help is a recognition of the fact that in addition to our strengths we have weaknesses. It is help from others that not only compensates for our shortcomings but adds exponentially to our strengths as well.

It really is true that a cord of many strands is not easily broken.

When we choose not to work as a team, we will almost assuredly lose.

The same is true in our tire selling life. When we ask for help and return the favor by assisting others, we combine the talents, energy and dreams of 2,500 associates. Doing so, we will accomplish great things. We will form a force too great for our competitors to overcome. We will hit our marks more because when one individual or group on our team is down others will pick them up. We will create a more positive culture that is not only the envy of others but one that is enduring and self-sustaining.

Help each other.

And win

* * *

Caring, winning teams look out for each other and take care of one another.

Once teams are fully connected, trusting and mutually respectful of one another, the true, caring leader must insist that they look out for one another. That's because a leader, no matter how energetic cannot be everywhere at once. People make mistakes every day. I do. It's the way we were made. To reinforce that point, I remind others often that in all of recorded world history, only one person was perfect. I then rhetorically ask, "You know how that ended, right?" I then suggest that we seek no part of perfection. But it's true that we are not perfect. It's also true that the pursuit of perfection is dumb, the prospect for death by crucifixion notwithstanding. But that's been covered elsewhere. But because we will all make mistakes every day, we need others around us to look out for us when we are about to fail and to pick us up when we do.

Teams that look out for each other are faster, safer, and higher functioning. As a result, they win more often, and they are significantly more profitable. What's more, they have far fewer grievances, less turnover, and fewer incidences of employee vs. employee conflict. Michael Hyatt, CEO of leadership consulting firm Michael Hyatt & Co, sums it up perfectly, "I believe your teammates are your most important priority. If you take care of them, they will take care of everything else." (Hyatt, 2020) It is a simple matter of watching out for and over others, ensuring that they do things safely and that they don't make decisions that will be harmful to their physical, economic, or emotional security.

Getting there, practicing The Not So Subtle Art of Caring, is no harder than demanding that you do and refusing to accept anything less. Push the curve to the right and chop off the left-side tail. Talk constantly about it. Tell folks, in the context of your business what it looks like and ask for it. Model the behavior. Catch people doing it and reward them. Often, it's as simple as one associate seeing another about to perform an unsafe act and telling them to stop. It's a simple matter of human protecting human, motivated by love and care. When you've arrived, you will know it. Someone will tell you without telling you by looking out for you one day. So pay attention for that; when someone catches you before a fall, you will know that what you are doing is working.

A TV commercial was enough to remind me to make this important point a few years ago.

March 25, 2011

This week I watched a Liberty Mutual commercial, again, for the first time.

You've probably seen it, or one of the other two like it. The spot begins and ends with a woman grabbing a distracted stranger's arm before he steps into a busy intersection. In between is a series of vignettes of people helping others in simple, everyday ways. In each, a third person observes the act of kindness then turns up as the performer of the good deed in the next scene. The cycle continues until we see the woman from the first scene observing an act of charity just before the initial scene is repeated at the end of the spot.

Implicit is a sort of "pay it forward" theme which suggests that one good turn begets another.

I say that I saw the commercial again for the first time as, in each prior viewing, I focused more on the contagious nature of courtesy - the truth that individuals who see others acting in responsible ways are likely to act accordingly when given their own chance to choose between doing the right thing or doing nothing at all.

This time, though, I was struck by the first (and last) scene and others in between which portrayed strangers looking out for others, preventing them from doing something hurtful.

These actions, which in and of themselves required almost no effort and occurred in scarcely more than the blink of an eye, prevented others from suffering significant emotional, physical or financial harm.

The smiles on the faces of the helpees AND helpers were unmistakable.

The best reason to look out for others, though, isn't the personal satisfaction we'll feel inside but because we keep bad things from happening.

That's the point for the week.

At work, at home, and on the streets of our cities and towns we are presented with opportunities each day to choose between looking out for others or looking away from them.

When we rise to the occasion presented by impending doom, we change lives.

We alter events in time, stepping in to prevent inevitable pain, heartache, and loss.

It matters little whether we know the potential victim or not. Familiarity is not the principal justification for courage. A deep, abiding desire to spare others from harm, however, is.

By looking out for others, we produce bonds as strong as any found in human relations. Such is the glue that holds high performing teams together. Far beyond a mere sense of obligation or debt, these ties are based in trust, care and love. Accordingly, they are nearly impossible to break.

Combined across organizations - businesses, families and charities alike - these bonds form a shield of sorts, a barrier to dread behind which objectives are more quickly met, waste is all but eliminated, and life is more fully lived on the right, safe side of history

Look out for others.

And win.

* * *

Winning teams are focused on speed.

When I was with the team in Fort Smith, AR, I would tell

them that, like Dr. Pepper, we had become nimble enough that we could make a decision by 10:00 am, know by 2:00 pm if we had screwed something up, and have it fixed by 4:00 pm. It was because we placed a priority on speed. There are 86,400 seconds in one day. No competitor in a space can add more or take any away. Those who find ways to do more within those 86,400 seconds by being quicker will tend to win more. Speed is an absolute competitive advantage. Teams that make speed an identifying trait win more often. Execution is still critical. You cannot be fast and wrong. That's no better than being slow and right. But when you combine executional excellence with the competitive advantage of speed, the results can be mancentifical. In a study of more than 51,000 leaders, Zenger Folkman found that "those leaders rated highly at doing things both fast *and* right had a 96 percent probability of being an extraordinary leader." (Zenger, 2016) It's the ampersand again. It's both. You can't do OK work fast, or great work slow; it must be great work done fast.

The probability is likewise high that the biggest impediment to going fast are what I call human bottlenecks. These are not always the slowest person on the team. These are often the person who gets in the way of progress. Those who create needless steps in processes. Those who require antiquated or unnecessary approvals. Those who hold out for the perfect that never arrives. Or those who are purposely sabotaging you.

People like to go fast. Most love the idea of being first. When, in the practice of The Not So Subtle Art of Caring, you speak to people using wind in the hair, and crossing the finish line, head extended and arms back analogies, they love it. People want to win. No reasonable person, except for the 5% of truly deranged psychopaths like those who derail their own teammates, wants to lose, or go slow. No one wakes up and looks in the mirror and says, "I can't wait to go slow today" or "lose today." So, your biggest problem will never be slow people. It's going to be human bottlenecks. Find them, remove them, and win.

Ask yourself, who are my human bottlenecks? It could even be you. Regardless, isolate them and get them out of the way.

June 14, 2019

This week I was reminded of the classic episode of *I Love Lucy* where Ethel and Lucy were working in a chocolate factory. Their job was to take pieces of candy off a conveyor belt, wrap them and put them back on the belt. At first, all was fine, until the speed of the conveyor increased, then things went terribly wrong. Lucy and Ethel fell behind. Chocolates began slipping by unwrapped. The two started stuffing chocolates in their mouths and their apron pockets. They became the bottleneck in the process.

Regardless of the speed desired by the chocolate factory manager, with Lucy and Ethel as human bottlenecks, that speed would never be achieved. As humorous as this situation was on TV, in real life, human bottlenecks aren't funny.

And that's the point for the week.

Human bottlenecks can manifest themselves in many ways. Sometimes they are folks who take on too much and never get anything done. Sometimes it's the guy who's impossible to work with. Sometimes it's the associate who goes through life at a snail's pace, or the teammate who refuses to admit they don't know how to do their job. Often, it's someone who is working hard, but on all the wrong things; someone not living The Card. But in every case, the common denominator is this: these human bottlenecks impede progress and frustrate those around them who are committed to moving forward with speed.

We can all be a bottleneck occasionally. I've even recognized myself as one from time to time. The key is to know when it happens and fix it – fast.

Bottlenecks kill efforts to create speed. Imagine three lanes of traffic narrowing to two ... the process actually moves slower than two lanes normally would. And it's wasteful. That's the bottleneck effect. The fewer bottlenecks we have, the faster we will go, the less waste we will create, and the better morale will be – all because we removed roadblocks to our success – human roadblocks, who often weren't intending to stand in the way in the first place.

So, don't be a roadblock.

And win.

* * *

Caring, winning teams are resilient.

Included in resilience is courage. It's a recognition also that not every day will be easy. That life will include trial, hardship and failure. But the hallmark of winning teams, is not only acceptance of that fact, it is a resilience to the difficulties themselves, and an ability to roll right on past them. According to Fast Company, "Challenges are inevitable in any organization—whether they're an early-stage startup or an established industry heavyweight, and whether they employ 20 people or 1,000. For companies to maintain high-performance and well-being, they need to have resilient teams." (Davis-Laack, 2019) Winning teams, like the men and women that lead them persevere. They are not dissuaded by setbacks. They see them as opportunities to learn and grow, and often to create competitive advantage and to place distance between them and whoever happens to be in second place.

And winning teams persevere as one. When bad things happen, they do not look to blame a part of their team. As any portion of the team goes, so goes the whole – for better or for worse.

As suggested above, it begins with the leader. When the leader shows resilience, so will the team. When the leader refuses to give up, the team will, likewise refuse to quit. The foundation of resilient teams is, you guessed it, TRUST. Without trust, resilience is impossible. As a leader, model and build trust and resilience will follow. And communicate in word pictures about resilience; tell your team what resilience looks like and what you expect. Finally, take opportunities before things go wrong to boost the confidence of your team; tell them a lot that you are proud of them, that there's no one besides them that you'd want to walk into a fight with.

When in the practice of The Not So Subtle Art of Caring, you build a resilient team, there's very little you won't be able to do.

How resilient is your team? Will they fight through adversity? Or do you get weather reports and other excuses when numbers are missed? What example are you setting for never giving up?

A story from an actual story was perfect for setting a tone from the top on resilience.

June 6

Last week I read a novel called *Out Stealing Horses*.

It is the story of an old man who has retired alone to a cabin in rural Norway recalling a summer with his father along a river near the Norway-Sweden border. Near the end of the book, the man, named Trond, remembers falling from a horse while on a ride with his father. What Trond's father said to him at that moment was unforgettable.

"Just let it sink, Trond," he said. "Just leave it. You can't use it for anything."

I stopped reading for a moment, then. It seemed to me, at once, that this was a way of saying, "shake it off, son", not unlike something our fathers might say to us after a fall from a swing or a bike. A bit like our dad's telling us to "Rub a little dirt on it."

But there was more to it. Trond's father's advice went beyond ignoring the physical hurt. It was more about the emotional hurt and the uselessness of carrying it forward.

There's good advice here for us.

In the course of our work-a-day lives bad things are going to happen. We will fail trying. Customers and our fellow associates may bruise us. It's important to let it go.

Here's the point for the week.

Carrying around emotional baggage is a useless endeavor that serves only to weigh and slow us down.

This is a difficult economy. As we drive to continue taking share some of what we will do will work. Some of it won't. Some things haven't. How we deal with these small failures says more about us than the failures themselves.

This team is winning this year because we win more than we lose but more because we believe we can and because we don't ever let difficulty hold us down.

So, shake off failures and forget them.

Be like Trond. Just leave it. You can't use it for anything.

And win.

* * *

Winning, caring teams win without their leader around.

According to Jaquelyn Smith, writing for Forbes, "In an ideal culture, the boss's absence should have a minimal impact on the day-to-day ability of a team to perform at its peak." (Smith, 2013)

As discussed elsewhere, making this happen has a great deal to do with having the right people in the right slots (including a true, caring leader vs. a micro-managing, authoritarian nutjob) trained correctly to do the right things operating in a process enabled environment where everyone understands the destination and knows their lives will get better when it is achieved. If you as a leader don't have that much done, forget leaving the building. But let's assume you do ...

The rest is on your team itself. The team has to have, yep, TRUST, in you and each other. In you that when you say they are in charge you actually mean it; and in themselves, that they can function as a unit without supervision, without killing one another. Next, they need the self-confidence to be able to deliver without direction. This is on you. If you have anyone in your organization who still relies on you for marching orders, STOP IT. People will never grow up and learn to take full responsibility for themselves or their roles as long as they are getting notes in their lunchbox from mom or dad.

Finally, they need to practice. Try it a few days before you actually leave. Tell them, "tomorrow we're going to pretend I'm gone, I'm not answering any questions, I'm not telling anyone what to do; you're on your own." See how they do. You don't need to go straight to live ammo; let them build their confidence. But be sure to build them up; tell them how well things go when they do. Managing a business without you isn't easy; it's why you earn what you do. Invest, in the practice of The Not So Subtle Art of Caring, the time and energy to make sure that your team has the trust, knowledge and confidence they need to excel without you.

Seeing a perfect example of just what I'm talking about day in and day out in my favorite restaurant gave me a perfect opportunity to reinforce the point one Friday.

26 October 2018

Nearly every day since I arrived here in August, I've eaten lunch at the same little Mexican restaurant in Fullerton. It wouldn't be an exaggeration to say that I've eaten there at least 30+ times already. I have the menu mostly memorized. I know what's going to be on the TVs on either wall each day. I'm getting to know the staff by name. And I know exactly what my bill will total each day.

Upon leaving today, something occurred to me about the place that I hadn't considered before though: I've never noticed the presence of anyone in charge. I've never seen a manager. No one is giving orders. The place seems to run itself. Everyone in the place seems to know their role, exactly. They work as a team, pitching in to bring things to, or take things away from, each other's tables. At the counter, whoever is available will ring me out.

And I've never had a bad experience. All without anyone seemingly heading up the show. With process, commitment to each other as a team, and tremendous execution like that, El Farolito Jr. does not require a taskmaster to be present all the time. Add in trust and self-confidence, and a place can run itself when the boss goes away.

And that's the point for the week.

As I shared with all of you during our last all-associate meeting, I want this place to run better when I am not here than when I am. I can see the start of that already. It's happening because we are putting processes in place that make work better, simpler, faster, cheaper, more customer-friendly, but above all, easily repeatable. It's happening because all of you are stepping forward with ideas to make work safer and more efficient. But more than anything, it's happening because you all are behaving more and more like One Team.

At El Farolito Jr., one never gets the sense that there is a wait staff team, and a cashier team, and a busser team, and a kitchen team. Nope. One gets the sense that there is an El Farolito Jr. team. One Team. That's what we are well on our way to. No more office team and receiving team and shipping team and B&B team, etc, etc. Nope. We are One Team.

We're on a path to doing things in the best, safest way possible, so that if someone is watching they won't be able to tell if anyone is in charge around here. Like at El Farolito Jr., they won't see anyone yelling orders, directing traffic, offering criticism, or otherwise getting in the way. What they will see is the pure magic that happens when 75 people come together as One Team, aligned around the growth of this business and the subsequent betterment of themselves – performing work in better, simpler, faster ways which delight our customers. What they will see is what defines winning.

So, execute as well when I'm gone as when I'm here – as One Team.

And win.

* * *

True winning and caring teams act world famous.

Because they almost always are.

When teams believe they are world famous, their mindset changes dramatically and along with it, their behavior. But the horse before the cart is changing the mindset. The shift is from not thinking about one's standing in the world to always thinking first about one's world fame and letting it guide one's actions. The trait of winning caring teams is that they make the shift; they think of themselves as world famous.

When they do, almost everything changes. Not just behavior, which becomes conspicuously more professional, but every aspect of the business. The thoroughness and timeliness of response to customers will improve. Product quality and delivery timing will improve. The cleanliness and housekeeping of your facilities will improve. The manner in which people speak to one another will improve. Customers will be attracted simply by virtue of the associative effect. Your people will even begin to walk differently (true story). Almost no part of your operation will remain unchanged. Doing this one thing, whether it seems silly to you or not, will change your life forever.

Making the shift requires a simple mental leap. For those who practice The Not So Subtle Art of Caring, it's a hop. As the world-famous American author Neville Goddard wrote, "Dare to believe in the reality of your assumptions and watch the world play its part relative to its fulfillment." Like anything else in life, making the leap is a choice. Once made, actually bringing the change about is no more than a matter of having leaders who talk about it almost every day, and who refuse to accept anything less in their results. See, being world famous is first and foremost a mindset. It simply starts with believing it, then putting it on the bottle.

Try it tomorrow. Tell your team they are famous. Ask them to start acting like it. Then watch the difference in behavior.

November 13, 2020

For years and years, first with my father, then with my wife, I would come to Indianapolis for Indy 500s and then Brickyards. No trip was ever complete without going to St. Elmo's. Their cocktail sauce has become a staple in our home. Grabbing a bottle this week, I noticed two small green words on the label: "World Famous." I don't doubt it. The stuff is incredible. When you put the words, "World Famous" on your label, it better be. When you put the words, "World Famous" on your label, you better act like it.

And that's the point for the week.

Whether St. Elmo's cocktail sauce is world famous or America famous or Indiana famous doesn't matter as much as they *believe* they are world famous. See, they put it right on the bottle. Because they do, it changes how they think about who they are and the kind of product they deliver. We are world famous y'all. Get ready for something spectacular.

Contrast that way of thinking with someone not so special. We're not famous, y'all ... we're nobodies ... get ready for something mediocre.

To me, life is a self-fulfilling prophecy. St. Elmo's is world famous because they believe they are world famous. Because they wake up every single day intent on being world famous, they are, and it's reflected in the product they put out each and every day.

We are world famous.

Without a doubt there are people from all around the world who have heard of us. By that definition, we are world famous. We should act like it.

Everything we do, every decision we make, every person we hire, every dollar we spend and every word that comes out of our mouths should come from a place where being world famous is top of mind.

Before doing anything. Before making any decision. Before making any hire. Before spending a thin dime. Before uttering a syllable. We should ask ourselves, will what I'm about to do add to the goal of making this company world famous?

Remember, we already are. We should act like it.

We should put it on our invoices. On our trucks. On our uniforms. On our business cards. "World Famous Truck Service & Maintenance."

How would you act then?

I want to challenge you to act like you are world famous. Because you are. Act like everything you do has to be done in such a way as to maintain that fame. Because it does.

When we all choose to behave like we are world famous (because we are), something astounding will happen. Mediocrity, indifference, slow pace, missed steps, or poor attitudes will never be tolerated ever again. Because there's no room for any of that on world famous teams. There's only room for outright excellence, an obsession with safety, a fascination with speed, and an absolute dedication to exceeding the customer's expectations every single time. Because that's what being world famous is all about.

So, act like you're world famous (because you are).

And win.

Chapter 4, Part II

The Behaviors of Great, Caring Teams

Marcus Aurelius wrote, "That which is not good for the beehive cannot be good for the bee." A key attribute of great, caring and winning teams is that they behave as One Team and chase One Number. Most teams are traditionally organized around separate business units and/or channels. These teams struggle with intramural competition, resource rationing, and customer conflicts. In a One Team, One Number culture, every part of the organization is oriented around (and paid around) one goal, eliminating friction, building trust, and creating dynastic winning potential. Nick Andriotis, writing for eFront Learning, says, "Companies where employees have a common purpose are easy to recognize – their employees are happy, have high energy and morale, and speak the same organizational language. Common purpose defines the quality of leadership that impacts a company's culture and spirit – its soul, if you will. This drives success beyond financial statements." (Andriotis, 2017)

Too, part of practicing The Not So Subtle Art of Caring is knowing that inherent in One Team, One Number is the acute understanding not just of the fact that one is part of a larger team but the complete knowledge of exactly how one fits into the wider team and how what one does contributes to the attainment of wider team goals. Within the One, Team One Number economy, everyone's numbers add up to the whole. Even a tire builder understands how many tires he needs to make each day to meet the overall goal for his plant which ultimately connects up to the objective for the whole company for the period. Again, Amy Morin from Forbes helps put it in perspective. "If an employee works on an assembly line connecting two pieces of plastic together without any knowledge of what those pieces will become, he'll never be invested in the organization. Similarly, if an employee doesn't know anything about his fellow workers or what they do, he'll never develop faith in their ability to do their part." (Morin, 2017)

What steps have you taken to connect every single person up to the wider goals of your organization? Can each person recite from rote how what they do contributes to the total? If not, get busy.

June 2, 2012

This week, I attended a farewell mass and recognition ceremony for my oldest daughter's graduation from elementary school. As part of the recognition ceremony, principals, admission directors and others from various local high schools congratulated and welcomed those graduates set to attend their particular institution. The event quickly took on an air of cross-town rivalry. In the process, the dynamic in the room changed, as then current schoolmates aligned with their future alma maters...until one of the high school representatives reminded the crowd that all were playing for a larger, and ultimately more important team.

Just like that, the sense of separation evaporated. Students then celebrated each other's achievements en masse, without regard for their future school affiliation. As I reflected on what I had witnessed, a paradoxical truth emerged. By maintaining a focus on the whole, the contribution of any individual part is magnified and made more significant.

That's the point for the week.

Our effectiveness as individuals is directly proportional to the degree to which we associate ourselves with something bigger than we are. By keeping a steady focus on the goals of the wider team, we are reminded that it isn't about us and that personal success matters little if the entire enterprise fails.

When we allow our point of view to narrow to our individual needs or smaller factions within the whole, we bring something less than our full weight to bear on the forward motion of our organization, while simultaneously missing opportunities to grow personally. Worst of all, we create snags and tears in the fabric of our relationships with others.

But when we dedicate ourselves, each day, to the notion that we and our immediate teams will win only when the entire organization prevails, we'll create greater alignment to the mission of the whole. We'll more often reach our own full potential. And we'll build trust with those around us who, by our actions, see that we can be counted on to endeavor for something beyond our own self-interest.

Caroline's graduation was another reminder to me that basic human nature doesn't change much as we age; only the situations do. Whether a 14-year-old rising freshman, or a 44-year-old tire seller, the degree to which we believe in, associate with, and fight for things greater than ourselves will have a factorial impact on our own success and that of our wider teams.

In the economy of the human enterprise, the smaller we become, the greater the whole will grow, its potential nearly unlimited, and bound only by the muchness of ourselves we're willing to surrender to the greater good.

Focus on the larger team.

And win.

* * *

Winning, caring teams cheer for each other, not against each other.

Those who have ever worked with me know that I have a very short list of things which will immediately disqualify you from being any part of what I am trying to accomplish. One of them is rooting against a teammate. In every place I have been,

I have made it clear to people: "If you cheer for a competitor or against one of your teammates, you cannot work here." It doesn't have to be active enablement of the competitor. Just the simple act of opening one's mouth and rooting against a teammate is enough to get you gone, for good. Do not pass GO, do not collect $200.

On winning teams, there can be zero tolerance for anything resembling acrimony, competition, back-biting, back-stabbing, or any other acts of skullduggery between teammates. As I have written elsewhere, I do not believe in healthy tension. Healthy tension is a term coined by someone somewhere who failed to build a cohesive team. Debate and disagreement during the process of decision making and discernment are hallmarks of great teams. Having someone on the team play the role of devil's advocate or to purposely ask "how do you know that?" each time a statement is made are great tools to get at the best result. But once the team has arrived at the answer, every hand goes on the rope and pulls in one direction. That's how great, caring teams win.

Losers encourage "healthy tension" and ongoing debate. They suggest that bitter competition among peers for future promotions is good for the company. They believe that the loss of good people because succession fights are badly managed is just a cost of doing business. These people also sit by quietly while one player roots against another. "She was a college athlete," they'll say, "It's just what competitors, do." False. It's just what highly dysfunctional teams do.

According to Tom Zender, writing for The Business Journals, internal competition can kill a business. He writes:

"When employees compete with each other for their own gains rather than collaborating with each other, there are great costs, including:

- Teamwork dies

- Conflicts flare
- Confusion ensues
- Progress slows
- Morale dissipates
- Good people leave
- Weak people stay and poison others
- Creativity caves
- Finally, operations slow down, costs go up and profitability bleeds red. Death is near."

(Zender, 2015)

Winners don't root against one another. Those who practice The Subtle Art of Caring cheer for one another. And because they do, they win more often. It's no more complicated than that.

Do you tolerate internal competition? Have you fallen for the "healthy tension" gag? What steps will you commit to taking tomorrow to ensure that your team cheers for each other, not against each other?

July 26, 2019

This week in sports saw one of the most celebrated missed dunks in history. Yes, *missed* dunks.

The dunk was attempted by LeBron James, Junior. The son of LeBron James, multiple time NBA champion and Akron, Ohio native. The dunk attempt itself was remarkable. Bronnie, as he is affectionately known, left roughly at the foul-line and was head high with the rim when he brought his arm down with the ball, barely missing the shot over a player easily a head taller than him.

Gasps were heard from the stands. And cheers were heard from the opposing sideline and cheering section. Groans and other signs of dismay were heard from LeBron Jr.'s side of the court. No cheers were heard from Bronnie's bench, not one, as no one on his team was celebrating the fact that he missed the shot. See, on winning teams, players don't celebrate the failures of their teammates.

And that's the point for the week.

The example above was from a real live basketball game. But the situation could apply to any sport. Imagine players on the sideline of a football game cheering when their tail back gets tackled behind the line of scrimmage. Or think about the home dugout erupting in applause when their star hitter strikes out. Or in business, imagine when one member of a team relishes in the failure of a teammate to finish a project on time, hit an objective, or reach and expected milestone. As crazy as these things sound, they happen every day on teams all over the world and in companies all over the world, including this one. It is a great disappointment to me when I see it. It's why I don't tolerate even one instance of it. Because behavior like this has no place on winning teams. To root against a teammate is to cheer for the competition. It is exactly the same thing.

Our competitors are outside the building not inside the building. Any time spent internally competing is waste. It is effort which holds us back from achieving our goals. It creates negative morale issues which further complicate our ability to move forward with pace. And, to me, this behavior is tantamount to stealing from the company.

When all hands are on the rope, pulling it in the same direction, we will almost always achieve our goals. But when even one hand is off the rope or pulling in a different direction, a self-interested direction for example - we will less often, if ever, achieve our goals.

And so, for me, I would prefer to have 100 B players committed to working together than 1,000 so-called A players, so in it for themselves that they would root against a teammate. Those B players and I will go to the moon. Self-interested A players will go nowhere.

So, for anyone interested in cheering against a teammate please understand that you can't work here. That's only because we have tremendously important work to do, work that requires everyone to pull the rope in the same direction, and to cheer loudly for each other as they do it. And ultimately, because I want you to be happy.

Those who prefer to cheer the failure of their teammates are invited to find a place to work where that sort of thing is encouraged, because if that's the sort of thing that makes you happy, you're not going to be happy here. What makes us happy is nearly 100 people working together and encouraging each other as we move ever closer to our destination – a destination where the life of every person here becomes better. Better because the dreams we have for ourselves and this company are achieved. Achieved because we believe in each other, fight for each other and cheer for each other.

So be like Bronnie's fans. Cheer for each other, not against each other.

And win.

* * *

Winning, caring teams defend what is theirs.

Evan Roth, writing for Forbes says that, 'I have your back' is one of the six things that great teams say to each other. He goes on to add that saying so is "a statement of trust, confidence and safety." (Roth, 2016) "Great teams defend their business and they defend each other. This is not a difficult concept to understand. Anyone can grasp the notion of preventing someone from causing harm to something or someone we care about. Therein lies the hard part. To defend something, one must care about it. One must be committed to it.

As a leader your job isn't to elicit a reaction from your team when something bad happens, but to guide them to a place where they understand that the loss means something to them personally. That what was taken was taken from them. That when a teammate is hurt, they hurt. The reaction will come when these things are truly believed and felt.

It begins with you as a leader practicing The Not So Subtle Art of Caring and first modeling the commitment – by NEVER missing an opportunity to defend what you are a steward of. Almost every day in business will present you with an opportunity to defend what's yours, what's right, or what's in your care. How you behave will largely determine how your team will learn to behave. If you pass the buck, so will they. If you step into the breach, so will they.

Great teams defend what's theirs. And it begins with great leaders who defend what they care for modeling the behavior for others. What example are you setting?

May 14, 2009

Imagine pulling into your drive tonight and finding someone you care little for walking out of your home with something that belongs to you.

How would you react?

Doubtful, you would let them just wander away with your belongings.

I wonder why we are willing to do that here.

This week, Cooper alone announced that they had signed not one, not two, but THREE of our large tire retailers. These signings come on the heels of other recently announced Cooper wins.

Someone we don't care much for walked into our house and walked out with things that belonged to us.

How we choose to react to these events will determine not only whether we keep what is ours but also how we are viewed by others in the future.

Here's the point for this week.

Winners defend what is theirs.

I expect news like I have just shared with you should infuriate you. I expect that you should want to do everything in your power to strike back. I expect that you would fight light a crazed lunatic to keep what belongs to you.

Defend what is yours.

Early this year I shared with all of you a blinding flash of the obvious ... that the only possible way to grow in a down market is to take something from someone else.

If we are not the takers, we will be the takees.

There is almost nothing I like less than losing. Allowing what is ours to be taken is no different than losing. In fact, it's worse.

A culture where we fail to protect that which is ours will quickly become one where no one wants to be. It's a culture built on apathy and unkept commitments. It's a culture where others cannot trust one another to keep what matters to them safe. It is a culture of loss, populated by losers.

This is a team of winners. This is a team that should wake up every morning intent on kicking the hell out of someone. This is a team that defends what is theirs.

So, get out there and take it back. Then go out and take something of theirs. And keep taking what is theirs until they don't have anything left.

And win.

* * *

Great winning teams communicate, then they communicate again, then they communicate some more.

These teams understand that saying something once is never enough. Research actually says the right number is actually in the neighborhood of three, seven or even something higher than that. In the 1930's, the movie industry settled on what it called then, "The Power of 7" having determined that it took a consumer being exposed to a brand message a minimum of seven times before they would make a decision to buy. The whole concept is based on something called the "Mere Exposure Effect" which simply says the more times someone is exposed to a message the more likely they will be to take note of it or act on it. Mark Cenedella, CEO of the Ladders uses a slightly less scientific method. He says, "Until they start making jokes about how often you repeat it, they haven't internalized it" (Bryant, 2018) Whether three, seven, 14 or until people start laughing at you, the point is one and done don't cut it for winning teams. Great teams are fanatics about communication. They believe that overcommunicating is impossible.

SkillPath lists eight characteristics for great teams. One is "All team members practice open communication with each other." (Rose, 2019) Effectively communicating across teams ensures alignment of thought and purpose. It helps eliminate errors and instances where part of the team goes zig while the other goes zag. The most important part of team communication though, is in the facilitation of forward progress. I say a lot that the greatest ideas for moving a business forward always come from those closest to the customer and those actually doing the work. It is crucial to get those folks talking, to get them volunteering thoughts and ideas. Those who practice The Not So Subtle Art of Caring not only foster cultures of communication, but cultures of trust and mutual respect as well, where no idea is a bad idea and where every associate feels safe to bring thoughts forward. At the moment this occurs, organizations will begin leaping forward and never looking back.

Use a communication journal. Start counting how many times you communicate things. If it's ever less than three, keep going. Try for seven. Once you're on a roll, make a run at "I'm sick of hearing myself talk." If you get there it's all good.

March 13, 2010

This week, I traveled to Bentonville, Arkansas for the Sam's Club supplier summit.

Sam's recently moved into spectacular new digs. Throughout the expansive, atrium style lobby, the walls are adorned with the guiding principles and key milestones of the organization.

Among them are Sam Walton's 10 Rules of Business.

No doubt, many of you have seen them before. Sam Walton, founder of Wal-Mart, is literally a legend.

As I stood there looking at Sam's rules – all of which are near timeless and universal in their applicability - there was one I kept returning to and reflecting upon.

Rule number 7.

"Listen to everyone in your company and figure out ways to get them talking."

Sam Walton understood a few things. While I'm not sure he ever articulated them just so, he knew that no one is as smart as all of us. He knew that no one knows a job better than the people doing it. He knew that the best information about their stores, their customers and their partners came from the people closest to them.

So, he encouraged everyone to talk – to contribute what they knew, saw and heard about their business.

By knowing more and better about what worked in their stores and what did not, what customers liked and what they did not, and what separated winning partner relationships from losing ones, Wal-Mart grew to become the largest company on the planet.

It happened because people were talking.

Widespread associate input enables, accelerates then magnifies success.

That's the point for the week.

The more we talk and listen, the more information we have

available to make better and faster decisions – and to act in like fashion.

What's more, as communication increases so does engagement, and with it, success.

We can't talk too much.

If you see something that needs improved, say something – so we can fix it.

If you see a mistake about to be made, say something – so we can avoid it.

If you see something that is going well, say something – so we can keep doing it.

On webcasts, in my skip-level roundtables, and at staff meetings speak out more. But don't limit speech to just these formal interactions. Use the blog more. Talk to each other and to Akron whenever you have something to say.

When you do, not only will Goodyear achieve more, but you'll feel more involved in our business, more like part of a team, and more successful as an individual.

Talk more.

And win.

* * *

Caring and winning teams operate on a rhythm.

I don't play the guitar (yet) but one of my best friends, Richie does. What I have learned from him is that, in a band, the rhythm guitar is the backbone of the operation. The rhythm guitarist plays chords and riffs in such a way as to provide a foundation for the song, a groove if you will. For those of you who are old enough, imagine the familiar riff from the Deep Purple song "Smoke on the Water", or just Google it.

You can think of things in a similar way for a business team. Without rhythm, there is no groove thing. Those who practice The Not So Subtle Art of Caring keep their groove thing on.

Rhythm is the purposeful establishment of meetings, planning cycles, deadlines, and other regular calendar events which happen repeatedly on a regular and predictable basis, without fail. Some of these items will be set for you, like the S&OP cycle, the financial/annual operating planning calendars, board meetings, quarterly and other reporting deadlines or other covenant demands. To these, you should add staff and other regular meetings with and among your team(s), team reporting requirements, routine calls, and any other recurring events.

But it's not just about meetings. It's also about the flow of information. Each day, week, month, quarter, and year, certain information is required to be in certain places – on a rhythm – either for others or for you to use to make decisions. Map it out. Then, work backward to determine what data or information is required when and from whom. Develop a cadence for receiving the necessary reports or grabbing the needed data, leaving enough time to review, question and reformat the information as needed. Be mindful also of the time you are giving others to complete tasks; your people are likely super, just not super-human. The internet is full of helpful suggestions for establishing a battle cadence or rhythm of business. The key isn't to be perfect, it's to get started and get better in time.

It's important to keep the why of this in perspective. Building cadence should never be make-work. The goal of this effort should be to drive efficiency and simplification in your life – not drudgery or the alienation of your team. Lisa Quast, writing for Forbes, put it well. "The goal for using this tool is to ensure everyone on your team knows what to expect and when, and to ensure individuals are focused on the most important activities at the appropriate times." (Quast, 2015) Rhythm helps those on your team know what's required each period, how to plan their time, and how to allocate resources. It tells your team what's important, enhances collaboration, and reminds everyone about how score is kept. You'll generate discipline out of thin air, hold fewer meetings for the sake of having meetings, and see problems coming well before they find their way to your door.

And remember, don't allow black holes or one-way flows. The information that will be generated as part of the cadence you develop will be interesting for everyone in your organization. Share it. Be transparent. Using the same cadence, keep everyone aware of the status and progress of the organization relative to its goals.

June 4, 2010

This week, I spent some time out west, fly fishing with a customer.

I was at once reminded of the importance of rhythm to winning with a fly rod.

With it, the fly travels cleanly, more quickly and with less effort to the intended spot in the river. With rhythm, the fish are more often fooled into thinking that your "fly" is an actual fly and will be more likely to lunge at it. With rhythm, everything stays in order; tangles are far less frequent and the likelihood of catching a friend's cheek goes down exponentially.

Without it, more effort is expended, the fly travels erratically, and time is wasted, often with lost flies, ruined line, and buddies with new face piercings adding to the misery.

Naturally, I found fly casting a natural metaphor for our business.

Rhythm in business, as on a trout stream, enables winning.

That's the point for the week.

Rhythm is achieved through, among other things, regular team meetings, communication, reporting, and contact. These things should all occur on a predictable, repeated basis – a rhythm.

When we have rhythm in our business, we achieve our goals

faster, more easily, and with improved result. With rhythm, tangles and lost opportunities are less frequent.

When teams operate on a rhythm, everyone in the enterprise better understands what is required, knows better how progress relates to plan, and can better react to changes in environment.

With rhythm collaboration is enhanced, trust blossoms, and less time is wasted in the mind-numbing meetings that used to be required to find out things that the cycle tells us without even having to ask.

So, find a rhythm.

And win.

* * *

Great, caring and winning teams never stop learning.

These teams know that the ability to learn and to continue learning can create sustainable competitive advantage. So, they see learning not as drudgery or worse, a punishment, but as something of value, a personal investment in them as a unit and as individuals. Rosabeth Moss Kanter, former Editor of the Harvard Business Review and one of the world's greatest mind's on leadership lists learning as one of 10 reasons winning teams keep winning. She says this specifically about winners, and losers: "Losers get defensive and don't want to hear about their many failings, so they avoid feedback. Winners are more likely to voluntarily discuss mistakes and accept negative feedback because they are comfortable that they can win." (Moss-Kanter, 2012)

These teams take an active role in their learning plans. For these teams, their education plans are something they take an active part in; they are not pushed on them by HR or prescribed by a Learning & Development Organization. For these winning teams learning is not haphazard nor accidental.

That's because teams that practice The Not So Subtle Art of

Caring understand their talent gaps.

Talent gaps are the missing capabilities in any organization. They are – or should be – identified relative to the specific written plan of the team. The great teams compare their planned objectives to their current capabilities and note the gaps which exist. They then identify those which can be addressed by training existing team members. Subsequently, specific Learning Plans are developed for each associate. The completion of these plans become part of the leader's and the associate's annual performance management targets. Using a talent gap approach, training dollars per capita are used far more effectively than could ever be possible under a one size fits all approach to L&D.

As a result, associates grow faster. They understand why they are being trained, see the goal they are working for and work hard to attain it. By tying training to skill gaps and tying achieving gap closure to advancement, winning teams help ensure retention but also, more importantly to them, more often ensure promotion from within which is significantly less expensive, less disruptive and less risky than having to hire from the outside because an internal hire is not available or ready when needed. Plus promoting from within vs. too much hiring from the outside has a significant positive impact on associate engagement and again retention.

Best of all, these teams, including the leader, constantly expand their knowledge base to a greater and faster degree than their competitors. Customers view learning and development as an investment in them as well which adds to the stickiness of their relationships too. But more than anything, the bonds of connected tissue formed by love, trust, and mutual respect are made even stronger – bonds which enable these winning teams, over time, to accomplish almost anything they put their (expanding) mind to.

November 12, 2010

Like many of you, I have watched with interest the continuing coverage of the recent mid-term election.

I've been struck by the repeated rhetorical questions about what each party will/should/might/won't learn as a result of the election outcome. Most alarming to me have been the number of pundits – from both sides – who are suggesting that little will be learned and, in essence, acted upon by the leadership in either party. If true, it suggests that these so-called "leaders" really aren't leaders after all.

One of, if not THE, key traits of successful individuals is the desire and ability to learn.

And that's the point for the week.

The notions that leaders are born (vs. made) and that talent is the number one determinant of success are pure myths.

When we believe solely in the power of genetics and talent, we tend to wait for the world to come to us, convinced that it is only a matter of time until the world recognizes our genius. It rarely does, resulting in resentment and a heap of wasted moments.

While people with raw talent spend time trying to look intelligent and avoiding mistakes, those with a desire to learn are trying new things and actually making the mistakes that make them better.

Accordingly, learning requires risk. It starts with the risk it takes to admit that we don't know everything. Learning then requires the risk to try something different with the inherent knowledge that we may fail. Finally, learning requires the risk to objectively and with feedback from others review our performances at their conclusion to identify what we could have done better. But the risks are worth taking.

We won't always do things perfectly and almost never on the first try or after reading something once. That's OK. We're imperfect creatures. But when we take the time to learn, we grow and become better – as tire sellers, spouses, parents, friends, and citizens of our communities. We develop skills that can never be taken away and that make us more valuable to those around us.

How we learn is less important than that we do so. Whether from a book, or a class or from just trying something you've never done before, learning can take a myriad of forms. One is no more important than another, but ALL contribute to the creation of better human beings.

Finally, nothing is more important than believing we can. Like any sort of winning, learning begins with a conviction that we can. When we believe we can learn, we will.

Remember that, as strange as it sounds, learning IS just for leaders. It's how leaders get that way. Anyone can become a leader. It starts with learning.

Learn …

And win.

* * *

Great, caring and winning teams do the little things well.

They almost innately understand that those who do small things with excellence will be assumed to perform similarly in the big things. So, they make it a point to attend to the details. They know likewise that the details, the last 1% to 5% is what sets people apart; because often almost everything about one's product or service compared to a competitor's is the same – except the little details. That's why winners sweat the small stuff.

It's the same even in sport. Take baseball for example. Bleacher Report writer Christopher Connors looked at World Series and playoff winners over a couple decades and determined that what separated the winners from the others wasn't big payrolls, or big pitching, or big sluggers. It was the little things, what's known in the game as "small ball." He summed it up this way, "But come October, it's the scrappy base hits, walks, sacrifice bunts, and high choppers that you need to bust your tail on to beat out at first base that are the new chic. Those are the plays that help you win." (Connors, 2012) Business is no different. Winners win playing small ball.

It shows in the way they dress. It shows in the way they talk. It shows in their proposals that they pore over, looking for alignment, font and typo issues. It shows in their products, that are just that much better. It shows in their vehicles, which are always clean. It shows in their facilities which are never cluttered, and never have trash on the floor. It shows in the time it takes to turn around credits and other disputes. It shows in every tiny little detail.

See, those who practice The Not So Subtle Art of Caring know that little things translate to big things. It shows in the culture, usually one of winning and mutual respect. It shows in their turnover and associate engagement numbers. It shows in delivery times. It shows in dock to stock performance. It shows in EBITDA. It shows in cash flow. And it shows in customer satisfaction.

All because the culture of the team is oriented toward an understanding that even the smallest detail matters, that every stone should be unturned, and that walking past a piece of trash on the ground is no different than ignoring a request from their largest customer.

Often the only thing that separates a little thing from a big thing is time. And all that separates great companies from losers is caring about little things.

Leaders too often segregate little things out of their lives believing they are too unimportant to trifle with or that they are below their pay grade. However, for most people, little things can have a big impact. So, if you are avoiding little things because you think they don't warrant your time, please think again. These things matter. So, ask yourself what you can do to spend more time paying attention to the little things in life.

November 11, 2011

As most of you know, I am an aficionado of chicken fried steak. To me, it is culinary perfection. For those unfamiliar with this gastronomical jewel, chicken fried steak is a piece of sirloin pounded with a mallet to ideal tenderness, and a fourth of its former thickness; battered, breaded, then deep fried to a rich golden brown, and finally smothered in white pan gravy.

Shortly after arriving in Fort Smith, I happened upon a version of the delicacy that has remained for me, despite samplings at a dozen or so other local establishments, the premier example of chicken fried steak in a five-county area, or on the continent for that matter. Until this week.

This week, I found a new favorite. As significant as that seems though, it isn't the fact that the prior champion was dethroned that is the most significant aspect of this story. Why it happened, however, is. The single factor that separated the new leader from the old was the spice in the batter. An element that by weight comprises well less than 1% of the dish is what put it over the top. In further considering this fact, it occurred to me that we all have a little something to learn from a piece of golden fried meat. Often, the smallest details make the biggest difference.

That's the point for the week.

For the most part today, competing products or services laid side by side will reveal considerable similarities. Take our business as an example. In comparing us to another commercial dealer, one would find tires, trucks, tools, techs, and buildings to house it all. What differentiates us from others are more subtle things that when weighed in time, energy, money or mass against the total offering would pale in scope and scale. Small, but not insignificant things like the attitude of our people, our torqueing program, the age of our vehicles, the uniformed appearance of our team, the cleanliness of our locations, and other "little" details place great distance between us and our competitors. These things command the confidence and loyalty of our customers. They enable us to charge a premium for what might otherwise be viewed as a commodity. They are the things customers tell others about.

Each of us has an opportunity each day, to add the nuance and spice to our version of chicken fried steak. We choose whether to toss in the extra dash of friendliness. We choose whether to add love and care to every job we do. We choose whether to wear a uniform, or not, and whether it's tidy and tucked in, or not. We choose whether to keep our location clean and neat, or not. You get the idea.

When more of us make a choice to do so, we'll win more. We'll do so by creating distance between ourselves and others in our field, by commanding greater share, and by collecting more for the work that we do.

By the way, the steak at the new favorite was three bucks more than its now second place competitor. I gladly paid it and will again and again. It's proof that little things, that seem meaningless in and of themselves, are worth their weight in gold. What on its face might not appear to pay the bills, actually does.

More than that, these little things create opportunities for each one of us to have more, be more, and achieve more by helping create a business that people will beat a path to find. All because we chose to add just a little more something than the other guy.

Do the little things well.

And win.

* * *

Winning, caring teams innovate.

These teams understand two things in their bones. One, you innovate, or you go out of business. Two, the best ideas for innovation will come from the people closest to the customer and closest to the work.

Most companies do things entirely wrong, entirely upside down. They create innovation teams, "special project" groups, complete with cute code names and the whole nine yards and challenge them, with great fanfare, to come up with new ideas to "save the company." Oh oh. This won't end well. Here's why. First, you just told a bunch of people that they are "special," that they are the saviors of the species. How well is that going to go over with the people actually saving the species? Whatever these people do, any idea they have will be DOA; they will be vehemently disliked for no other reason than someone told them it was their job to "save the foundering masses from themselves." Because that's what everybody heard. Second, the ideas they cook up will be cooked up 30,000 feet from the people who use them and sell them; what could possibly go wrong???

Those that practice The Not So Subtle Art of Caring know the best ideas come from the people who know the business best. It's the people who wake up each day and make the stuff, sell the stuff, and deliver the stuff or, if it's a service, actually deliver the service. It is NOT some guy in a C-suite who last saw a customer on a "Win with the Winners" trip on some island in the Mediterranean. And it is especially not some outside hire, here to save the day like Mighty Mouse with ideas that when implemented will probably kill your core line anyway.

Nope. Even Greg Satell, writing for Harvard Business Review says, "the simplest answer is that you need to start by empowering the people already in your organization." (Satell, 2018)

You must build a culture where ideas for innovation come from your own people. Encourage them to look for problems in search of solutions. Visit often. Give them confidence. Build an engine of growth and competitive advantage right on your own front line. And use it to kick the heck out of the competitor whose CEO just hired Mighty Mouse.

February 1, 2019

Last week, a contingent of our leaders and members of our ownership group visited an organization in Cleveland that specializes in helping companies innovate. They do so by spending a tremendous amount of time with potential customers. This firm is responsible for some very well-known commercial innovations, like the Spinbrush, and has a remarkable success rate when looking at the commercialization of their patents. In listening to them and learning from them throughout the day, a number of my own guiding principles kept coming to the front; among them that innovation is driven by people who connect up customer needs, problems, and wants with solutions their company can uniquely provide. Accordingly, innovation is most likely to come from those closest to the customer.

And that's the point for the week.

Often firms rely on their leadership to drive innovative change – people like me – people furthest from the end user. Or they form innovation teams, similarly staffed with leaders, or worse, people from the outside, people who don't completely understand the work or the customer. I happen to believe in the innovative power of those associates closest to our customers. Those who know them, who talk to them, who see them, who pack their orders, and process their returns. It is from these folks that the next great ideas to make our customers lives better will come.

But it starts with every associate knowing that it's ok to, as I say, step out on the ice, or touch the wire, or come out of the forest. All of you should know that your ideas will be valued. That our leadership is looking for new, better more innovative products and ways of doing things and that there is more safety in stepping out and speaking up than in sitting back and keeping your head down.

For us to attain the growth we aspire to achieve, we must find more innovative ways to do things. We must disrupt our industry. We must rock our competitors back on their heels. You all will lead those efforts – by speaking up and putting forth ideas you already have in your minds and hearts to make this business better. By looking for problems in search of solutions. And when you do, we will move forward with unfathomable speed and force toward the destination we all dream of today.

So, step out on the ice. Innovate.

And win.

* * *

Great, caring teams, those that practice The Not So Subtle Art of Caring, do epic stuff.

These teams understand that big ideas can lead to big separation between them and their competitors and can likewise generate huge amounts of economic value for associates and shareholders alike.

Great big things inspire enthusiasm, engagement and even retention – of both associate and customers. People love to be a part of something big. They love the status, the fame, and the halo effect that goes along with being part of something big. People rally around big things. They tend to stick with big, exciting things, and they will fight for big things that matter to them. Craig Ross, one of the authors of the book, *Do Big Things* says, "The teams that are doing extraordinary work have team members that practice this: They stay focused on what they collectively care about and even more importantly, they stay focused on *why* they care." (Richard, 2017)

This is different from innovation, though something big can be the result of innovation. This is a mindset. A way to focus your associates on doing things that create big news. I would tell my teams that I want us to do things that cause others to say, "They did what???" That's what doing epic stuff means. Causing people to say, "Wow! They did what, now??"

Doing so is a matter of encouraging ideas at all levels of your organization and likewise being bold in your own actions. Do things on your own that cause people to take notice. Confidence is contagious. As you project it, they will catch it, and you'll be off to the races.

Encourage your folks to do the same. Remind them regularly that they will live through failure. Remind them also that with big moves often come big pay days and better lives for everyone who works there.

March 15, 2019

I collect novelty desk plaques designed in the fashion of the old-style name or info plates, you know, the ones that looked like woodgrain, with white letters, in little brass holders. You'd often see them at the bank when you were a kid, or in fancy office buildings.

Well, the ones I collect have humorous sayings on them instead of things like "Next Window Please" or "Mrs. Gerstenmaier." One of my favorites offers encouragement to, paraphrasing now, "Do Epic Stuff" (except it doesn't say stuff, hence the paraphrasing).

I was looking at it the other evening and thought to myself that, if HR would actually let me, I should buy one of these little plaques for everyone here. For I can think of no better admonishment to each of us than to strive to accomplish extraordinary things.

And that's the point for the week.

It really matters not a lot what it is you are doing in life or where you are doing it, those watching and depending on you are, by definition, hoping for something extraordinary from you. See, it's beyond question that our spouses, our children, those in the community who depend on us, our customers, or those in the hobby who are watching to see what we will do are not hoping for something ordinary. No one looks at any of us, or the combined group of us and says, "Gee, I can't wait for those guys to do something commonplace, something usual, something utterly forgettable." Nope. People come to see, and they remember the extraordinary.

March 10 was this year's first Hot VW's Drag Day event. Two years ago, we weren't even on the poster. This year, we were the presenting sponsor of the entire event and a joint sponsor of the three-event racing series. And the industry noticed. Because we did something extraordinary. We did something they deemed epic. Then, at the event, in the Real Street class, our sales manager spent the day standing his Buggy on its T-Bars in wheel stands which can only be described as EPIC. In extraordinary fashion, he went on to set the low elapsed time for his class for the event and, while he didn't win the class, no one can tell you who did – because all anyone was talking about for five days after the race was Fast Jesse and his fly wheel stands. See when you do something epic, people remember.

No one wants ordinary. No one remembers ordinary. We don't show up here every day to be ordinary. We come here every day to do something epic. Because when we do, customers will seek us out, the industry will tell our story to more people accelerating the pace of our change, and the lives of those who work here will become more extraordinary faster – which is why I show up here every day.

So, live the plaque ... Do Epic Stuff ...

And win.

* * *

Great, caring and winning teams, those that practice The Not So Subtle Art of Caring not so subtly celebrate their wins.

These teams recognize that recognition matters. They know that there is a reason that 40 and 50-year old human beings involved in sport still jump around and behave like children when something good happens. It's because people thrive on positive reinforcement. People are also tremendously social creatures. And nothing speaks more directly to the social and reinforcement needs of the human id than a party.

Find me a losing team that occasionally wins, and I will give you Ivory Soap odds, 99 and 44/100ths percent to 1, that there are no celebrations when they win. That's because traditional, authoritarian micro-managing stooges view winning as people's job, not something to be recognized or celebrated. These guys unfortunately are the norm. According to Gallup, only one in three US workers agrees that they've received praise for work in the last seven days. (Mann, 2016) The good news for caring leaders is there is an opportunity here to differentiate yourself from these ogres and to improve not only the morale of your team but your business results too.

According to Atlassian who surveyed over 1,000 workers and found that public celebrations improve a team's sense of well-being by about 16%, concluding that these celebrations "can make a huge difference in the morale and performance of a team." (Boogaard, 2019)

Celebrations are another one of those discomfort generating behaviors and traits, like love and hope. It's like, "I'm all for love, hope, and celebration, I just don't want to get caught engaging in them." Sound familiar? Well, snap out of it. If not you then who? Your people want a true, genuine caring leader who is willing to do the right thing regardless of what the authoritarian quack upstairs has to say. Be unsubtle and let your results speak for themselves.

A story about my wife's and daughter's alma mater, the Ohio State University was a great opportunity to reinforce the importance of celebration to winning, caring teams.

January 1, 2021

Tonight, my wife's, and now my daughter Chuck's, Ohio State Buckeyes destroyed Dabo Swinney's allegedly #2 ranked Clemson Tigers, beating them by three touchdowns in a game where Swinney, and his much-ballyhooed defensive coordinator, Brent Venables, were terrifically outcoached, and outclassed.

But as much as this could be a letter about execution, or about not saying stupid things, or about maybe coaching your players to stop hitting with the crown of their helmets, it's not about any of those 3 things. It's about what happened after the game.

As the clock hit 00:00, the entire Buckeye squad ran onto the field, celebrating, hugging each other, fist bumping, jumping up on each other, heading to the stands to whoop it up with family and friends and tossing gear high in the air.

I wasn't struck so much that celebrations in athletics are unusual, but that celebrations, like these, that occur outside of athletics are what separate winners from losers.

And that's the point for the week.

Celebrations in athletics are commonplace, even at the grown adult, professional level, where it's not uncommon to find middle-aged men dousing themselves with expensive Champagne after winning a significant championship or series.

But in business celebrations are rare. I suppose celebrations are viewed as something childish. Or maybe revelry is perceived as lacking decorum. Or it could be that the stick in the mud leaders that populate most C-suites today truly believe that fun has no place in the "serious" world of big business. It's more my sense, actually, that these people don't celebrate because they don't have much *to* celebrate.

True, caring leaders magnify success by rejoicing when they see it. They miss no opportunity to recognize team wins. They may not chase their players around spraying them with booze, but they do find ways to make a big deal out of even little accomplishments.

Leaders that celebrate success, tell others they care without saying a word. They tell their teams that winning matters, that achievement is recognized, that accomplishing things gets rewarded. Oh, and that theirs is a fun place to work, where laughter, cheer and joy are not only OK, but are encouraged and modeled by the boss.

These events create camaraderie, and opportunities for teams to replay the victory in their own words, to learn again what went well, and to reinforce the positive behaviors that led to a positive outcome. In these environments, trust blossoms, love springs forth and a kind of brotherhood and sisterhood form that results in a nearly impenetrable mesh between teammates that defies competitive assault or other intrusion, and ultimately yields an associate body of such incredible speed, force, and focus, that losing eventually becomes universally unthinkable.

So, celebrate victories.

And win.

* * *

As we depart the topic of leading teams, remember, your role, as a caring leader, is to demand great things of those you lead in the accomplishment of great deeds which result in great things happening in the lives of them and others. This work requires courage, perseverance, and love for other human beings. In doing research for this project, I came across a lovely quote that I believe sums things up quite perfectly. It's from Mr. Luke I.

O'Neill, a Harvard MBA graduate who decided to open a school in Boston dedicated to the leadership principles of the famed explorer Sir Ernest Shackleton. O'Neill says, "Never give up, don't be afraid to lead, follow your gut, and remember, it's about people." (O'Neill, 1999)

Yeah, what he said.

In the next chapter, you'll see that stewardship is the ultimate measure of the winning, caring leader. We'll show what differentiates the steward from a mere servant and of course, the ineffective traditional, command and control tyrant. You'll learn why the steward is uniquely equipped to lead and win and why, as study after study has shown, the steward consistently delivers results while Ken Doll sits haplessly alone, staring at underwater stock option grants, and sadly sipping coffee from the "World's Best Boss" mug he bought five years ago as a gift to himself.

Chapter 5

"Steward" Little and Other Stories

"If you devote yourself to more than yourself…you will have more than yourself to show for yourself."
Andy Stanley
1958-
American Pastor

True, caring leaders are ultimately stewards. Beyond acting as a mere servant, those who practice The Not So Subtle Art of Caring engage in the stewardship of that which is entrusted to them.

Stewardship is most commonly thought of in a religious context, or more recently in connection with save the planet virtue signaling. As a result, when suggested as a practice for business people, all but the most devout, run for the exits, anticipating a recruitment speech from either group. Steward leadership, like virtually all forms of leadership does have its roots in ancient traditions, some of them religious. For example, Regent University's Jeremy Kamer writes that, "Joseph is a prime example of a steward in the Old Testament. Genesis 39:4-6 recounts Joseph's appointment over Potiphar's house, and in 41:38-57 the later appointment of Joseph as the Pharaoh's steward of Egypt where He was in charge of everything except when Pharaoh was on his throne." (Kamer, 2018) In business, Edward Boyd describes cultures dating back to Hammurabi referring to stewards in regard to the keeping of accounting and other records. (Boyd, 1905) But to speak of a contemporary business leader as a steward is to speak of one in terms of the simple definition of the word, "a person morally responsible for the careful use of money, time, talents, or other resources, esp. with respect to the principles or needs of a community or group." (Collins English Dictionary)

The definition is rooted in the care of others. The steward leader is above and after all, a caretaker. While there is a hint of service to stewardship, to act as a steward is to be more preoccupied with the care of that which we are in our charge than mere service. It is not sufficient merely to serve. One engaged in The Not So Subtle Art of Caring must act as a steward.

Think of George Toma who at 91 has served as groundskeeper for every single Super Bowl. For those counting at home, that's 54 of them. George is a caretaker. He is a steward, of grass. But he sees his role as much more than that. "We're here to help have good grass, so we give the players a safe playing field and give the fans in the stands and on TV a field of beauty." he says. (Toma, 2020) For George Toma, while he is primarily charged with caring for the turf, he abundantly understands that his role is one of stewardship, of care, of providing abundantly for others.

See, to live as a steward requires a multiplier mindset.

Caring leaders are preoccupied with growth – of both the enterprise and of each individual assigned to their care. Their role is not simply to oversee the maintenance of the status quo, but to advance the well-being of the organization.

A perfect illustration of stewardship, and of the multiplier mindset, appears in the Gospel of Matthew in the Parable of the

Talents. (Matthew 25:14–30) It goes like this: A wealthy young man, upon departing for a trip, leaves his fortune in the care of his 3 stewards. To the first, he gives five talents (a talent was an historical measure of weight used for precious metal), To the second he entrusts two talents, and to the third he leaves a single talent. Upon his return, the master asks for an accounting of his fortune. The first two servants report that they have doubled their master's money; they give him their original stake plus the profit. The third slave, however, having buried his talent out in a field rather than trying to make a profit, returns only the single talent to his master. The master is pleased with the first two stewards, but he is disgusted with the actions of the third. He severely reprimands this steward, awards his talent to the first to invest, and casts the third out into the night (to the proverbial wailing and gnashing of teeth).

The lesson of the parable is about multiplication and about the expectations that others have for a steward to deliver it. The steward is expected to actively manage the affairs entrusted to him/her and to return them in better condition than they found them. The steward is not a retirement age volunteer from whom performance is neither expected nor required. Nothing could be further from the truth. Inherent in the steward model is not only a focus on the active management and growth of that which has been entrusted to their care, but also a sense of accountability. The steward has a distinct understanding that he or she is answerable to a higher authority to deliver on expectations. It is for these reasons that the Matthew story is so fitting.

The conventional wisdom surrounding steward leadership is that stewards are unpaid, twilight of life types who spend their golden years, answerable to no one, giving back by generously donating their time and talent to organizations in need of their unique gifts. While the assembled library of literature on the topic of steward leadership is not great, what does exist is not always helpful in dispelling incorrect stereotypes. Take the following passage from a 2013 book on the topic, "Many senior leaders ... appear to move into a steward leadership mindset when their careers have matured...." (Kukard, 2013) Mark Murphy, a senior contributor at Forbes, likewise wrongly generalizes that Stewards are plodding and slow and that working for stewards "may not offer ... an adrenaline rush." (Murphy, 2015) The truth is that steward leaders come in all ages, shapes, sizes and colors. They are not simply a bunch of old people, and the best of them are not plodding or boring. Quite to the contrary, the archetypal steward is foot-forward, accountable, and focused on growth.

What all stewards share is that they are multipliers. Implicit in the notion of multiplication is that which does, in fact, differentiate a list of steward attributes from a list of those for the servant – a focus on results. Missing from all of Greenleaf's, Russell's, Stone's, Patterson's, McNerny's, Spears', Blanchard's and Hodges' (and others') lists of attributes/traits of the servant leader is any mention of the word results. However, an early article from IEDP lists "Delivering Results" as one of nine components of Stewardship then goes on to say that "the true mark of a steward leader, however, is his or her ability to engender trust in the members of the organization and empower them to operate with flexibility to achieve the goals of the organization. (IEDP, 2013)

Too, stewards are accountable. The steward leader recognizes that they are employed to deliver results and will stand to account for their performance. They likewise build a culture of accountability within the organizations they are responsible for leading. They understand that growth and multiplication are not possible without clear performance management metrics tied to its attainment. In fact, researcher David Birkenstock Ed. D., Rector of Helderberg College, South Africa, confirms that steward leadership, "recognizes the role of manager and of being fully accountable, responsible and reliable. (Birkenstock, 1993)

Also differentiating stewardship from other forms of leadership is the leader's point of view in regard to time and possession. True stewards understand that their role, in any capacity is not permanent. According to The New York Times, "At its most basic level, success in stewardship requires an understanding that leadership is a temporary role which is outlasted by the lifespan of an organization." (Churchill, 2015) Stewards have an absolute comprehension of the fact that their role in any situation is temporary.

As such, they do not think possessively in regard to the teams or people that they caretake. No doubt, each of the parable stewards would have referred to the investments they made as "my master's money" not "my money" or, "my talents." Those leading modern-day teams will not be caught saying, "my team" or, "my people." The principle is the same. When we view our role as being charged with taking care of something vs. owning something our world view changes. We go from seeking to maximize our own utility to maximizing the wealth of the business and those who work in it. Our own wealth is maximized as a by-product of the growth of others'. This is not a socialistic concept. Capitalism is still alive and well in Stewardship. The leader is still very much in charge; there has not been a full redistribution of charge or control to those being led. What changes is the perspective on job and people ownership. When we mature enough to let go of the requirement that we must "own" our job, or "possess" the people who work for us, nothing short of amazing will begin to happen. We will start to focus on the multiplication of value for the entire enterprise and for every person in our care, not solely for us and our individual good. The difference is as striking, and it can produce extraordinary results in your organization.

A May, 2020 article from the Schuitema Group sums it up perfectly, "Effective business leadership has two essential

elements. The first is Care and the second is Growth."
(Schuitema, 2020)

Like anything else, moving from being cared for to caring for is a choice. As a leader, it is your decision to make. Imposing the traditional, command and control, authoritarian orthodoxy is a choice. As is imposing a steward orthodoxy. It begins with declaring, as a leader, what rules you expect people to live by, and more importantly, those you will live by.

For most leaders, the transition is made difficult by the fact that they are used to being cared for and being served. They are accustomed to sitting at the heads of tables, being the first in lines, getting the best rooms, and sitting in the front of a plane while their people sit in back. Stewardship flips the model on its head. In this chapter, we'll describe that mindset shift by detailing twelve key aspects of Steward Leadership. You'll see that stewardship is a full-time proposition and requires a new way of thinking about possession and permanence. Next, we'll talk again about the critical importance of belief then look at what a steward takes from any position and what she leaves. Then, we'll see how stewards focus on what people do, not who they are, how they fade heat for those they lead, and how they build first transparency, then trust in the organizations they lead. Finally, we'll end by describing how stewards walk around their putts, mind the back of the house and pay heed to the point of diminishing returns.

So, the question becomes, can you make the transition? Can you make the switch from being served, to serving? For those you lead, the transition is easier. Remember, more than anything, they want to believe.

And so, with that, we have come full circle. Remember, most everyone simply wants something bigger than them to believe in and fight for. Those you lead will do almost anything you ask them to do, provided that you are clear in your expectations, provided that they understand why you are asking them to do something, provided they know how to do the things you are asking them to do and provided they believe their lives will improve when they do them. People also want to know what to expect from those they follow; they want to understand what the rules are and what principles will guide them. More than anything, they want leadership, they want respect, and they want someone who cares. And when they find it, they will run into a burning building for the leader who gives it to them. Your job is easy. All you have to do is choose.

* * *

Stewardship is a full-time, lifetime proposition. It is not a hobby. It is not something to be done one day a week, or outside of business hours, or late in life after a full career of beating the heck out of people who trust us to do the right thing. Nope. It's an all day, every day, this is what the rest of your life looks like thing.

Unfortunately, the conventional wisdom views stewardship in a different light. "The model of stewardship that dominates the literature conceives of stewardship as largely ad hoc and situational." (Segal, 2012)

However, true, caring leaders do not turn their true selves on and off with whimsey. They are who they are. For as Dave Ramsey puts it, the key to building true caring stewards "is to change not just peoples' behavior but also their hearts." (Ramsey, 2019)

In teaching others about principles, I do this thing with my wedding ring. I got the idea of it from another amazing human being and leader named Andy Stanley. He's the pastor of the North Point Community Church outside of Atlanta. Anyway, I start sliding my ring off as I say, "Hey, babe, if you don't mind, this morning when I leave for work, I'm going to leave my wedding ring right here on the nightstand. It's OK, because when I get home tonight, I will put it right back on. But for the next 10, 12 hours or so, we just can't be married." I ask the audience to imagine what that might be like, how that might be received. The punch line is this: when we fail to be true to our principles in our whole life, it is the equivalent of telling our spouse that we don't want to be married in our whole life. That if we want to be somebody untrue during the workday, it's no different than wanting to be untrue to our spouse during the workday. See, what Jesus Christ says in Matthew is true, "No one can serve two masters." (Matthew 6:24) It's not religious; it's just a fact.

And like anything else in life, it's a choice. And once made, our choice to be a caring leader – to be a steward of our position and those we lead – is a commitment like any other. It's not a technique. It's not a style. It's not a method. It's an all day, every day, this is what the rest of your life looks like thing.

A story about a character from a very popular children's book enabled me to make the point a very long time ago.

October 22, 2004

This week, I've been reading the story of Stuart Little to my kids. For those not familiar with the tale, Stuart Little is a fictional mouse from a children's book of the same name written by E.B. White. Stuart is born into the Little family and raised as any other of their children, despite the fact that he is quite clearly a mouse. The book tells the story of Stuart's wild adventures, many of which center around him protecting (from a cat named Snowbell), then searching for, a bird named Margalo when she comes up missing. In the end (spoiler alert), we are left with Stuart still on the hunt for Margalo, but hopeful, in fact quite sure, that he will find her.

As I ended the book, the girls already asleep, I began to think about Stuart in the context of real life. First, I wondered about the etymology of his name. Stuart, I recalled, is the French modification of Stewart, a surname which was crafted in 14th century Scotland from Steward, a designation for he who was assigned to serve a ruling monarch as the supervisor of their estate and household. So, even today, a steward is one who serves. And Stuart = Steward.

And Stuart is Little. Stuart is not a giant. He is not even human size. He is tiny. But he does big things. At one point in the book, Stuart wins a major boat race in Central Park, NYC – a big deal. Returning home, his brother asks Stuart where he's been. Instead of making a show of his conquest, Stuart simply says, "knocking around town," as if it were nothing at all. For Stuart, it wasn't about Stuart. The etymology of "Steward" Little personified him as a character, always looking to serve others, including the grand search for Margalo, which consumes the entire second half of the book. Finally, White's leaving the search undone, was I believe, purposeful. It was a way of saying, "The servant is never finished."

And that's the point for the week.

There are lessons everywhere. Often, we find them in unlikely places, sometimes in little children's books. True caring stewards are like that too. They are found in unexpected places. That's because they endeavor to make themselves small, or like Stuart, little. They know that the smaller they become the larger others can get. And they know that the work of getting small is never done.

The stewardship of others is not a part time avocation. It's not a boat race in the park to be run and done. It's a lifetime commitment, to others. Stewardship does not take a day off. Or, as I'm fond of saying, "every day, means every day."

But the paradox of stewardship is this, when we make ourselves really, really small, so that others can get really, really big, that's when very large things start happening in our own lives. The path to achieving that which we deserve in life is through the service of others. The greater our service, the greater will be our reward. Best of all, like little Stuart, our greatest adventures will be found in a life devoted to others, of countless lives touched, and an endless horizon stretching beyond the limits of our human sight.

So be a stuart of others.

And win.

* * *

The biggest mental impediment to fully understanding the stewardship mindset has to do with possession. We are conditioned from a very young age to understand the concept of ownership.

According to researcher, Lauren Fasig, "understanding of ownership emerges around 2-3 years of age, when children begin to make inferences about who owns what" (Fasig, 2001) Try it for yourself sometime. Find a toddler, take something out of their hand, and say, "My (object in hand)." Chances are extremely high that the child will, scream, "No, my (object in hand)!" or "Mine!" in a pitch one octave shy of glass shattering. See, we are wired to think in terms of possession. We play board and card games as children that teach us whoever ends up with the most wins. And it just keeps going.

So, imagine getting our heads around a form of leadership that requires us to check our concept of possession at the door in favor of simply watching over that which has been temporarily entrusted to our care. It's what author Ashley Hodge calls the number one "stumbling block" to the Stewardship Mandate: "*the possession obsession*." (Hodge, 2005)

But it is the central point of it all. The recognition that we don't own our position, or the people who report to us. Both are merely entrusted to us to care for, and to multiply. When we can fully wrap our head around this simple concept, our entire universe takes on a completely different complexion.

The goal doesn't change much; we are still oriented to maximize the achievement of the objectives of our firm. It's the why that shifts. We swing around from seeking to maximize our own utility to maximizing the value for our organization and for each of the people in it. As a result, our own utility is magnified greatly. It's the fundamental paradox of stewardship; that by making ourselves really, really small, our ultimate reward is really, really big.

To be clear, stewardship is not a game of wealth redistribution. The child doesn't stop screaming, "Mine!" and start yelling, "Ours!" It doesn't work that way. It works more like, "mine!" and "yours" and "yours" and "yours" and etc. But everyone recognizes a number of very important points. First, none of us get to take a stick of it with us and second, for me to get more doesn't mean you get less. If you can get right with those two things, the stewardship thing will be a breeze.

See, The Not So Subtle Art of Caring, is an ampersand proposition. Like Coke Zero. It's And. The tide rises, *and* all boats get lifted up.

A seasonal hiring ad from my favorite home improvement store was a great reminder to make the point.

November 3, 2017

While shopping on the website of my favorite home improvement store this week, I noted that their landing page included a help wanted ad for temporary seasonal associates, for both part and full-time positions. At first, I didn't think much of it and went about my e-commerce adventure. But later on, I started thinking about temporary versus permanent in a more literal way. It occurred to me that while the conventional lexicon makes it very clear what is meant by a "temporary hire", in actuality, there really is no such thing as a permanent position.

In each of our positions, we are all temps.

And that's the point for the week.

None of us takes a job expecting to have it for life. In any role, we are a temporary occupant, filling the seat until the next temporary occupant takes the wheel.

The trouble is, few among us think this way.

When asked, most people refer to the job they hold in the possessive; they say, "my job" or "my position." They even refer to those they have the privilege to lead in a similar fashion: "my people" or "my direct reports" as if they own them.

When people start to attach possessive significance to things, they create unhealthy emotional attachments to them. They see encroachments on "their" turf as threats. They believe any interference into "their" business or "their" team is an affront.

But when people regard their stays as temporary and their roles as mere stewards, something extraordinary happens, that few imagine or bargain for. People begin to act more fully in the best interest of the wider organization and the people in it. They recognize that people are not their property but that they are gifts, on loan to them and subject to their care. Those being led will immediately detect the difference and will look for ways to maximize their contribution. Those being led by stewards will naturally seek to do more, to return more and to give every bit that they get.

Those acting as stewards will likewise seek to return that which has been entrusted to them in a better condition than they found it – because they will feel obligated to do so. All because their perspective correctly changed. From owner to steward. And from permanent hire to temp.

So, think like a steward.

And win.

* * *

Remember, Rule #1 is Believe. Recall it's a two-part deal. One part has to do with believing in some power greater than yourself. This is not evangelization. I prefer, in a paraphrased attribution to St. Francis, to let my actions do the preaching for me. Whether it is someone you call God, or a god by another name, a bolt of electricity, or a star in the sky, having something to believe in that you regard as a being greater than you is critical to your ability to lead. If you wake up each day firmly believing that your universe revolves around you, your ability to make others big will be greatly impaired, if not made impossible.

Even in the time of Plato, Socrates urged Alcibiades "to exercise due piety to the gods" – advice he ignored by the way, resulting in a string of unfortunate outcomes as the youth bade to rely on his own power.

Like Alcibiades, when you represent the upper limit of everything in your personal universe, the extent of everything available to you is bound by that which you can provide. Greatness. Comfort. Joy. You name it. When you are your own personal god. You are the end of the rope.

But belief in something bigger than you can also help remind you that you aren't alone, give you purpose in your life and give you the confidence to dream big. As Peter Economy put it, writing in Inc., "Big dreams come from a big God." (Economy, 2015)

Doing so also reframes our perspective on ownership. By believing in something bigger than ourselves, we know (and love) the source of our talents to whom an accounting for our harvest will ultimately be made. This enables us to more fully and joyfully grasp our role as a steward and caretaker of bounty which has been temporarily entrusted to our care, bounty which we are obliged to grow for the primary benefit of others, and which we have no option of taking with us when our time here is over.

Our ability to produce greatness ourselves and through

the care of those entrusted to us is directly proportional to the degree to which our source of strength is found in something other than ourselves. My hero John the Baptist understood this completely. The source of his strength came from a man whose sandals, he said, he was not fit to untie. John the Baptist achieved his mission by declaring whenever asked, "I am not." When each of us wake up each day intent on making ourselves really, really small, so that whatever or whoever we believe in can get really, really big, we will be well on our way to winning. The first step is no harder than simply believing.

If you can do that, you're better than half-way there.

August 26, 2016

Some time ago, I wrote about the death of my father, who died right in front of me after the CPR I tried did not work. You've also learned about the birth of my daughter, Caroline, and the miracle that resulted in her still being here. While these stories may seem to bear absolutely nothing in common, in fact, they do – more than one thing. They both have to do with believing in something bigger than ourselves; and both have to do with stewardship.

See, shortly after Chick was born, and having gotten her to Ann Arbor, Michigan for care for a potentially disastrous heart defect, I had one of many conversations I had those few weeks with the greater power I happen to believe in. It was a shorter conversation than some. Like most, it was one-way. In it, I told Him that Caroline belonged to Him, and that if He wanted her, He could take her. I told Him I'd prefer to keep her for a while, but if it was His intent to take her back, He could have at it.

Three years later, my father died. It took me two years to have that conversation with my God. Two miserable years where I nearly destroyed everything meaningful in my life – in bitterness because something that belonged to me was taken from me.

After the conversation with Him in Ann Arbor, I was at peace with what was happening in the life of my daughter. I didn't find that peace regarding the death of my dad until I had that same talk some 24 months after his passing.

By the way, just before we found out Will was coming, Annie and I lost a child. The night it happened I had a conversation with a certain larger force than me where I gave him back to whom he belonged. And I found peace.

See, when we recognize that we are merely stewards of things, the loss of them finds the proper perspective.

And that's the point for the week.

This letter is not evangelization. It's not a call for you to believe in anything. If you believe that you are the greatest thing in your universe, OK. It is a call to recognize that your possession of anything in this life is temporary. The exchange rate, at some point, for everything you have here will become zero. You will leave and not one bit of it will come with you.

I choose to view my role in that reality as one of stewardship, as having an obligation of care. It is my duty of care to leave things better than I found them. The home I live in, this position, you, others in my life, and all of the stuff in my life that I won't take with me.

When we view our role in life as stewards, one very important dynamic changes – we go from being so-called owners, to being caretakers. When that happens, our entire perspective spins on its axis. Our goal changes from enriching ourselves to enriching others. From ensuring our own well-being to ensuring that of others. From putting ourselves first to putting others first. From being served to serving.

And in doing so, we find great peace.

So, shift your thinking. From ownership, to stewardship.

And win.

* * *

What did you take with you when you left your last position?

A heart full of reminders of all of the lives that were made better because of your stewardship?

Or a box of golf trophies, pics of you and the missus with famous people, shots of the fam on high-dollar vacations, a die-cast model of your $125,000 Range Rover, a signed football from your alma mater's national championship season, and other evidence that you are the most important person in your life?

If you are a true, caring leader, you've got a heart full to carry out. If you are a traditional command and control, authoritarian narcissist, you're walking out with a box full of meaningless, self-aggrandizing stuff that never mattered to anyone in the building but you, kinda like your tenure.

But that's the difference between those who practice The Not So Subtle Art of Caring and those who don't.

Those who don't leave like a hand straight out of a bucket of water. No one notices. No one cares. But when a true, caring steward walks away, it leaves a hole. Because stewards focus on making others big, not on putting things on their credenza that make others feel small. So, ask yourself, "If I left tomorrow, would I leave a hole?" If the answer is no, start caring about others more, and take the self-aggrandizing vacation photos home.

Oh, and if you feel a need to decorate your office with stuff, here are some ideas. Include items that celebrate team accomplishments, not your own. If you have a personal item or two, have them say something about who you are as a leader, what's important to you, what you value. Think about adding a puzzle for times folks need to wait. Put a map of the world on the wall or a globe on your desk; let folks expand their horizons. Put something useful out for others to use, like a lint roller. Think of others first, think of the heart, and take my dad's advice; never have more than you can carry out under one arm.

A recent episode of the TV show *Industry* reminded me to make these points.

January 8, 2021

Over the long holiday break, our family likes to binge-stream TV shows on networks like Prime, Netflix and Hulu. One of the shows, we started this season is called *Industry*. It's a fictional drama about a bunch of young British folks working for a prestigious firm in "The City," London's equivalent to Wall St. The show is directed by Lena Dunham, so you're going to get what Lena Dunham gives. But all in all, it's not bad TV. The issues are by and large, real. And the storyline is compelling. In any event, at one point in the show, one of the old lions of the firm is let go. He's a man in his 60's. He's been with the firm his entire career. As he's leaving, he's packing his few things in the proverbial copier paper box. In doing so, with an air of bitter resentment, he mutters, "Not much for a life." I was struck by the scene for a number of reasons. But mostly because the man's words echoed in my ears. "Not much for a life." See, the man was measuring his life in terms of things, in terms of possessions. He wasn't thinking about the things he couldn't put in the box. He was thinking about whether he was better off, not whether others were better off, or if that place was better off. He was thinking as an owner of his life, not a steward of his life. The truth of the matter is this: when we think of our life in ownership terms, we are in for a long, lonely, and unhappy road.

And that's the point for the week.

See, none of this is ours. Wherever you are that you are reading this, look around you. None of what you see is leaving this earth with you. You are merely using it for a while.

Same for the people in your life. They are not yours. You

own no one. You have the privilege of employing some, raising some, teaching some, maybe even mentoring some. But you don't own any of them, and ultimately, all of them are free to do whatever they will.

The fundamental truth is this. We are stewards of everything in our lives. We are caretakers of everything in our lives. Our purpose in life is to leave that which we encounter better than we found it. Stuff and people alike.

This fundamental truth is the very basis of caring leadership. It is at the root of The Not So Subtle Art of Caring. And it is the glue that forever bonds leaders to those they have the privilege to lead. Because when those being led realize that their leader is 100% committed to their care and the betterment of their lives, they will make a decision to follow that person almost anywhere. And when they do, nearly anything becomes possible.

For these leaders then, a life is not measured by what can fit in a ridiculous copier paper box, but by what has been poured into the hearts of others, and by the immeasurable gratitude of those whose lives became irrevocably better because those they follow chose to care more for others than themselves.

So, choose to be a steward.

And win.

* * *

What would happen to your organization if you left tomorrow? Not for a day or two, I mean really left.

Depending on your management style, research has already given us an insight. If you are a traditional, micromanaging authoritarian type, it's going to be a dumpster fire. According to Yale University, "When a leader tells the team what to accomplish and how to accomplish it, the team loses autonomy. It can't really use all its members' resources. (Hackman, 2011)

Conversely, for the true, caring leader, things operate as well as or better without the boss around than when he or she is there.

First and foremost, that's because the caring leader wants a team that will function better when he or she is not around. But mostly, it's because steward leaders understand two things well: one, that they won't be there forever and two, that it's their responsibility to ensure that their organization thrives once they are gone. Like anything else in life, it's a choice. The traditional, authoritarian narcissistic leader is too insecure to tolerate a team that doesn't need them and he or she doesn't particularly care what happens after they leave. For the micromanager, success without their heavy hand would be a blow to their ego, and a suggestion that the contributions of the team are not the direct result of their greatness. So, when they leave, the wheels come off – by design. When these terrible bosses take off, their folks bury their talents in a field. These old-school managers get that because they choose that.

On the other hand, having a team with the character and capability to stand on its own and, more importantly, win on its own simply begins with a decision to do so. According to Sue Andrews, an HR consultant at KIS finance, speaking to Business News Daily, "A boss will need to give orders to instruct others what to do, but a leader can inspire others to find the best way forward, whilst motivating them to maximize their potential." (Schooley, 2019) See, it's a mindset. The steward well knows that someday they will be gone, for good – because everything is temporary – and so, they plan accordingly.

It's not just succession planning. Though, tactically, the steward must ensure that he has identified and trained his replacement. But his or her succession is a single detail in a much larger effort to ensure that the organization they leave behind is capable of functioning at a high level autonomously. It's never as simple as just saying it. It's hard work. Choosing the caring way, the road less traveled, is never easy.

Remember, like anything else, it begins with a choice. The first step is to choose to act as a steward of your team, to care about outcomes, and to then take the steps to ensure that when you are gone things will go even better than when you were there. One of my favorite descriptions of a lasting, autonomous team is from leadership expert Glen Llopsis who said,

"A team should operate as a mosaic whose unique strengths and differences convert into a powerful united force."
(Llopsis, 2012)

Remember, you don't own that team. Changing that point of view will change everything – even the way you think about what happens when you won't be there – especially the way you think about what happens when you won't be there. As in the Parable of the Talents, if you want your team to turn five talents into 10, you have to make a choice to enable them to do so.

Receiving a shiny new gold level card from a hotel chain one week spurred me to remind my team of this fundamentally important choice.

October 28, 2011

I received a letter of congratulations and a shiny new gold affinity card from one of the major hotel chains this week, recognizing my move up to their next level of status. As I replaced my old silver card in the stack of airline, car rental and hotel plastic I keep rubber-banded together in my briefcase, I noted that I have achieved gold level or better with as many as four different hotel chains this year. While some might take pride in such a changing of the affinity card guard and the recognition of one's loyalty by these national chains, to me it meant something altogether different. That I'm away a lot.

I was saddened at first by the thought. Being in hotels well over 100 nights a year, I miss a lot at home and with the folks in Fort Smith. It also reminded me that I won't be here forever. But as I considered things further, I was reminded of something positive and a key principal of leadership.

When gone, I'm not able to be intimately involved in every detail of life at my house or at 1000 S. 21st Street either one. But that's OK. Because even when I'm here I'm not. Things go about pretty much the same in both places when I'm here as when I'm gone. They should. If the show can't go on without its leader, it isn't much of a show to begin with.

That's the point for the week.

The true measure of one's effectiveness as a leader is better made by watching what happens when they are not around than when they are.

Leaders are by definition not individual contributors. Their greatest gift to any organization and to their own legacies and advancement is the quality of the teams they assemble. Leaders who create excellent teams achieve more than their counterparts who rely on their own wits, sheer power, or strength of will. That they do so is purely a matter of physics. People run faster without someone hanging on their back.

I can be gone for tens of nights per year and feel OK about leaving for good because the tremendous teams I have at home and at work don't become paralyzed without me. Annie and my kids at home and Martha and the entire gang at Wingfoot can be counted on to deliver outstanding results no matter where I am. This happens for a few simple reasons. One, because no one, let alone me, knows their jobs better than they do. Two, because they understand the vision for our organization. Three, because they are free and empowered to be and do their best, unencumbered by meddling on my part. Four, because there are replicatable processes that guide the way this place does things. True stewards take care to ensure that things work as well as or better without them than with them.

See, effectiveness gained through omnipresent micromanagement is a short-term proposition. It's unsustainable. If the entire operation depends on the leader, then the moment he leaves, it becomes a train wreck. Worse, when leaders do the job of those most capable of doing them, good people run off in search of more empowering environments where they can thrive. When the boss never leaves his desk, customers are never seen by the leader; the biggest and most important eventually leave in search of more attention. Too, associates in the field are never met and told how much they are appreciated; as a result, the brightest will at some point just go away in search of proper care and feeding. Worst of all, by micromanaging the present, these old-school authoritarian managers ignore the future, leaving the organization to drift without a vision.

Often, it's simply our own conceit and insecurity that keep us from empowering our teams to run without us. We wrongly think that we'd be somehow unnecessary. We mistakenly believe that something done right requires us to do it. We labor under the misapprehension that our value is defined by the extent that our own fingerprints are plastered all over the work product of the team.

When teams are set up to function as well without their leaders present as with them there, the worth, regard for, and capability of every member, including its leader, skyrocket for no other reason than these teams win more. They achieve great things all the time, not just when the leader is present. The individual parts that comprise them reach their true potential unencumbered by the constraint of an over-controlling boss. Most importantly, trust blossoms between leader and team helping to create a virtually unbreakable bond that enables these organizations to climb any mountain or ford any stream – whether their leaders are at their desk, a Holiday Inn Express 700 miles away, or gone for good.

So, be a steward of your business. Set your team up to prosper without you.

And win.

* * *

For years, I have counseled groups I have worked with that people are who they are by about age six, then, after that, only the situations change. It turns out I was right. A study by Christopher Nave, published in the journal, Social Psychological and Personality Science, found that the personality traits observed in individuals as first graders remain predominant throughout their lives. According to Nave et al.,"the same individual even in two vastly different contexts separated by many years – such as his or her classroom as an elementary school student, or a clinic interview room as a middle-aged adult – remains recognizably the same person." (Nave, 2010) So what's my point?

My point is this. Caring leaders recognize that the individuals they have the privilege to lead have been WHO they are for virtually their entire lives. True, caring leaders, those who practice The Not So Subtle Art of Caring further recognize that any effort on the part of the leader to fundamentally change WHO a person is is akin to tilting at windmills, or for those of you opposed to Don Quixote references, substitute beating your head off a wall. What true, caring stewards fundamentally get is that what can be changed is what people do – how they behave. Trying to change who someone is will be a long, futile and fruitless process. But working to change what a person does; now that's the stuff of leadership.

The base question is this. Are you comfortable with the idea of changing what a person does vs. who a person is? If so, you'll fit right in with this stewardship gig. Most traditional micromanagers struggle. They'd rather try to drum the who right out of someone.

I used a story about a tree, grown from a sapling for my oldest daughter, to make this point for my team at Goodyear a few years ago.

August 29, 2014

I have no less than two dozen large, mature Oak trees on my property. You know, the ones that reach 80 feet in height and twice that from leaf to leaf. Well, with oak trees come, you guessed it, acorns. Each year, most of the thousands of acorns that fall in my yard are either gathered up by squirrels or eaten by my dog Moses. Those that aren't are left to potentially germinate.

One popped up the week my daughter chick was born in 1997. I decided to dig it up and pot it. I took care to ensure that it had everything it needed to flourish – water, light, fertilizer. As it outgrew a pot, I'd transplant it to a larger pot. The tree moved with our family to Georgia, then back to Ohio. In 2010, when the tree was 13 years old, some 8 feet tall, and in a very large pot by then, we learned we were moving to Arkansas. I decided it was time to put the tree in the ground. We moved away and came back. From time to time, I go check on the tree, which is now taller than two of me. It's 17 now. Coincidentally, my daughter is 17 today also, which is why I thought of the tree.

That tree grew to be the mancentifical Oak tree that it is today because I nurtured it and cared for it and recognized it as an Oak. I never bent over it as a seedling and muttered to it, "Hey little seedling, when you grow up you are going to be a breathtaking Redwood; you're going to be so tall, and so big around that five men won't be able to put their arms around you." Nope. I told my little seedling that it was going to become a ginormous Oak, because it was growing from an acorn, and from acorns come Oaks, not Redwoods. People are the same.

People born Oaks will never be Redwoods, no matter how hard we try. See, as leaders, we can't change what people are, we can change what people do.

And that's the point for the week.

People are like trees. If as a leader, I'm given an acorn, there is no amount of nurturing that will ever amount to that little acorn becoming anything other than an Oak. Period. It won't ever be a Maple, or a Redwood, or a Birch, or a Hickory. It's going to be an Oak. And the kind of Oak and the height it reaches will depend on the stewardship it receives from me.

Despite every effort on my part, there is nothing I can do to change WHAT that Oak of mine is. But I can provide the best possible condition for the acorn to thrive and produce. I can provide care to ensure that its needs are met. I can help guard against that which threatens its growth. And I can have an impact on what that Oak does.

When we reject our hard-wired inclination to try to "fix" what we think is wrong in others and concentrate more on creating the sort of environment they can thrive in and on providing them the nurturing and stewardship they require to achieve their maximum potential, they more often will – and we along with them.

Doing so requires little more than understanding their unique needs and responding appropriately.

People cannot be "fixed." They *can* be placed into situations where they enjoy a greater likelihood of success. They *can* be provided the counsel, learning, and development to enable them to reach their greatest potential by ensuring that they perfect the behaviors which will guarantee the greatest likelihood of their success. They *can* be protected from internal and external factors which threaten their progress.

When they are, they and the teams they comprise will thrive, reaching levels of height and beauty that all the fixing in the world could never produce.

Nurture what they are. Be a steward of what they do.
And win.

* * *

True caring leaders fade heat before it reaches their people.

If we've established nothing so far, it's that things will go wrong sometimes. When they do, true, caring leaders, as stewards of the business, step to the front – into the fire – while traditional narcissists scramble to the back, looking for human shields to place between them and the heat. Evan as stewards of their organization, these leaders understand that any difficulty in the business is a potential for loss of value: for customer defections; for associate resignations; for stock price or rating devaluation; and for sullying of the firm's image. So, as a caretaker for the value of the business and the well-being of its stakeholders, the caring leader has an absolute interest in becoming quickly and directly involved in confronting downside when it happens.

According to researchers from ghSmart whose CEO Genome research includes assessments of over 20,000 C-suite executives, "The best leaders take personal ownership in a crisis (and) quickly process available information, rapidly determine what matters most, and make decisions with conviction." (Nichols, 2020)

By decisively and quickly confronting difficulty when it arises, caring stewards not only nip problems in the bud, before they become full blown disasters, but they also set a positive example for and earn the trust of those they have the privilege to lead who see a leader who accepts personal responsibility and never, ever uses others as scapegoats when things explode.

How do you react when things go wrong? Do you step to the front and stand in front of your people? True leaders do.

A simple, but significant customer explosion was a great

opportunity to make this point with my team.

July 12, 2019

This week, I had the opportunity to make a solo visit to a customer who is rather upset with the performance of one of our products. It wasn't a brief visit. It wasn't a particularly pleasant visit. At times it was embarrassing. But I learned a lot. I was able to come up with an idea or two for how to move forward. And I received straight up props for owning up to and confronting the issue versus a close competitor with similar issues, whose chief had never been to or called the customer and whose key people have yet to take responsibility for their product failures. This competitor he criticized roundly.

See, when as stewards of our business, we take our medicine, positive things happen. And that's the point for the week.

Avoiding problems, sidestepping or denying them will never make them go away. In fact, the original mess is usually compounded by any such moves to get out of the way. But when we step up to the issue early, take our lumps, and deal with things head on, not only do things get cleaned up more quickly, enabling us to get on with life, but we generally get positive recognition from those involved for having taken responsibility for the issue. What's more, we set a positive example for those paying attention to us as role models.

Certainly, we don't want to invite trouble for the purpose of looking good getting out of it. But when trouble finds us, our best option is to deal with it, openly, honestly, and as quickly as possible. Doing so is never fun. It's never easy. And it's never going to become something we look forward to. But when we choose, to act as stewards, to stand up, we will win more often, as a company and as individuals, because we will be seen as people who can be trusted, even when things go wrong. So that even when mistakes happen, one thing that will never be considered a mistake is doing business with us.

So, deal with trouble head on.

And win.

* * *

To the caring steward, transparency matters.

One of my favorite scenes in all of cinema is the one toward the end of Adam Sorkin's film, *A Few Good Men*, where archetypal command and control authoritarian manager, Jack Nicholson screams at his replacement generation counterpart, played by Tom Cruise, "You can't handle the truth!" What Nicholson's character, Colonel Nathan R. Jessup (a narcissistic villain name, second only to the equally vile, micromanaging, and untruthful redneck Roscoe P. Coltrain from the Dukes of Hazzard) is actually saying, is that he prefers a lack of transparency, that as a leader, he's keeping information back for others' own good. The trouble is, when managers behave like Jessup or Coltrain, they stymie progress, stifle trust, and sow the seeds of suspicion and doubt. When leaders promote a lack of transparency, they create impediments to winning and the growth of their people.

Imagine going through life with a layer of fog over everything, so thick that it was impossible for you to fully identify or discern one object from another, let alone see details or a clear way forward. When leaders fail to create a culture of transparency, this is what every day feels like for those in their organization. Mired in a fog, they stand in place waiting for their Dear Leader to show them the way. According to leadership expert Glen Llopsis, "The reason most leaders are not transparent is because they believe they will be viewed as less authoritative; that the credentials they worked so hard to attain will lose their power, leverage and gravitas." (Llopsis, 2012) As if ... Right?

The caring steward promotes absolute transparency. He or she believes that the quality of decision making and the results they deliver are directly proportional to the information that is available to their team. Llopsis agrees. Not only does he say that teams will solve problems faster and achieve higher levels of performance, but he believes that maximizing transparency "will not only build trust, but more importantly set-forth a precedent that will transcend through team(s), and establish a new type of loyalty and attitude that will ripple throughout the organization." (Llopsis, 2012) Caring leaders cannot imagine hoarding information as a weapon or as leverage. The concept of other adult human beings "not being able to handle the truth" is laughable to the steward leader. Of course, the steward leader believes that to whom much is given, much is required. But in an organization where trust is shown, trust is given. And winning becomes a way of life.

The more comfortable you are sharing information with your team the more comfortable you will be as a steward of your team. If you believe information is power or that people should have limited access to information you're going to struggle. Ask yourself how transparent you're willing to be.

A man who, in Amsterdam, had recently completed a very interesting renovation project provided the basis for a story that reinforced the value in transparency.

January 14, 2011

This week I heard a story about a man who had renovated a home along a waterway in Amsterdam, installing a large, uncovered window at street level. When asked why he had installed the window on the first floor and not an upper level thereby enabling an even better view of the water, he replied that, the window had more to do with the view in, than the view out. He went on to say that his home stayed cleaner because of the window.

Upon a first hearing of the story this seems odd – both in

terms of a view in vs. out and how a window has anything to do with keeping one's home clean. But after further reflection, it makes perfect sense.

It's about the importance of transparency, both literally and figuratively.

Because the man's home—its contents and the activity that occurred there - were in plain view to those outside, he was more likely to keep everything inside in proper order. In his stewardship of the home, the more that was openly visible to others, the more effective was his stewardship. When all have a view to the works, things work better.

That's the point for the week.

Transparency matters.

Every aspect of our lives—at home, at work, in our communities—improves when transparency is part of the equation.

When we act with transparency – by creating a culture of max communication and extreme openness – we'll be more apt to do the right thing. We'll more likely welcome input from others. We'll enable others to see things that we don't. And we will take great pains to ensure that anything that reflects on us reflects well.

Our level of care for anything increases directly with the level of sunlight that shines on it.

A greater degree of openness will also yield operational improvements.

Transparency ensures that people have all the information they need to make better decisions. Transparency provides an implicit invitation to others to participate in the big picture. Transparency uncovers new opportunities – that otherwise may have remained hidden.

Transparency, like sunlight, is a natural antiseptic.

When we provide and expect transparency, we'll have greater credibility with those around us. We'll develop stronger relationships with others. And we'll more quickly fix that which needs fixing. In short (you guessed it) we'll win more.

So, build big windows.

And win.

* * *

While we're on the subject of Jack Nicholson films, the notion of the importance of trust to the typical steward leader makes me think of a scene from the Martin Scorsese film, The Departed which also starred Nicholson. At one point in the film, the character played by Nicholson, Francis Costello, looks at his goons and says, "No tickie, no laundry." This idiom, popular in the 60's and 70's was a way of saying, without one thing, none of another. In the literal sense of the idiom, without your receipt, you cannot have your dry cleaning. The point of applying the idiom to leadership is this: without trust, there is no leadership.

An absence of trust has long been identified as a leading cause of unhappiness among disengaged associates and those who hate their bosses. In fact, according to The Predictive Index, a survey of over 4,000 workers, among the traits consistently chosen to describe a horrible boss, "Betrays trust" made the top 10 and was listed by over half of those surveyed. (The Predictive Index, 2018) "This lack of trust is typical among command and control bosses and has caused many to rethink whether traditional, authoritarian management styles still apply in a world where trust is valued higher than almost any other attribute.

In the economy of the true, caring leader, trust is the currency upon which everything moves. Without trust, nothing happens. No tickie, no laundry. No soul, no service. According to recent research "Increasingly scholars have identified the leader-follower relationship as a series of psychological contracts that rise to the level of a "covenantal relationship" and that "Leaders earn the trust and followership of others by being trustworthy and accountable." (Caldwell, 2011) In order to be trusted, leaders must first prove that they are trustworthy. This is accomplished by engaging in behaviors that prove to associates first that the leader is committed to earning their trust and next that the leader can be counted on not to betray that trust. Ultimately though, by developing a trust-centered relationship with those they have the privilege to lead, the caring steward can lead their organization to higher levels of long-term associate engagement and shareholder value.

What specific steps do you take each day to ensure that you earn and keep the trust of those you lead? Is your word as good as gold? Are you accountable for the commitments you make?

My own experience with and a reminder from the television show *Undercover Boss* formed the basis of a story about trust-centered stewardship.

April 8, 2011

Sunday, I watched the latest episode of *Undercover Boss*. Many of you have probably seen or heard about it. The premise is simple. The leader of a major organization goes undercover to learn, as the show's intro sequence suggests, "what is really going on inside their company."

I'm a fan of the show. Having had my own similar experience at our shop in Brunswick, I can relate some. The notion that leaders should be spending time where the work actually occurs is something I strongly believe in. As I've mentioned to a number of you, it's almost impossible to manage what you've never seen before.

But leaders shouldn't have to go undercover to find out what's really going on.

That's the point for the week.

The implication the show makes is that associates won't be open and honest if they know who they are actually talking to.

I get it. But it doesn't need to be that way.

It's all a matter of trust.

Organizations of any stripe work best when trust is found among their guiding principles. Without trust, people hold back – in how they work, what they say, and who they confide in.

Trust is enabled when associates know they can speak up without fear of reprisal or ridicule. Trust is fostered when associates know they can try something new without fear of discipline when they fail (because sometimes they will fail). Trust is nurtured when associates know they can share things in confidence without fear of them coming back around. You get the idea.

See, trust and fear are mutually exclusive. More of one means less of the other. Without fear, human beings are liberated – to dream more, achieve more, and become more than they ever dreamed was possible. Because they trust.

Now, the truth about trust is that it must be earned. It can't be demanded from, bartered for, or beaten out of others. Nor will folks be scared into trusting; people won't trust because they are afraid not to. Remember, more fear equals less trust.

Trust takes time. That's OK ... as long as it is being relentlessly sought after by leaders intent on its achievement.

Too, achieving trust is like a card game; associates won't show their hand until their leaders show theirs. Until we trust those we have the privilege to lead they'll never trust us as leaders.

But when they do ... those we lead will move Heaven and earth for us. They'll watch out for us. They'll do more and give more for us. They'll do so faster, better, and with love. Because they trust.

Go over-cover. Foster trust.

And win.

* * *

Stewards walk around their putts.

Those who walk around their putts gain maximum information and in turn, maximum advantage – simply because they know more, because they've seen more, because they have more insights into what's coming. Though, like anything else, subject to diminishing returns, as the quantity and quality of information increases, so does the quality of decision-making. So too, the relationship between decision making and winning. So, it stands to reason that those with better information win more.

Like most everything else in life, having more information is a choice. Taking the time to walk around a putt is a choice. Taking the time to look at a decision from all angles or to put oneself in the shoes of another are, you guessed it, choices. David Angel writes in Medium, "So how do I usually fail at being a good steward of risk? It's usually being lazy: I either don't try to truly understand the situation or I fall back on convenient heuristics." (Angel, 2016) The Not So Subtle Art of Caring includes making the choice to walk around your putts. To, even if you are highly intuitive, as I am, to look both ways before you step into a crosswalk. To always put yourself in the shoes of the other parties. Always. To also determine what information, what looks, what insights yield advantage, then take the time to get them.

I tell people all the time to do things as if their lives depend on them – because they do. The life you want to have depends on what you do today. If you make better decisions today, by taking a bit more time to walk around the putt, your life tomorrow gets measurably better. So put the time in today. Walk around the putt.

July 15, 2011

On Monday, So Yeon Ryu won the 65th Women's US Open at

The Broadmoor in Colorado. She didn't win with her driver – Ryu was tied for 43rd in fairways hit for the week – but won on the green. Ryu carded twelve birdies in the tournament, none more important than one on the final hole of the final round to force a play-off with fellow Korean, Hee Kyung Seo. That Ryu made twelve birdies is not what struck me most about her win; it's HOW she made them. Ryu spends a considerable amount of time looking at putts from all angles and discussing them with her caddie. As a result, she rolls more in.

It occurred to me that what propels Ryu's performance on the golf course applies in almost every aspect of life. The more we know about any circumstance the better we'll respond to it.

That's the point for the week.

Things are almost never exactly as they seem at first glance. Like stories, situations have more than one side. When we evaluate them based on a single look or from a single direction, we miss things. As a result, we make poorer decisions. When we do, we win less often. But when we take the care to ensure that our decisions are based on the most complete and up to date information available, we'll more often make better choices. In short, we win more.

In any situation, it's important that we know what we don't know, then find the answers to fill those gaps. Implicit in doing so is an admission that we do not have all of the answers. Like much else in leadership, good decision making is rooted in humility. When we freely admit we don't know everything we open ourselves up to more, and usually better, options. Moreover, we open ourselves to the participation and input of other human beings, the net result of which is geometrically better decisions made faster.

Certainly, what we do with the information once we collect it – that is, how well we execute – matters a great deal. But terrific execution based on incomplete information can be as or more devastating than even the poorest execution properly aligned.

Taking time to learn all we can before making a decision shouldn't slow us down either. In fact, the contrary is true. We'll still make decisions by their deadlines – we have to; we'll simply spend the time before the bell sounds gathering all the facts we can. But because we'll make better decisions, we'll actually end up with MORE time in the end. That's because whatever time we invest in learning will pale in comparison to the time we'll save by no longer having to clean up the literal and figurative messes that result from poor, ill-informed decisions.

By investing the time to collect as much information as possible, we'll not only make better decisions in less time, we'll also strengthen our relationships with those we have the privilege to lead. See by factoring in all inputs we'll less often jump to conclusions – a practice which does more to destroy trust than almost any other managerial shortcoming. Too, when we seek out all available information, we'll naturally ask others for their input, resulting in not only better decisions, but associates who feel better about the choices we make and their jobs for being asked – associates who choose to stay HERE cheering as our ball finds the bottom of the cup and knowing they were part of making it so.

Make better decisions based on better information. Walk around your putts.

And win.

* * *

Careful stewards pay attention to the back of the house.

For many leaders, the front of the house is where all of the glamour is found. When visitors come, it's to the front of the house. It's the part of the house that attracts attention. It's shiny. It's fun. Those laugh-a-minute sales and marketing folks hang out in the front of the house. There's PR to be had in the front of the house. And don't forget those all-important photo ops. The back of the house? Who cares? No one ever sees that. Besides, it's dirty back there. Do you have any idea how much I paid for this suit??

Every business has two parts. The parts customers see, and the part they don't. The part you talk about with customers, and the part you don't. The part that's shiny, and the part that's not. Here's some news. Caring stewards pay attention to both parts. They work to make the less shiny parts more shiny. They work to make more of the business something to talk about. They work to make more of the place something to be proud of. That's because they are stewards of the entire enterprise – because they care about the entire enterprise, and everyone in all parts of it.

The careful steward can be trusted in big things because they can be trusted in small things. Things like housekeeping. Things like bending over and picking up a piece of trash on his or her way into the building. Things like refusing to believe that things people can't see don't matter, or worse, that people who can't be seen don't matter. Michael Holmes, writing for Life of a Steward says, "Faithfulness in the small things is the surest sign of a good steward. It's more important than talent, skills, vision, or anything else." (Holmes, 2012) See, when a leader believes that everything matters, nothing gets missed. And when nothing gets missed, when no one gets missed, the organization races forward like a gleaming orb, full of people who couldn't imagine working anywhere else and customers who wouldn't leave you on a bet. All because of a single steward leader, who chose to pay attention to every part of the place, and every person in the place.

What does the back of your house look like? Would you be willing to give guided tours of it tomorrow? If not, it's time to get to work.

February 6, 2009

As I rode the bus from the airport to the Gaylord Resort last week, we passed a number of shopping malls and strip centers which lined the interstate.

I was struck by the sharp contrast in many cases between the front of the stores and the back.

In nearly every case, the fronts of the stores were neat, colorful and inviting while the backs were unkempt and unappealing. A few, though, managed to project a positive image on both sides.

It occurred to me that these were more productive retailers, more attractive places to work, and more satisfying stores to shop.

I thought about our business and each of us as individuals.

Are we as concerned about the things others, like our customers, can't see as we are with those they can?

When we spend equal energy on what our customers don't see and what they do we win more.

That's the point for the week.

Making certain that every aspect of our business and behavior projects a positive image is a key to our success as individuals and a company.

What we do when no one is looking says more about us as a company, a sales team and individuals than almost anything.

The notion that things our customers won't see don't matter has no place in a high-performance team.

Every detail is important.

When attention to that which is less visible is discovered by others it leaves a significant and lasting impression. People reason that when care is given to the apparently unimportant that tremendous attention has been given to that which matters.

Pay attention to the front AND back of the store.

And win.

* * *

Earlier in the chapter, I referenced diminishing returns in regard to information support for decision making. Just as the plotting of almost anything in life along a single axis will reveal a bell curve, the plotting of anything with a measure of input and output will reveal a point of diminishing returns where each additional unit of input yields output at a lesser rate than the prior unit of input.

As stewards of the enterprise, caring leaders are particularly aware where points of diminishing return exist and are careful not to throw good money after bad. Caring servants view their role and purpose to maximize the economic value of the enterprise for which they show care. To persist at anything beyond the point of diminishing returns is to destroy value, an activity which holds no level of interest for the steward.

This extends to everything from market share to change management. There is a cost to every point of share gain and to getting every hold-out associate on board. The thoughtful, caring leader is astutely aware of both the cost of each incremental unit of gain as well as the benefit of each. Once the incremental benefit compared to the cost to achieve that added gain begins to turn back, the steward must rethink their investment and investigate other ways to multiply the resources of the firm.

For the caring steward, The Not So Subtle Art of Caring is entirely about multiplication, about dramatically expanding the return on every investment – in both real and human capital. As renowned leadership expert John Maxwell puts it, "The highest level of influence you can have in others' lives is at the multiplication level." (Maxwell, 2018) Leaders fixated on multiplying their value, the value of others and the value of the organizations they care for will be astutely aware of the top of the value curve and will seek to shift resources and effort whenever a point of diminishing returns is reached.

Are you acutely aware of the point of diminishing returns for every activity in your organization? If not, you should be. Here's a hint: your people are. They know when good money starts to follow bad. Ask them; they will tell you.

A story about a speaking engagement at a cross-state university was a great set-up for a discussion about diminishing returns.

November 14, 2009

This week I had an opportunity to speak to a group of students at the University of Toledo about our company and our selling strategy.

While there, I had a chance to learn about a sales simulation that teams of UT students run aimed at maximizing the total portfolio value of a territory or channel.

In it students decide how to allocate units of time to different accounts. As they play, the kids learn that their accounts have varying total lifetime values to their fictional companies (just like real life).

The first reaction of the teams after they identify the most high-value accounts is to allocate gobs of time to them and little to any others.

Over time they slowly realize, usually when it's too late, the lesson of diminishing returns. After a certain point more time added to high value accounts produces no more yield. Meanwhile, other accounts quickly suffer.

The heart of their lesson, my speech to them and the point for the week is that it is possible to have too much of a good thing.

Are you spending too much time with too few accounts? Or do you have a balanced attack that maximizes return on your efforts?

This lesson doesn't begin and end with the way we manage our territories and channels. It is certainly true for virtually every aspect of our lives.

Individuals who win, like the leading Toledo sales teams, are those who figure it out. They learn when the top of the return curve has been achieved for any activity – in business, at home, or socially.

It is possible to have too much of a good thing.

Find the top of the curve.

And win.

(Go Rockets!)

* * *

It is without question that the top of the curve on traditional micromanagement has long since been reached. These mostly narcissistic authoritarians are dinosaurs whose time has come and gone.

There exists a significant and growing incongruence between the generations now comprising the majority of the workforce and the management style being used to direct them. According to researcher Mark Emmons, just Millennials by themselves, already 50% of the workforce, will comprise 75% of working adults by 2030. (Emmons, 2018) But, sadly, according to Gallup a whopping 55% of Millennials say they are not engaged. Similarly, 50% of GenXers are not engaged. (Gallup, 2016) Worse, Udemy Research reports that a huge 67% of Millennials believe there is a gap between what they think they are capable of and what their boss believes they are qualified to do. (Udemy Research, 2018) "These disconnects are the result of managers who are using a century plus old leadership style on people who want nothing to do with it.

There is a clear solution. Steward leaders, those who practice The Not So Subtle Art of Caring. These leaders have an intrinsic motivation to maximize the output of the corporation while also ensuring that the multiplicative value of the combined human resources under their care are likewise optimized.

So, there's hope. And for each of you reading this book, a choice: between the old broken-down way of hurting others, or the new, better way of making them really, really big.

I trust you find the decision as easy as it's always been for me.

Next, in the final chapter, we'll end with a few last letters, offering insights into a handful of this, a handful of that, and a little of anything else I could find – 12 additional leadership traits which separate the caring steward from everyone else.

Chapter 6

A Dog's Breakfast of Things

"Now that, my dear James, is what I call a Dog's Breakfast..."
Ralph Hagen
1959-
Canadian Cartoonist

I was born in 1964. As you might imagine, as the son of a truck dealer, I grew up learning a fair repertoire of colorful sayings, many of them not suited for mixed company. I've spent a lot of my life cleaning up things my father said to enable me to use them again, because at their root, they had value. Choosing a career in the truck and tire business, things got worse not better. I picked up some doozies from one of the best bosses I ever had, a wrestler, like me, from upstate New York, named Jack Winterton. Jack was another storyteller. And a teacher. Like all of our best teachers, he quit before I was done learning. I miss him a lot. But better too few years with the best of something, than none at all.

One of his more descriptive terms was Dog's Breakfast. I loved it. It's a way to say, "a handful of this, a handful of that, and a little of anything else you can find." But you can say it in two words, not 17. Plus, there were zero curse words in it, so it was perfect. Or so I thought. Later in life, I used it in a board meeting. I'm the CEO of a company making a quarterly earnings presentation, and I toss out "Dog's Breakfast." I'm thinking, "Jack would be cracking up right now." I almost did. Then I look at my boss, and he's not pleased. He immediately starts cleaning it up, "What Phillip meant was _____" (fills in the blanks with 17 words).

So now you know what a Dog's Breakfast is. Whether you use it in a board meeting is entirely your call. You know what I'd do.

The following stories don't fit neatly in any earlier category, or there's not enough of their brand to fill up a chapter. So, there's a handful of this, a handful of that, and a little of anything else I could find that I thought truly mattered. They are stories about:

- Making Every Day Different and Better
- Learning from Those Who Came Before
- Remembering What You Can Endure
- Bringing the Yellow Broom
- Not Lifting the Lid
- Measuring What Matters
- Learning to Let Go
- Having Vision
- Locking Up Your Goat
- Getting the Whole Picture
- Recognizing Feedback as a Gift
- Being Someone Who Does Something

Some of these letters are about not being subtle; some are about the art of it all. Others are truly about caring. But what they all have in common is this: they are lessons from unlikely places, lessons that teach us about a better sort of leadership. It's a kind of leadership that puts care for others first, before anything else

– before the first number, before the first customer. It's a sort of leadership rooted in the love of others that teaches us that the smaller we make ourselves, the bigger others can become. And that somehow, paradoxically, when that happens, when we get really, really small, and others get really, really big, the most ginormous things ever start happening in our lives. All because we made a choice: to start practicing The Not So Subtle Art of Caring.

* * *

The sunrises I saw out of my window each morning while living in California were a fitting basis for a story about recognizing and creating difference. True, caring leaders focus not only on making each day better than the one before, but also on the beauty of the world around them. They can find something breathtaking even on the grayest day or in the most dilapidated cityscape; because they look for it. To the servant leader, every individual is different just like every sunrise is different because they look for and notice goodness in everything.

It is that ability and desire to choose the better part which enables these leaders to create sequential "betterness" day after day. According to Harvard Business Review contributor, Bill Taylor, founder of Fast Company magazine, "the best leaders see things that others don't see." (Taylor, 2018) As French writer Marcel Proust wrote, "The only true voyage of discovery, the only fountain of Eternal Youth, would be not to visit strange lands but to possess other eyes, to behold the universe through the eyes of another, of a hundred others, to behold the hundred universes that each of them beholds, that each of them is." (Proust, 1923) These best, caring leaders, whether innate or learned, share an ability to, in my view, not see things differently so much as to see things entirely, then to identify both the good and the points of opportunity and leverage both in each frame. And while traditional command and control authoritarian managers predictably home in on the negative, these caring visionaries gain minutes, hours, or days in competitive advantage on their prehistoric counterparts who are left behind stewing over a view of ugliness they can do nothing to change.

What is your natural orientation? Do you immediately notice and focus on the good, or do you isolate on the negative? Winning, caring leaders spend their time on all that's right and good. Practice doing so by writing down the good you see in every new situation, starting the moment the sun comes up.

November 16, 2018

The sunrises I have seen from my house this week have been fantastic. Maybe spectacular is a better word. Every day, streaks of color have run North to South across the sky in mixed hues of blue, pink, orange, purple, yellow, and red; always followed by a piercing dome of white, then the appearance of the sun – sometimes orange, sometimes yellow, sometimes pure white for an instant. See it occurred to me that while the sun rises every day, each sunrise is different. No two are ever the same. The more I considered this, the more it seemed there was a message in there for us; that what we do and try each day should be different than what we did the day before.

And that's the point for the week.

Every day presents us with a choice. A beautiful, wonderful choice. A choice between happiness and sadness, a smile or a frown, selfishness or selflessness, helping or hurting ... You get the point. It's also a choice to do things differently and better than we did the day before. Every day is like a do-over. With every sunrise, every yesterday is gone forever, never to come back no matter how hard we try. But it also means that yesterday can't keep us from doing something more remarkable today. Whether here, at home, or in your communities, when you wake up every day firmly believing that each day presents you with the opportunity to do something spectacular, you more often will. We more often will. When more of you walk through the doors here intent on making each day better than the one before, we will create an incredible momentum here that will soon become unstoppable. Everything about this place will become better. Because the people who work here wake up each day wanting every day to be better than before.

I have told many of you before that I don't care much about what happened before. I truly don't. It's because I can't change it. What I can change is my todays and my tomorrows when they become todays. I came here choosing to make every day better than the day before so that together with all of you we could create something fantastic here for all of you, for our customers and for our stakeholders. And I have loved to see the sunrises here every day. I've seen the streaks of light in your faces, in your work, and in our improving numbers. And I can't wait to see the brilliance of our different, better tomorrows ... when they become todays.

So, make every day different and better.

And win.

* * *

You should have, by now, started to see a common idea emerging. Leaders who practice The Not So Subtle Art of Caring, make each day different and better because they do things that are different and better.

Like choosing to learn from the past and from those who came before them. Great leaders do that. Pantsuit Barbie and Ken Doll don't. Someone confided in me once that the chief of our company was making changes solely for the purpose of NOT having it appear that he was doing anything like his predecessor, the guy who fixed the place. Does that sound familiar?

It's not just my former chief. Among the traditional management set, failing to learn from the past is commonplace. And it's a problem. But why? According to Harvard lecturer Tony Mayo, "They failed to seek advice or (they) actively discourage differences of opinion when they move up the organization." (Mayo, 2007) Whether it is casual indifference to or an outright careless disregard for the teachings of the past, when we as leaders fail to take the time to be informed by those who have done this before, we are leaving a trove of knowledge untapped. The great American author, Pearl S. Buck, once wrote that, "knowledge of history as detailed as possible is essential if we want to comprehend the past and be prepared for the future." (Buck, 1954)

I have said for years that every significant problem in American business has in the course of some 250 years, been encountered and solved – only the players and circumstances change. But the base issues are little different. The problem is two-fold: no one ever writes down what happened before, and even where they do, no one bothers to learn from it. Because every generation must learn the hard way. That's crazy. To be a better leader, spend time with those who did it before. Write down what they say. Learn from them. Avoid the mistakes that they made. Double down on the goodness. But begin by simply sitting down with those older than you, and wiser than you, in all facets of your life, and write down the things they tell you, or type it in an iPad, or record them on your phone. But capture it somehow, for posterity, and for your own darn good, lest your stock end up at $3 again.

The sad occasion of my father-in-law's passing presented an opportunity to make this point (mostly to myself).

November 30, 2018

As many of you know I lost my father-in-law on Thanksgiving. So not much more significant than that happened in my life this week. My father-in-law was one of my heroes. He taught me a lot about being a husband, a father and the businessman, and I became better at all three because of him. The day after his funeral I learned that one of his former employees had compiled a collection of his wisdoms and sayings over the years. She wanted the family to have it. There were dozens of items on her list and I recognized every one of them. But I had never written them down. So, some I had forgotten to practice. Here's this man who I idolized, and I had never bothered to take notes on anything he had taught me. I suppose that the closer something is to us, the more we take it for granted, when in fact it should be quite the opposite. The closer something is to us, the more we should find great treasure in it.

And that's the point for the week.

We all have people or things, like my father-in-law, who are just there, have always been there, can be counted on to be there, or who we never think of not being there. And so, we go on, day in and out, without recognizing the remarkable that's right in front of us – until it's not. We benefit greatly from having these things in our midst, but because their presence is so commonplace, we don't often think of how tremendous they really are – until they are gone. We learn priceless lessons from these unpaid teachers, which at the time don't seem to hold much value – until it's the last day of school. And we are left wishing, among other things, that we had taken a note or two, or written some things down.

Whether a parent, an in-law, a spouse, a great boss, someone in the community, or just a wise soul you work beside, those we might take for granted are abundant in our lives. I know that my life is full of them. And I know that the rest of my life will be a lot better if I start taking notes, if I start writing down what I'm taught, so that I more often put into practice what I learn. Imagine if we all did that. Imagine if we started writing down and learning then acting on the wisdom of those close to us and wiser than us. Imagine how great our homes could be, our community could be, our company could be. Simply because we bothered to write down and remember what the people who were the most important people in our lives taught us.

So, write down what wise people teach you.

And win.

* * *

In addition to learning from those who came before them, the best, caring leaders are certain to learn from life's trials too, especially what these hardships teach him/her about the things they are able to endure. The caring leader does not become bitter as a result of difficulty, but sees each life experience, good or bad, as an occasion to learn from, even if only about our own capabilities or of those around us.

Having lived through a number of awful personal and professional difficulties, like my father dying after the CPR I tried failed, or the financial crisis of 2008, I have told people on the other side of each that while I would not want to go through the trial again, I am thankful for the opportunity to have done so; for I learned a great deal – about life, about business, about myself and my own capabilities, and about others. But in every case, I also share with people that having confidently led people through the mess with a caring heart and watching the desk-pounders and cutters do their thing, I'd do it my way every single time.

The following letter could have shown up in a number of places in this book. It's here for that reason. It's here because it's about tone, and making it personal, and expectation setting, and what happens (or should) when things go wrong. It's about all of those things for sure. There are other points that could have been made that I didn't, maybe some you'll immediately take away – some about love and possession. But tucked in the middle of the letter is an explicit point about what we let rise beyond the limit of our own self-confidence.

None of us escapes loss, trial or hardship in life. The things we endure teach us what we are capable of living through. The trouble is, that many of us forget. We'll walk through a full-on, level 8 back bender, then lose our minds when some clown hits us with a level 4, in our face confrontation.

This discussion goes well beyond giving others control over your life. By this point in this book, you should know better than to ever do that again. This is also about more than courage or perseverance. This is about what you have inside of you before the courage comes out and before you persevere even one day at anything. This is about knowing that you can endure and having the self-confidence in yourself to stop acquiescing.

I tell my people all the time that short of doing something truly stupid, there is almost nothing we can do in our work that will cause any of us to stop breathing; we are business people, not soldiers or police or other uniformed heroes (whom I thank God for every day, by the way). I go on to remind them that there is also no single act, again shy of absolute stupidity or calculated criminality, that they can commit that will place our business into bankruptcy. Therefore, I tell people: because the odds are extraordinarily high that you will end the day both alive and employed, please, for the love of all that is holy confront risk and anything else that frightens you. It's not about being fearless. Fearlessness is synonymous with stupidity. It's symptomatic of narcissism. Fear is a natural human emotion and should not be discouraged in others. It should be recognized and empathized with but rationally managed to yield forward progress through the recognition of all that the human spirit is capable of enduring.

The point of all of this is simple then. You can endure much more than you can imagine. And once you do, it should serve as a reminder to you that there is almost nothing you cannot survive. So, learn what you can live through and remember it. Nothing about fixing what is broken in your business will kill you or put you out of business, so choose The Not So Subtle Art of Caring – remind yourself on the occasion of each difficulty that you have endured far worse, and fix what needs fixing.

August 31, 2018

Twenty-one years ago, this week, my first daughter, Caroline, was born. At first, she appeared to be perfect. She was big: 8 pounds, 14 ounces. Her color was ideal. And she could scream like a banshee. But a few hours later, she started to turn blue. We learned that she was born with a very rare heart defect called transposition, and she might die. That night, she was flown 200 miles in a Citation jet to Ann Arbor, Michigan where she would have a very complicated open-heart surgery.

During those weeks in Michigan, I learned an awful lot about the human heart. But I also learned about my own heart too. No doubt, I will share a few of those lessons with you during our time together, but the most important one came at the end, when it occurred to me that we – Caroline, my wife, Annie, and I – had all survived it, mostly unbroken, with the exception of a rather large wound down the chest of my little girl.

And what I took away from that experience is this: that I had seen the worst that life has to offer and lived through it. I realized that the things that used to cause me to become agitated, scared, or worried didn't anymore – because I knew that I was capable of outlasting the most horrible thing I could imagine. I realized that unless an awful boss or customer or situation in my life or work could duplicate what I just lived through, they/

it better pack a lunch, or back way up. I also realized that anger, anxiety, or other negative energy, either directed at me or from me is both unproductive and ineffective.

And that's the point for the week.

Things go wrong in life. Because we are not made to be infallible, humans make mistakes. We aren't perfect. My own daughter wasn't made perfectly. I mess things up every day – here at work and at home. People around me don't always get things right. When others around us let us down, we have a choice: to react poorly, or to respect the dignity of the human being in front of us and work with them to make sure that things are better next time. And when we are on the receiving end of negativity we also have a choice: to first and foremost never give the abuser control of our own perception of ourselves, next to recognize but we are capable of withstanding any petty trial, but most importantly when we err, to recognize our faults, ask forgiveness and work hard to never make the same mistakes twice.

On our way to building the sort of business we want for our futures here, things are going to go wrong. People will make mistakes. I want people to try things and to fail. But when things go awry, I likewise expect that we always treat people the way we want to be treated. That the leaders here never overreact to setbacks, and that all of us recognize that any difficulty will be temporary on our way to something better.

Pretty much all I ask is that when we mess up, because we will, that we be kind to each other, and that we all work very hard not to repeat the same errors. Because when we do these things we will more often win, for no other reason than we will not waste time on the negativity that most companies invest when mistakes occur. because you see, when things go wrong there's a right way to react.

So, choose the better way.

And win.

* * *

The consistency and steadfastness described in the last letter must spill over into all aspects of the steward's life both at home and at work. A steward must be viewed as dependable.

The next letter is about keeping your word. For caring, steward leaders, integrity matters. In winning, integrity matters. As a boy, I overheard my father telling a young salesperson that their objective was their commitment, their word. (See, in my dad's business, he did not just dole out objectives, his salespeople were part of the process of setting their goal each month then committing to them. My father knew that in doing so, he would avoid the "That's not my number" syndrome.) He went on to explain that the sum total of everyone's commitments became his commitment back to them, and that when anyone failed to keep their word it put pressure on his ability to do the same. I never forgot it.

And so, in any event, throughout my career and to this day, I have spoken to my teams about their objectives as their commitments and as their word, and about the importance of keeping it. As obvious as it sounds, teams that make the connection between goals and word keeping / integrity are more profitable. Several studies bear it out. (Guiso, 2013 and Simons, 2008)

But creating an integrity culture doesn't just impact profitability. Foremost, it impacts culture and associate engagement. Workers want leaders they can trust. Unfortunately, among the current crop of traditional top-down, command and control CEOs, they aren't finding many. For example, in a recent Gallup study, when participants were asked what CEOs could do to improve trust, a sickening 72% of respondents said, "Do a better job of keeping your promises." (Gallup, 2008)

Leaders don't need to exceed associate expectations. They simply need to meet them; to do what they say, or when they can't to tell people, and to tell them why. I learned this lesson as a young boy and never forgot it.

I wrote about it in a letter more than a decade ago.

November 19, 2010

This weekend I was in Lowe's grabbing a few things to help get our house ready to sell. As I traversed the cleaning products aisle, I passed the broom section. One of them was yellow. It reminded me of my dad and a lesson I learned from him four decades ago.

It happened like this:

One day while working in my dad's shop he walked up to me and asked for "the yellow broom." I was, if memory serves, fifteen.

By way of background, our brooms were known by their color. Each had different bristle strength. The yellow broom was soft-bristled, suitable for use in the showroom or for removing snow from cars in winter.

I allowed to my dad that I'd go get it right away. However, when finding it in use, by one of my porter brethren, I returned to what I was working on prior to the interruption from my dad.

Some 30 minutes later, my dad returned, looking for the yellow broom. He wasn't happy. I told him that I had gone looking for it but found it being put to good use. My dad asked me to please tell him what it was he asked me for. (My dad was a master of the obvious question.) "The yellow broom?" I answered, as I often did, in a mix of cautious interrogative and snark.

Then came the lesson/rant. "Yes, the yellow broom. When I ask you for something, I expect one of two things – either that you deliver what I asked for or that you return to tell me that you can't deliver it, why you can't and when you expect to do so." He went on, "When others ask you for something and you agree to deliver it, you've given your word." (In an earlier lesson I'd learned that one is born with their word and their back and neither should be broken for anyone. So I understood the importance assigned to the giving of one's word). He finished by repeating, "Keep your word or tell people when you can't."

That's the point for the week.

When we give our word, others plan accordingly. When we fail to either keep it or come back to say we can't, bad things happen.

While it is never optimal to not deliver on our commitments, things will end up in a better place when those we've made promises to know it before we break them. That's what my dad was saying.

We won't keep every commitment we make. That's because we aren't perfect. It's OK. As long as we let those counting on us know beforehand, so that, together, we can seek the next best solution.

When we do, we'll spend less time in the unproductive effort of sweeping up messes (sorry, couldn't resist). We'll more quickly find another way. Most importantly, we'll protect vital trust between ourselves and others.

So, bring the yellow broom – or say you can't.

And win.

* * *

But while your people want to know you can be counted on to be there, they don't want you hovering, or doing their work for them.

In survey after survey after survey of what makes traditional command and control types horrible bosses, common to virtually every study is their predilection to micro-manage. In a 2018 survey of 2,000 employees by Comparably, 39% said micromanagement is the worst offense a manager can commit.

(Comparably, 2018) These folks can't help it though. They tend to be narcissists who believe they are the smartest person in any room. It's a dangerous cocktail. Mixed together, a desire for control and to prove their intelligence will drive the autocrat to be deeply involved in any situation. Well ... almost any situation. While it's true that the micromanager will always find a way to involve himself in work that ends well – even work he or she wasn't actually involved in – he or she will rarely be found anywhere near work that ends poorly. They will always have some plausible reason for denying culpability when things go wrong, which is the sick underbelly of micromanagement. The narcissism of the autocrat fools him into thinking he is a great boss though (remember, he has the mug – which he bought for himself).

However, he couldn't be more wrong. In their book, *The Progress Principle*, Amabile and Kramer show that this micromanaging style, "has a negative effect on the four dimensions of performance: people are less creative, less productive, less deeply committed to their work, and less collegial to each other when their inner work lives darken." (Amabile, 2011)

Unfortunately, Pantsuit Barbie's behavior is costly to the company too. The Journal of Experimental Psychology found that workers who say they are being micromanaged perform at significantly lower levels. (DeCaro, 2011) Too, a 2019 study by Robert Half found that Micromanagement was #2 of 12 top reasons that quality employees leave their jobs, resulting in losses to competition, increased hiring costs and lower productivity. (Half, 2019) But the good news is, it doesn't have to be that way. There is a much better alternative.

One of the things I love about leading businesses is that I get to hire grown adults. Accordingly, I'm able to leave them alone to do their jobs, jobs which, by the way, they tend to know how to do far better than me. It's been my experience that grown adults want to know where the destination is and where the boundaries lay. Then they want to be left largely alone to do their work. I find that they are happier that way. Teddy Roosevelt did too. He once said, "The best executive is one who has sense enough to pick good men to do what he wants done, and self-restraint enough to keep from meddling with them while they do it." (Tulia, 2005)

Cooking a few dozen chickens one day reminded me of the point. Before you get to that, and lest the more lighthearted nature of a bar-b-cue somehow not cast sufficient weight on this issue, I want to remind any of you working for an ogre of my advice from Chapter 1: Leave. There is no good reason to continue to work for a jerk for one day longer than is absolutely necessary. Give these people the absolute minimum required; and spend the balance of your waking hours finding a path to the door. Now ... chickens.

May 5, 2009

This weekend I was asked to help head up the cooking for a charity event for my daughter's school.

Beer-can chicken was the bill of fare.

Twenty-four birds needed to be ready to serve at 6 pm.

For those not familiar with barbequing (which is different from grilling) this is a game marked by flurries of activity at the beginning and the end with not a great deal to do in between. Kinda like childbirth for us fathers except that the chickens don't scream at you.

Anyway, barbequing two dozen chickens at a tad over 225 degrees is a four plus hour proposition. At any point in between it is hard to resist the temptation to speed things up by adding more wood or even to open the lid and check things as if by sheer will the birds will cook faster. Jacking up the lid just adds more time to the process. More wood chars the outside before the inside is completely cooked. Patience is rewarded. The best result occurs when everything is properly set up then left to run as planned.

Here's the point for the week.

Business can be a lot like cooking chickens. The best result occurs when we have a well-prepared plan then stick with it. The chickens around us cook better when we leave them alone to do what they do best. Chickens, like people, don't do well when micromanaged.

How often do we lift the lid on our plans before they are fully done? How often do we add more fire when the fire we have is just hot enough? How often do we poke at things just for the sake of poking?

Think about your own chickens.

If your team has a plan in place and no evidence that it isn't working, leave them be.

The end result will be better, and all involved will be happier.

So, don't lift your lid.

And win.

* * *

The first cousin to not micromanaging is ensuring that you are involving those closest to the work in defining initiatives, policies, and also KPIs.

I speak and write extensively about the importance of involving those closest to the work and closest to the customer in fashioning the initiatives, policies, and other significant output that drives your business. Try including customers themselves, and if that's not possible, put an empty chair in the meeting to represent the customer or make a teammate play the role of the customer. Then watch how different your meetings become. But most organizations don't even get as far as front-line associates, let alone the customer. Why in the world most businesses have this work being performed by senior executives who have not been within 150 miles of an average customer or front-line associate since they were one is a great mystery to me. Winning companies are pushing this work farther and farther down in their companies. According to Rosetta Technology Group, "(Servant) Leaders help the people they serve understand the why behind their work. They help them connect their own work to the overall vision. This is the antithesis of "do as I say" or "because I said so" or "it's not your job to know (management)". (Rosetta Technology Group, 2018) That's because winning companies are increasingly being run by caring, steward leaders who almost instinctively recognize the value in expanding the net when it comes to business planning.

Winners also use a similar process to establish key performance indicators for their teams. Not only will better metrics be chosen, but the metrics and objectives will have far greater buy-in from across the associate body. See, people almost never complain about soup they help make. It's critical though that the metrics chosen are those that have the most immediate connection to the 3-5 things you are trying to accomplish – and only those. Put another way. Measure the outcomes which will most immediately indicate (hence indicator) whether you are on track or off track relative to whichever goal you want an indicator for. "The test of a good process or behavior measure is that there is proof indicating that it predicts a meaningful outcome and that it drives the right behavior from employees." (Graham Brown, 2007) Going a bit further, I have advised teams that the best indicators are those that are instantly understood, can be measured daily and which are simple enough to display as a happy face or a frowny face. If you've chosen metrics more complicated than that, start over.

I was recently asked to come help a business which was being run by a classic top-down, fear-based micromanager. Under his guidance the business had gone backwards with remarkable velocity. He had come from outside the industry and had spent almost no time with those doing the work. As such, he had no notion what was actually occurring in the business. But he had just purchased a new $125,000+ sport utility vehicle shortly after laying off a large chunk of the work force so he had tone-deafness going for him. He was bound and determined to install KPIs used in his former life, a business with zero similarity to the one he found himself working in. He spent no time trying to gain buy in. Instead, it was, "Here are the KPIs we will be using." Worse, his preferred KPI which he clung to like a dog on a bone had nothing to do with people, was at best complicated to implement, and had zero buy-in among those he expected to use it. It was one of what Mark Graham Brown calls "stupid or superstitious process measures that do not link to important outcomes." (Graham Brown, 2007) Otherwise, things were great.

What this cat was missing, besides the part about people hating to be micromanaged, oh and the parts about maybe spend 5 minutes with the people closest to the work and a few more gaining buy-in, was the part about **measuring what matters**. KPIs must INDICATE. They must tell you whether you are gaining ground or losing it (happy face/frowny face) relative to the three to five things you are trying to accomplish. So always, measure what matters. Oh, and win.

I had enough fun with this ogre wanting to measure the productivity of cement across a network of entirely unidentical locations that I wrote about it to prove these very points.

Are you measuring only what matters? Are you keeping KPIs confined to the five or so things that make the most difference in your business? Remember, people have a hard time keeping track of more than about five things at a time. So keep your KPIs confined to the very few things that make the biggest difference and measure those things.

December 1, 2020

This week I was treated to a conversation regarding the wisdom of using sales per square foot as a key performance metric in the truck service business (for the first time in recorded history). The purveyor of the notion posited that if their shops could simply produce more per bit of floor space, they'd have it licked. As brilliantly obvious as it sounds, there's just one problem with the cement productivity theory. Just as I've never seen a spreadsheet produce one dollar of gross profit, I've likewise never seen concrete come to life and produce anything. It's the living, breathing people who walk around on cement that actually make things.

And that's the point for the week.

Much of what's wrong with American business today is that leaders measure the wrong things, and way too many of them. Everything that happens everywhere in any business anywhere in America happens because of people. Period. Successful leaders connect the dots between the human behaviors that deliver desired results then measure them and reward excellence.

Output per square foot is a useless measurement. Output per person? Now you're getting warmer.

When success is tied directly to human behaviors which can be taught, measured, and rewarded nearly anything is possible - because the human desire to succeed is limited only by its own imagination.

Concrete can't think for itself, act for itself, cheer itself on, or develop trust centered relationships with other hunks of cement. Only people can do these things.

When people understand what they are being asked to do, how to do it, why they are being asked to do it and, most importantly, that their lives will improve when they do it, amazing things start happening. Organizational goals start getting smashed. Bonds of trust between people form then strengthen. And business cycles and other adversity which once could have been significant setbacks become minor irritants as the organization races forward with speed and force.

So, measure people things, not stupid things.

And win.

* * *

The key to both not micromanaging and involving a broad coalition of folks in defining initiatives, policy and KPIs, is learning to and CHOOSING to let go.

Life is a choice. And one of the harder ones for leaders to make is to let go.

For those with children or who were ever a child, which is to say all of us, think back to the bike riding learning experience. At some point the teacher of the process had to let go. The child does not go through life with the parent jogging behind them holding on to the seat of their bike. That would be preposterous. But the autocrat does the managerial equivalent of it every day by refusing to let go of things which should be delegated.

He or she can also cling to old ways of doing things, even old products for way too long, well past the point of negative returns, simply because she cannot let go. Then there's the anger-filled, stubbornly clinging/proving a point version of won't let go; the worst kind of all, when way past the point of the point of no return (right or wrong, it matters not) she clings to a point, "on principle" or "I'm correct, insert expletive here" or some other coarse way of trying to camouflage her ridiculous, emotionally-charged behavior when, even her most loyal follower is telling her they'd have dropped it hours or days ago. But she holds on long after things stop working, mostly because she has a deep ego driven need to be right, always.

Most of what drives both of these unfortunate outcomes is ego. Traditional, command and control bosses tend to be narcissists with gigantic egos. Remember, it's why they are hired in the first place. According to Stanford researcher, Jeffery Pfeiffer, they refuse to let go of work, preferring to remain involved because of "a cognitive bias motivated by the desire for self enhancement." Similarly, Pfeiffer found what he termed a "faith in supervision effect" among these control-freaks which causes them to inflate the worth of work produced with their involvement, leading to a greater reluctance to ever back away. (Stanford Graduate School of Business, 1997)

Caring servants also recognize the folly in over imprinting themselves on the work of the team and, like the Stanford egomaniacs, in holding on to things past the point of any marginal return; they know there is zero to be gained from either. In short, servants know when to let go. Likewise, caring servants delegate, often, they let go of work they know should be being done by others. They recognize the value that comes from teaching work to those they lead and letting ideas spring forth from those who follow them.

Have you grown up and learned to let go before things become emotional? If not, invest some time here. No good will come of adding emotion to your processes.

I combined a story about the catching monkeys in the wild with one about the peeling of bananas as a bonus to make these points.

July 30, 2009

On the seventh floor of 1144 East Market Street is a sort of laboratory for the workplace of the future, called Innovation Station. The station is a collection of modern, even futuristic workspaces and meeting areas. It has been described as "a look at what could be for Goodyear's future headquarters." Prior to a customer meeting that was scheduled in the Innovation Station this week, I happened to reflect on this exhibition of the possible. To me the Innovation Station is most remarkable not for its post-modern technology and design but for the cultural shift its construction represents. The Innovation Station required our leadership to let go of long-held notions about how people work and from where. It required them to embrace what could be. Their openness to change made me think of "the banana."

If you've ever seen film of a monkey's capture, you know that it's really quite a simple thing. A clay jar or barrel, with a small round hole in its side, is placed over food – like a banana. A monkey will smell the food, reach inside the jar, and grab it. You might expect that what follows is the dropping of a net or some other snare over the monkey. Nope. The monkey is already caught. He does it all on his own.

See, monkeys for all their cleverness have at least one fatal flaw. They won't let go.

The hole through which they reach for the bait easily allows passage – in or out – of an open hand, but not a fist. With their hand closed around the food they cannot extract it. Easy enough, you might say, just drop the food, remove the hand and scurry to safety as the hunters approach. That would be true enough – if monkeys would let go. But they won't. They'll cling to the food even to their own peril.

Knowing when it's time to let go then doing so are keys to personal happiness.

That's the point for the week.

We can be a lot like monkeys.

We tend to cling tightly to things, ideas, even others for far too long. Mostly, we cling to the past – the way things were.

When we hold too tightly to anything, we prevent ourselves and, in many cases, others from experiencing a better way. We halt our ability to fit in. We damage relationships.

When we are open to the possibility that something better exists in change or in the future we win more. Teams value us more. We and others grow and learn. Relationships thrive.

Don't be a monkey.
Know when it's time to let go. Then do so.
And win.

* * *

By the way, most of us eat monkey bait the wrong way – literally – by grabbing onto that little handle at one end of the fruit and yanking away.

Peeling a banana the wrong way is something most everyone does. Almost no one ever even tries the other end. We have a notion of how a banana should be peeled and won't let go of it.

It's not really our fault. Parents, I expect back to Eve, have been teaching children the wrong way. Grocery store people further reinforce our wrong-headedness by displaying bananas upside down.

Still though, we don't even entertain that there could be a better way. We just yank away at the tough end.

But see, a banana is a flower. That tough little handle is the bottom – not the top. It's the stem. There's a soft, delicate end opposite ... on top. Look at a picture of how they grow. They grow like the flower they are, stem down, blossom up.

Next time you eat a banana, gently insert your fingertip in the correct end, the stubby little flower end, and pull ever so slightly. You'll be amazed – both at how easy it was to peel the skin away and at why you didn't let go of the stem a long time ago.

Remember ... let go.
And win.

* * *

True, caring and visionary leaders have vision. They see things that others can't, don't or won't. They see what's not there, or

274

said better, what's not there yet.

Though often, this capability is innate, those born without a natural talent for "seeing the future" can develop and hone this skill by engaging in behaviors which make it possible and also by making a choice to outwork their peers. In reviewing any situation, leaders should always ask themselves whether they have looked at it from every possible angle and/or constituency. Are there short-term trade-offs that could yield long term gains? Are there alternative markets or uses that are not being considered? Are folks looking beyond a thing's current condition? What wider trends are occurring in the world that could help or hurt? What if you scrapped everything and started over? What if you kept part of a thing but not all of it? Who haven't you talked to yet that might have an idea? Where are your competitors most vulnerable? What do your customers want you to do? What do your people want you to do? Who in the business haven't you heard from?

Most often people don't see things because they aren't looking for them. The motivation behind why matters little. Why the micromanager doesn't do what she should matters less than the fact that because she doesn't, she creates huge competitive opportunities for you to win at her expense.

Visionary leaders should teach those on their teams to think and act like visionaries. Also, when engaging in visionary behavior it is critically important that visionary leaders help others understand exactly WHY they are doing things. It is never OK to default to, "because I'm a visionary, don't you worry about it." Those you have the privilege to lead must always understand the rationale for every move they are involved in helping make; otherwise, buy-in will be zero. And when buy-in is zero, forward progress is zero.

But above all, the goal, as a visionary leader is for you and your team to learn to look at any situation and arrive at a condition where all are motivated to ask "what if?" and "why not" questions, challenging the status-quo in search of a better future where the lives of every single associate improve. Or as proffered by the team at Michigan State University, "In order to cast that larger vision for a team or organization, that often means having the ability to look at the situation – whether it's an organizational restructure or diminishing product sales – in a different light, even when there seems to be no light at all." (Michigan State University, 2020)

March 6, 2009

This week I had a chance to travel to New York to meet with Mavis Tire.

It was an action-packed day. We visited more than 10 of their stores across New York state covering over 500 miles in all.

About a year ago, Mavis completed an acquisition of Cole Muffler's 50 stores in upstate New York. Mavis is in the process of completely renovating these locations. During our tour, we saw them in varying stages, some complete. On the way to each, the Mavis team would share "before" photos to illustrate the extent of each transformation – all of which turned out to be absolutely remarkable.

The renovated stores were beautiful. They looked almost new. They were clean, shiny and inviting. Best of all they had become tremendously productive from almost the first day of their reopening.

Some of you may be have seen one or more Cole locations in your time with Goodyear. For the rest of you, let it suffice to say that were you to imagine a great place to work or shop, what you'd describe would be quite different from these stores.

I remember at the time of the acquisition many folks wondering if Mavis had lost its mind. A few asked, "Why in the world would Mavis want this business?"

The answer has to do with vision. Mavis saw these stores for what they could be, not for what they were.

This morning, I thought about this. It struck me that we all have something to learn from Mavis.

We are more likely to reach our greater potential when we see the good that can come from any situation.

That's the point for the week.

The way things are is far less important than the way things can become.

It's a matter of vision.

To see what is possible vs. what is ...

Where we can go vs. where we are ...

What we can sell vs. what we are selling now ...

What we can become vs. who we are today ...

You get the idea.

How are you viewing your world? As it is? Or, how it could be?

Have vision.

And win.

* * *

Sometimes having vision won't be enough. Sometimes, as a leader it's going to be necessary when someone shows up at your door with a gigantic offensive gesture, that you take care to ensure that your goat doesn't get loose.

We all have a goat.

It seems to me that the quality of one's leadership is exactly proportional to their ability to keep their goat safely tucked away. When we let others get our goat, bad things start to happen. We say and do things we almost always regret later. According to Princeton professor Christy Wampole, writing for the New York Times, "Getting flustered breathes life into other people's fictions. When your buttons have been pushed and your goat gotten, it is rare that you can act with composure in response. Instead, you react. Action derives from power, reaction from a state of powerlessness." (Wampole, 2014)

The fix is another one of those "it's not that hard, but it's not simple to do" ideals of caring, leadership. What's simple is this. The notion that true, caring leaders do not abide fools; they do not allow their goats to be gotten. What's hard is following through: When confronted by a goat getter, servants remain absolutely calm. They speak in a normal tone of voice. They never make it personal. They suggest to the offending party that goat getting is not helpful. Ideally, they walk away.

To help, from now on, try this: Your goat is being gotten. In that moment, ask yourself, "What is my primary role and purpose?" It likely has something to do with the leadership of your team, or attainment of its goals. It is NOT to engage with a fool. So, disengage from the goat getter right then and there. "Don't protest against what you disapprove, Do without it." (del Vasto, 1945) Focus instead on what you are actually there to do, which is anything but to wrestle with a pig.

There's an old saying, so old that it's been attributed to Mark Twain, George Bernard Shaw, and none other than NASCAR driver Cale Yarborough, that cautions against pig wrestling. It goes like this: "Don't ever wrestle with a pig. You both get dirty, but the pig will enjoy it." This is true of goat getters. They are pigs, and in the workplace, almost always, traditional narcissistic authoritarians. So, do yourself and your people a favor and stay out of the mud.

Nothing will frustrate a goat getter more than you refusing to tell them where your goat is tied. Silently smiling back at, wishing a nice day to, asking to change the subject to one of mutual interest or simply excusing yourself and walking away will do more to launch a traditional authoritarian goat getter into a second orbit than you bringing your goat out could ever hope to. Best of all, you will be setting a positive example for others which is largely what this whole leading others gig is about in the first place.

So, now that I've unmixed the metaphor, on to the story of the goat.

August 23, 2019

This week, in talking with an associate, I was reminded that each of us has a goat. And that it is best that our goats are kept safely hidden away. See, if we aren't that careful, others can get our goat; And bad things can start to happen

And that's the point for the week.

It's easy to give someone your goat. We all do it. I do it. Sometimes it feels good to let the old Billy Goat run loose. But it's always a dumb idea. See, every time we let someone get our goat, not only do we escalate tension, negativity, and hostility – but we give them complete control of our life. Once they have hold of our goat, they define everything about us – how we act, what we say, what we think, even how we feel about ourselves. Because we let them, because we choose to.

Sometimes people can get your goat without even knowing it. But because you gave them your goat, you gave them control. I often use a simple example of being cut off in traffic. In that moment, you have a choice: keep the goat locked up or let him run. The dude who cut you off is just driving on down the road. But the second you let him have your goat you give him control of your life. You'll get where you're going all hacked off, you'll impact everyone around you negatively, and crazy driver dude doesn't even know your name, but you gave him your goat.

Like nearly everything else in life, it's a choice – to hide your goat or let him roam free, for anyone to get. It takes discipline and conscious effort to lock your goat away. But the benefits are extraordinary. If nothing else, you'll enjoy the facial expressions of those who try to take little Billy away.

But far beyond that, when you keep your goat you stay in

charge of you, you remain calmly in control of your life. The interactions you have with others will become more productive. You'll feel better. You'll get more done. And when you get more done, we will get more done. And when we get more done, we'll win more often. Simply because more of us kept our goats locked away.

So, lock up your goat.

And win.

* * *

The time you save not reclaiming your goat can be better used ensuring that you are giving your team completely specific instructions.

One of the simplest but biggest mistakes a leader can make is to provide insufficient instructions. This can happen for at least five primary reasons.

Commonly, we as leaders fall into the trap of believing that if we understand it, everyone else understands it. Don't. Just because you get it does NOT mean everyone else will. There is a rather high probability that you are not the lowest common denominator in your organization. Find it and cater to it. When they are able to pick up what you are putting down, everyone else will too. A general corollary to the first reason is the fact that far too often, as leaders we assume that some instructions are implicit, obvious or self-explanatory. Don't assume.

Second, as mentioned earlier, we say something once and believe it indemnifies us from any further responsibility for communication. False. Communicate, communicate, communicate, until you are sick of the sound of your own voice.

Third, we as leaders believe that our people don't need, shouldn't have or can't be trusted with certain information which is actually vital to the task at hand. All wrong. Without complete information, people cannot complete their jobs.

#4, many people will never raise their hand and ask for help. Human nature dictates that many people do not like to (a) be the center of attention and/or (b) admit that they need help/ don't understand something. As a result, they won't do either. As a leader, you must compensate by over-educating then asking people to play back what you taught.

Five, what you say and what they hear can differ. Have you ever played the game of telephone, where info is passed along, becoming totally changed by the end? This happens in real life. This is why you must communicate, communicate, communicate in very specific terms.

The good news is that fixing problems related to insufficient or unclear instructions is not hard at all. I have used six simple who, what, when type news reporter rules for true, caring leaders interested in ensuring improved task execution between instruction and outcome. They are:

1. Tell people exactly **who** needs to be involved. If you've ever watched six-year-old children playing soccer, you understand the importance of role clarity. The need for it never changes.
2. Tell people exactly **what** you want to accomplish. When they know the desired outcome, they will deliver it.
3. Tell them **why**. People will more fully engage when they know why they are performing a certain task.
4. Tell them **how**, explicitly. People will give you exactly what you want when you teach them exactly how to do it.
5. Tell them **when** by giving clear deadlines. People will more often meet deadlines when they are made clear.
6. Finally, tell them how their lives will improve when the task is complete/ when the goals of the organization are met. People will more often buy in when they know there is something in it for them.

Research from the University of Rochester's Edward Deci and Richard Ryan shows that when leaders move beyond just telling someone *what* to do, to giving them the rationale for *why* they are being asked to do it, the level of associate engagement increases sharply as does the workers expression of choice to work on the project. (Ryan, 2000)

Simply following the traditional micromanager formula of barking orders while providing limited and veiled information will result in a mess. It is not surprising then, that many traditionally run businesses today are a catastrophe. Despite efforts around six-sigma, op-ex, lean, I/A and other process-oriented initiatives, these organizations continue to struggle. That's because if you are layering process over or automating organizations with fundamental communication and training gaps, you simply end up with more elegant versions of the same mess. It actually makes things worse. I've seen it happen. Until information flows freely and associates are fully informed, fully connected, and fully engaged, there will be fundamental breakdowns. Automation will simply magnify them, not make them better.

The point here is to ensure that you are sharing as much information as possible in as clear and concise a means as possible. Ask yourself, are you ensuring that your people are working with the best available information and the clearest possible instructions? If not, fix it fast. No one knows your organization better than you, or how best to ensure the fast flow of information around it. Take advantage of what you know to optimize information flow. Work from the outcome you want backwards; ensure that every bit of information is where it needs to be when it needs to be there.

I used a funny story about a photo opportunity in Brazil to make this crystal clear.

April 26, 2019

I have, in every stop in my career, found myself, at one point or another, reminding others in an organization, usually my superiors, that "our sales folks will do whatever we ask them to do." My remarks were almost always made in defense of teams of people who were not doing something they didn't know they were supposed to be doing. I was reminded of that this week in Brazil when I asked someone to take a picture of Todd W and I in front of a large São Paulo sign. He did. The next day, Todd and I got copies of the photos. It appeared as if we had visited someplace called "Paulo". In five photos sent to us, the São was chopped off. It occurred to me that our photographer had done exactly what we had asked: he took our picture in front of the sign. Had we said, "Please take our picture in front of the sign and be sure to get the entire sign in the frame," I'm sure the outcome would have been quite like what we had envisioned. We got what we asked for. To get what you want, ask for that – specifically. And that's the point for the week.

Reasonable people, especially those who believe in or have a vested interest in a particular cause will do almost anything they are asked to do – assuming it is legal and seems practically achievable. People who show up at any enterprise – for profit, not for profit, for the good of the family - believe they are good at what they are doing and believe they are adding value. (If you don't believe me, stand out by the front door or gate one morning with a clipboard and ask every associate that arrives whether they are: (1) good at what they do and (2) adding value. I promise the percentage of folks answering "yes" to both questions will be like Ivory Soap purity, 99 and 44/100%.)

So, if the goals of the organization aren't being met, it's usually not a worker problem, it's almost always a leadership problem. It's the result of a lack of specificity in regard to some goal or task. It's hey take our picture in front of the sign, instead of, hey, do this specific thing by this specific date or until this specific outcome is achieved.

See, when we provide specific instructions, we remove room for error which eliminates a giant instance of waste and a potential point of friction between human beings which, like in any machine, slows things down.

So, the next time you ask for something – or are the one asked for something, think about whether the instructions were specific enough. Or if you were asked to take a photo of Paulo. Get the whole picture.

And win.

* * *

True, caring leaders, those that practice The Not So Subtle Art of Caring, recognize feedback as a gift.

The giving nor receiving of feedback should ever be viewed as painful, ugly, confrontational, degrading, or otherwise negative. Feedback should enhance the organization and the life of the recipient, not take away from either. Too often, constructive feedback is viewed negatively by managers, as something confrontational and to be avoided; or by some leaders as a blissful opportunity to tear into someone and to show them who's boss. Either extreme is entirely unhealthy. Too, recipients frequently avoid conflict, viewing these events as opportunities for argumentativeness, defensiveness, or other close-minded behavior, which are neither helpful.

The answer lies in the recognition that feedback should be given and received positively – as a gift. Feedback should be intended to help another human being identify things that stand in the way of being great, which is, after all, what each of us truly desires. When presented accordingly, all but the truly irrational will welcome and embrace feedback as a means to a positive end, as a roadmap to a better them.

Feedback should never be given in anger or with a desire to belittle. True, caring leaders know that blowing out another's candle will never make theirs burn brighter. Those who practice The Not So Subtle Art of Caring are investors, and multipliers. Remember, they wake up every day with one thought – to make others really, really big. The caring leader will have no part of feedback that tears down. That's for managers whose low self-worth causes them to try to divest others of theirs. A recent article by Jim Schleckser, CEO of the Inc. CEO Project put it well. "Whenever and however you receive honest and open feedback, you should consider it a valuable gift. As Warren Buffet has said: *'Honesty is a very expensive gift; just don't expect it from cheap people.'*" (Schleckser, 2018) That's because insecure, traditional authoritarian managers believe that letting anyone get too big represents an existential threat to them. Show me a leader like that, and I will show you a losing team. But find a collection of people who view feedback positively, as a gift, that comes from the heart, with love, and I will show you a bunch of winners, bonded by trust and pushed ever forward by an intrinsic desire to be the best person they possibly can be.

Do you view feedback as a gift? You should. You should never get defensive either when giving or receiving feedback. It's a present. View it that way, and win.

A story about the annual Christmas present opening ritual in our house was a wonderful way to remind people that feedback is truly a gift.

January 6, 2017

Last week was, of course, Christmas. My kids, even now that they are older, I suppose because Annie and I have kept the traditions alive, still regard Christmas morning with a sense of wonder and glee. There are still full stockings, a plate left with only a few cookie crumbs and bits of carrot, packages in two distinct styles of wrapping paper – one for packages from Annie and I and one for those from the fat man. Though our children don't believe anyone actually comes down the chimney, they very much believe in the wonder of the day, and in the value of that very first gift 2,000 years ago and in each of those that they receive every year.

Invariably though, something isn't quite right. The size is off a notch. Santa got a navy one instead of black. "It's cute, but I don't think it's me." Immediately after comes the discussion of the dissolution of said items; to return, exchange, give to someone else possibly, or maybe just keep it after all.

This year, the annual ritual made me think of feedback. See, when we think about feedback in similar terms, life gets better. Because feedback, after all, is a gift.

And that's the point for the week.

For the recipient, to see feedback as a gift it must first be offered as one. Feedback should never be offered in a negative package. Feedback should be a present. It should enrich the recipient, not devalue them. It should build them up, not tear them down. It should add to their self-esteem, not destroy their dignity. Too often though, feedback given by traditional, authoritarian, command and control types is given harshly; it does tear down, devalue, and destroy. But when feedback is given positively, from the heart, the likelihood of acceptance goes up factorially, bonds between leader and follower form, and organizations move forward driven by the fuel of constant self-improvement.

Those receiving feedback given as a gift may, as with any other present, do with it as he or she wishes. Use it, put it on a shelf, pass it on, or even ask for an exchange (of ideas).

The manner in which feedback is both given and received though, like anything else in life, is a choice. But when the choice is made to give and receive feedback as a gift, barriers to trust are removed, dialogue blossoms, and organizations are transformed as individuals identify and address that which stands between them and individual greatness.

So, view feedback as a gift.

And win.

* * *

True leaders do not only tell, but they also do. Whatever they ask of others, they do. Whatever needs done, they do it. What others refuse to do, they do it. And what others say cannot be done, they do.

As I considered stories and letters to end this chapter and indeed this book with, it seemed more than fitting to finish with an epistle about doing.

For what separates the servant from the traditional leader is, above all, what they do – when no one is looking; when things get difficult, when the nattering nabobs of negativism are yammering on about what their spreadsheets say is or is not possible

The Not So Subtle Art of Caring is about action, which is by definition about doing things, important things, things that improve the lives of others.

There is no formula to becoming a caring leader, no series of 10 steps to follow, or boxes to check. In my life and experience, it has been a simple, binary choice; between putting others first, or putting yourself first. When you choose to make that seemingly small step, when you choose to do that one thing, everything begins to change.

But it starts with doing, because that's what those who practice The Not So Subtle Art of Caring are all about. Doing things.

For others.

So, go do something – for someone else, to make the lives of others better, to make this world a better place.

Do something someone said couldn't be done.

And win.

August 21, 2020

On the wall in the office at our shop in Baltimore is a sign with a quote from James Baldwin that reads:

"Those who say it can't be done are usually interrupted by those doing it."

I like that sign. Clichés and sayings that find their ways onto signs, and into books for people to read and be motivated by, end up that way because they are true. I can personally vouch for the truth in this one. It describes part of the experience in each of the many changes I have helped lead during my career. Saying something can't be done is just talk – usually by people who have never sold anything, ran anything, or turned a wrench ever in their lives. Proving whether it can or can't is the stuff of doing and the people who have the courage to do it. And that's the point of the week

Talk is cheap. So are theories and opinions about what will work and what won't. My personal favorites are: We tried that once. Or I ran the numbers on that, and the data says it won't work. Or my spreadsheet shows something different will happen. Or that may have worked where you came from, but that will never work here. Or we tried that in my prior life (in a completely unrelated business) and it didn't work. All of these, and more, are simply defenses from those who can't do, don't want to do, have never done, or don't want to see done by someone else. Progress without effort is impossible. Achieving anything requires doing something. In business, at home, or in any community endeavor, standing still, or any other defensive measure, will actually result in moving backwards. Because as one stands still, the rest of the world, those who actually do things, breeze by. But when more and more members of a team join the ranks of the doers, grabbing an oar and pulling on it with force, something fantastic begins to happen. Momentum is achieved. Progress toward the desired destination hastens. Rough water, which before seemed significant, presents little impediment at speed, and at a higher plane.

Best of all, the bonds that are built from the practice of doing as a team become nearly unbreakable with time, enabling us to achieve what only weeks before might have seemed unthinkable. All because we did. All because we defied the talkers, the doubters, and the never did one thing in their life crowd. Because we dared to grab an open oar and yank as if our life depended on it.

Because it did ... maybe not the one we're living today ... but the better one we want for tomorrow for sure.

So, be one of the ones doing it.

And win.

*　*　*

Thanks for reading my book. It means a great deal to me that you did.

Afterword

The Importance of Grace

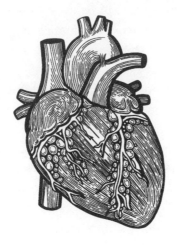

"And if by grace, then it cannot be based on works; if it were, grace would no longer be grace."
Romans 11:6

Grace. No other word has greater meaning for me, for my life or for my leadership of others than Grace. I have a daughter with the middle name, Grace. My business name even begins with Grace.

Among all qualities found in caring leaders, and in the practice of The Not So Subtle Art of Caring, none is more meaningful than grace. No quality will be (or should be) more recalled by those you lead than grace. Grace is at once a state of being and something to be given. But grace should not be confused with simple kindness. Or pardon. Grace borders on the ethereal.

In a famous case before the US Supreme Court, Jacobellis vs. Ohio, Justice Potter Stewart, at a loss to provide a requested definition, made history by instead declaring, "I know it when I see it." Grace is like that. It's hard to define exactly … but you know it when you see it.

And you remember it. For a lifetime. Because those who lead with grace lead with their heart and appeal to hearts. They believe that the connected hearts of those they lead create an unstoppable force for good that can accomplish anything, least of all the goals of the organization they lead.

Thought leaders in the discipline of organizational management are increasingly rejecting traditional command and control, fear-based management and coming to the conclusion that heart-centered, caring leadership styles are more likely to deliver results. According to Dr. Yu Sing Ong, Ph.D., Professor at the Elem Graduate School, HELP University of Malaysia, "The mindset of leaders must change to embrace a grace-based leadership approach (Ong, 2019)

Ong is, for the most part, simply reinforcing what most of us already know. That the old way of managing doesn't work anymore. It is also true that it's a binary choice. It's what the verse at the top of this chapter is about for me. It's a reminder that if I profess to lead by grace then I am to lead by grace; I don't default to the old way ("works") when things get hard or when I feel peer pressure, or when serving others seems unpopular or gets ridiculed. Ong says the same thing, though, albeit in a slightly different way: "Changing the hearts rather than merely modifying behavior or accomplishing tasks is the antidote to many leadership failures." (Ong, 2019)

See, leaders that practice The Not So Subtle Art of Caring know that grace is the reason for their success. Grace endures all and conquers all. They know that in grace there is redemption and second chances. They win with grace, lose with grace, struggle with grace, and lift up with grace. They believe with grace – and in grace.

They know that but for grace go they. And so, they go,

making the lives of those they lead better, day in, and day out. Until it's time to go. Until it's time for the next right moment to come.

Everything has a beginning and an end. Like this book. Like our time in stops along our way.

The letter below was the last one I wrote to the team in one of the most meaningful stops on my path. It was about grace. So, it is doubly fitting here.

Thank you for reading my book. I hope that you found something of help in it, something of hope in it, something of grace in it, and something to make the lives of other people better in it.

So, now read the letter, then put the book down, and go practice The Not So Subtle Art of Caring.

Oh, … and win.

December 22, 2011 (The Last Wingfoot Week)

Last Friday, as I did a year ago, I had an opportunity to say a few words before our Christmas luncheon here in Fort Smith. The act of speaking in this time slot is often referred to as grace. I did say, "grace," though not in the manner you'd expect. I spoke of grace.

Grace is often confused with forgiveness. Though while the latter is manifested in the former, grace is more than that. To me, grace is the recognition of the unlimited potential and value of other living beings and an allowance for the fact that along one's way to achieving the height of their own greatness, not every day will be a good one.

That's the (run-on) point for the week.

In grace is a fundamental belief that others matter. Grace recognizes that others aren't perfect and will let us down sometimes. Grace knows that imperfect effort deserves joy, not criticism for that which wasn't perfect. Grace leads us to find more joy in the contrition of an offender than anger in the offense. Grace truly believes that it's the thought that counts.

When grace guides our actions, we'll win more. We'll do so because those we have the privilege to lead – at work, at home, and in our communities – implicitly understand that they are safe: to try, to speak, to change without fearing the consequence of failure. These things are the fuel of progress and brighter tomorrows.

Accordingly, grace looks forward – to a point in the distance worth achieving – to something better than the present, and infinitely more appealing than the past.

Grace is unconditional. Grace doesn't judge. Grace is a purposeful commitment to give people more than we think they may deserve or even that they may think they deserve.

As a result, grace invites trust, faith, and devotion from others – things that are among the foundation stones of healthy and productive relationships. These human connections propel us forward at ever increasing rates of speed, forming blocs of human energy that can withstand virtually any setback, and enabling flight to summits never dreamed of. All, because of grace.

Until we meet again, be grace-full.

And win.

Phillip Kane
January, 2021
Akron, Ohio

Acknowledgements

I'd like to thank David Donovan Evans for his friendship and for the beautiful cover art and photography; it wouldn't be my book without you and to Paul Szentkiralyi for his input and guiding hand.

Read More Letters on Leadership for Free at:

https://AndWin.net

Follow Phillip Kane at:
@ThePhillipKane on Twitter
https://www.facebook.com/phillipmatthewkane
on Facebook
phillip_m_kane on Instagram

A Note from Phillip Kane:

Thank you for reading *The Not So Subtle Art of Caring: Letters on Leadership*. If you weren't already, I hope you are now convinced that there is a kinder, better way to lead people to accomplish extraordinary things than the authoritarian, command and control style of the last century. I hope you found more than a few things that will help you on your path to more effective caring leadership. If so, please tell others. Please also take a moment to leave a review on GoodReads, Amazon or the Apple iTunes store. If not, please contact me directly at phillip.kane@andwin.net. You can also learn more about The Not So Subtle Art of Caring at https://phillipkaneauthor.com

Warm regards,
PK

Bibliography

Preface

Botelho, E.L., Powell, K.R., Kincaid, S., and Wang, D., *What Sets Successful CEOs Apart*, (Harvard Business Review, May-June 2017)

Bower, G. and Clark, M., *Narrative stories as mediators for serial learning*, (Stanford EU, 1969)

Introduction

Comaford, Christine, *63% of Employees Don't Trust Their Leader – Here's What You Can Do*, (Forbes, January 28, 2017)

Denning, S., *The Leaders Guide to Radical Management*, (Jossey-Bass, 2010)

Greenleaf, R.K., *Servant leadership: a journey into the nature of legitimate power and greatness*, (Paulist Press, 1977)

Holy Bible (ESV) Mark 10:43

Krejcir, Rev. Richard J., *The Character of Servant Leadership*, (The Francis A. Schaeffer Institute of Church Leadership Development, 2000)

McCrimmon, M., *Why Servant Leadership is a bad idea*, (Management Issues, August 16, 2010)

Northouse, P.G., *Leadership*, (Sage Publications, 6th ed., 2013)

Oliver, S., *Companies Headed by Introverts Performed Better in a Study of Thousands of CEOs*, (Quartz, August 16, 2016)

Rentfrow, J. and DeVries, R., *A Winning Personality*, (The Sutton Trust, January 14, 2016)

Chapter 1

Beck, Randall and Harter, James, *Why Good Managers Are So Rare*, (Harvard Business Review, March 13, 2014)

Benincasa, R., *Mutual Respect is the Foundation for Your Team's Extreme Performance*, (Association of Talent Development,

January 31, 2019)

Breeze, Lauren, *Evidence Suggests Connection to Employee Performance*, (Perspectives in Business, St. Edwards University, 2004)

Fusch, G. & Fusch, P., *Leadership Conflict Resolution on the Production Line*, (International Journal of Applied Management & Technology, 2015 Vol. 14 Iss. 1)

Goleman, D. *The Focused Leader*, (Harvard Business Review, December 2013)

Hagley, A., *Innovation: Why encouraging mistakes fosters big ideas*, (Verb, June 18, 2019)

Holy Bible, (KJV) 2 Tim 1:6

Izzo, J. Dr., *Stepping Up*, (Berrett-Koehler, 2012)

Johnson, A., *Why Love is the First Skill You Should Develop*, (Benedictine University, Center for Values Driven Leadership, June 5, 2014)

Juneja, P., *Effect of Politics on Organization and Employees*, (Management Study Guide),

Kazimoto, P., *Analysis of Conflict Management and Leadership for Organizational Change*, (International Journal of Research in Social Sciences, 2013)

Kouzes, J. and Posner, B., *The Leadership Challenge*, (Wiley, 2017)

Kucher, C.B., *Four Reasons People Follow a Leader*, (CEO Think Tank, February 18, 2014)

Llopsis, G., *5 Ways Leaders Can Reclaim Their Identity*, (Forbes, April, 22, 2013)

Lynch, O.H., *Kitchen Antics: The Importance of Humor and maintaining Professionalism at Work*, (Journal of Applied Communication Research, Vol. 37, 2009, Iss.4)

Noe, R., *Leading Well*, (CreateSpace, 2014)

Porath, C. and Pearson, C., *The price of Incivility*, (Harvard Business Review, January-February 2013)

Zak, Paul J., *The Neuroscience of Trust*, (Harvard Business Review, January-February 2017)

Chapter 2

Bacal, R., *Common Leader Mistake – Trying to Treat Everyone the Same*, (leadertoday.org)

Cain, A. and Lebowitz, S., *26 signs you're a great boss, even if it doesn't feel like it*, (Business Insider, October 16, 2019)

Cuddy, Amy J. C., Kohut, Matthew, and Nefflinger, John, *Connect, Then Lead*, (Harvard Business Review, July-August 2013)

Geiger, E., *5 Great Things That Happen When Leaders Get Out of Their Offices*, (Facts & Trends, January 30, 2018)

Horwitch, M. and Callahan, M. W., *How Leaders Inspire: Cracking the Code*, (Bain & Company, Brief, June 9, 2016)

Lee, C.D., *Great Leaders Encourage the Heart*, (HigherEdJobs, July 8, 2019)

Leslie, J.B., *The Leadership Gap*, (The Center for Creative Leadership, White Paper, September 2015)

Liden, R., Wayne, S. Liao, C. and Meuser, J., *Caring leadership and Serving Culture: Influence on Individual and Unit Performance*, (Academy of Management Journal, 2013; 57)

Lipman, V., *New Employee Study Shows Recognition Matters More Than Money*, (Psychology Today, June 13, 2013)

Maxwell, J., *Everyone Communicates, Few Connect*, (Thomas Nelson, 2010)

Picoult, J., *Where Business Leaders Should Spend More of Their Time (But Don't)*, (CustomerThink, July 24, 2017)

Porath, C, *The Leadership Behavior That's Most Important to Employees*, (Harvard Business Review, May 11, 2015)

The Predictive Index, *The Predictive Index People Management Study*, (2018)

Tredgold, G, *The One Mistake Many Leaders Make That Disengages Their Staff*, (Inc., January 23, 2018)

Udemy Research, *Udemy In Depth: 2018 Employee Experience Report"*, (2018)

Chapter 3

Bohn, R., *Stop Fighting Fires*, (Harvard Business Review, July-August 2000)

Emmons, R.A., PhD, *Gratitude is good Medicine*, (UC Davis Health, November 25, 2015)

Forsey, C. *What's Authentic Leadership, & How Do You Do It?*, (blog.hubspot.com, February 13, 2019)

Griffin, T., *5 Character Traits of Great Leaders*, (thomasgriffin.com, November 13, 2020)

Gurteen, D., *Conversational Leadership*, (conversational-leadership.net, 2020)

Hayes, R.H., *Why Japanese Factories Work*, (Harvard Business Review, July-August 1981)

House, R., Spangler, W.D., and Woyke, J., *Personality and Charisma in the US Presidency: A Psychological Theory of Leader Effectiveness*, (Administrative Science Quarterly, 36, 1991)

Kriz, Scott, *For Better or Worse: A Consistent Leadership Style is Key to Success*, (Fortune, July 31, 2016)

Llopsis, G. *5 Reasons Leaders Are Afraid to Challenge the Status Quo*, (Forbes, August 12, 2017)

McCloskey, C., *The Value of Acknowledging your mistakes*, (The Public Manager, Association for Talent Development, August 2016)

Porath, C., 2015, *The Leadership Behavior That's Most Important to Employees*, (Harvard Business Review, May 11, 2015)

Quiocho, C., *Don't Ask Anyone to Do Anything You Wouldn't Do..." Military Leadership Lessons for Business with Tony Cole*, (Authority Magazine, May 24, 2018)

Schultz, P., *Hire Character. Train Skill*, (TriSoft, October 7, 2019)

Shankar, Y., *Character Not Charisma is the Critical Measure of Leadership Excellence*, (Journal of Leadership and Organizational Studies, November 2003)

The Predictive Index, 2018

Vergauwe, J., Wille, B., Hofmans, Kaiser, R. and De Fruyt, F., *Too much Charisma Can Make Leaders Look Less Effective,* (Harvard Business Review, September 26, 2017)

Y Scouts, *10 Charismatic Leadership Characteristics, Attributes, and Traits,* (Scottsdale, AZ, June 11, 2020)

Chapter 4

Andriotis, N., *What Embracing Shared Purpose Can Do to Benefit Your Organization,* (eFront Learning, July 2017)

Boogaard, Kat, *Found! 6 research-backed ways to make your team more effective,* (Teamwork, November 5, 2019)

Bryant, Adam, *How to Build a Successful Team,* (The New York Times, 2018)

Connors, C., *Major League Baseball Teams Know the 'Little Things' Matter Most in the Postseason,* (Bleacher Report, October 4, 2012)

Davis-Laack, P. and Westfahl, S., *5 things that resilient teams do differently,* (Fast Company, June 15, 2019)

Grant Halvorsen, H. and Higgins, T., *Do You Play to Win — or to Not Lose?,* (Harvard Business Review, March 2013)

Hoppen, D., *How to Align Individual, Team, and Organizational Goals for Success,* (Quantum Workforce, November 26, 2018)

Hu, J., Liden, R., *Making a Difference in the Teamwork: Linking Team Prosocial Motivation to Team Processes and Effectiveness,* (The Academy of Management Journal, January 2014)

Hyatt, M., *Why You Need to Take Care of the People Who Take Care of You,* (Michael Hyatt & Co., February 24, 2020)

Mann, A. and Dvorak, N., *Employee Recognition: Low Cost, High Impact,* (Gallup Workplace, June 28, 2016)

Morin, A., *3 Core Beliefs Individuals on Winning Teams Have,* (Forbes, March 21, 2017)

Moss-Kanter, R., *Ten Reasons Winners Keep Winning, Aside From Skill,* (Harvard Business Review, August 1, 2012)

O'Neill, L.I., *Never Give Up, Don't Be Afraid to Lead,* (The Irish Times, August 23, 1999)

Pedersen, P., *Out Stealing Horses*, (Picador, 2008)

Quast, L., *New Managers: How to Establish Your Rhythm of Business' Model*, (Forbes, October 12, 2015)

Richard, S., *How a Team can Do Big Things*, (skiprichard.com, December 6, 2017)

Roth, E., *Great Leadership Teams Say These Six Things About Each Other*, (Forbes, Nov 8, 2016)

Satell, G., *4 Ways to Build and Innovation Team*, (Harvard Business Review, February 13, 2018)

Skill Path, *8 Characteristics of an Effective Team*, (April 29, 2019)

Smith, J., *"How to Thrive When the Boss is Never Around*, (Forbes, July 3, 2013)

Zender, T., *"The worst competition is internal competition*, (The Business Journals, January 16, 2015)

Zenger, J., *Great Leaders Move Fast*, (Chief Learning Officer, November 30, 2016)

Chapter 5

Angel,D., *Be a Good Steward of Risk*, (Medium, November 5, 2016)

Birkenstock, D., *Leadership: The Key Dimension in Adventist Tertiary Educational Administration*, (Institute for Christian Teaching, 1993)

Boyd, E., *A History of Accounting and Accountants*, (Richard Brown, Edinburg, 1905)

Caldwell, C., *Leadership, trustworthiness, and ethical stewardship*, (Human Resource Management International Digest, March 2011)

Churchill, A., Barney, B., Hazel, A., Kelsall, D., Mouch, S., and Verdun, D., *What is Stewardship, and should all great leaders practice it?*, (The New York Times in Education, 2015)

Collins English Dictionary, HarperCollins Publishers

Economy, P., *5 Ways Faith in Something Bigger Than Yourself Can Lead to Startup Success*, (Inc. August 13, 2015)

Emmons, M., *Key Statistics About Millennials in the Workplace*,

(Dynamic Signal, October 19, 2018)

Fasig, L., *Toddlers' Understanding of Ownership: Implications for Self-Concept Development*, (Social Development, December 2001)

Gallup Workplace, *How Millennials Want to Work and Live*, (Gallup, 2016)

Hackman, R., *Do Teams Need Leaders?*, (Yale Insights, March 1, 2011)

Hodge, A., *Stewardship Mandate*, (iUniverse, 2005)

Holmes, M., *Stewardship: Small to Large & Things to People*, (Life of a Steward, October 13, 2012)

Holy Bible, (NIV) Matthew 6:24

IEDP Editorial, *Steward Leadership*, (IEDP October 9, 2013)

Kamer, Jeremy *Steward Leadership and Paul*, (School of Business & Leadership, Regent University, Journal of Biblical Perspectives in Leadership 8, no. 1, Fall 2018)

Kukard, J., *Steward Leadership: A Maturational Perspective*, April, K., & Peters, K., (UCT press, 2013)

Llopsis, G., *6 Ways Successful Teams are Built to Last*, (Forbes, October 1, 2012)

Llopsis, G., *5 Powerful Things Happen When A Leader Is Transparent*, (Forbes, Sep 10, 2012),

Maxwell, J., *Mark Cole: How to Grow Your Influence*, (johnmaxwell.com, December 8, 2018)

Murphy, M., *Which of These 4 Leadership Styles Are You?*, (Forbes, July 9, 2015)

Nave, C., Sherman, R., Funder, D., Hampson, S. and Goldberg, L., *On the Contextual Independence of Personality: Teachers' Assessments Predict Directly Observed Behavior After Four Decades*, (July 8, 2010, Social Psychological and Personality Science)

Nichols, C., Hayden, S.C., and Trendler, C., *4 Behaviors that Help Leaders Manage a Crisis*, (Harvard Business Review, April 2, 2020)

Ramsey, Dave, *A Call to Stewardship*, (Ramsey, October 15, 2019)

Schooley, S., *Are You a True Leader or Just a Boss*, (Business News Daily, October 17, 2019)

Schuitema, A., *Success in Leadership Starts with Care*, (Schuitema Human Excellence Group, May 13, 2020)

Segal, L., & Lehrer, M., *The Institutionalization of Stewardship: Theory, Propositions, and Insights from Change in the Edmonton Public Schools*, (Organization Studies, February 23, 2012)

The Predictive Index, *"The Predictive Index People Management Study*, (2018)

Toma, G., *This Groundskeeper Has Worked Every Super Bowl. He Turns 91 On Sunday*, (NPR, February 1, 2020)

Udemy Research, *Udemy in Depth: 2018 Millennials at Work Report*, (Udemy, Inc., 2018)

White, E.B., *Stuart Little*, (Harper & Brothers, 1945)

Chapter 6

Amabile, Teresa and Kramer, Steven, *The Progress Principle: Using Small Wins to Ignite Joy, Engagement, and Creativity at Work*, (HBR Press, 2011),

Buck, Pearl S., *My Several Worlds: A Personal Record*, (1954)

Comparably, *Study: The Worst Traits in a Boss*, (March 28, 2018)

DeCaro, M.S., Thomas, R.D.,Albert, N.B. and Beilock, S.L., *Choking under pressure: Multiple routes to skill failure*, (Experimental Psychology, July 2011)

del Vasto, Lanza, *Principles and Precepts of the Return to the Obvious*, (1945)

Gallup, *Trust in Business Index*, (BBB/Galup, April, 2008)

Graham Brown, Mark, *Beyond the Balanced Scorecard*, (Productivity Press, 2007)

Guiso, Luigi, Sapienza, Paolo and Zingales, Luigi, *The Value of Corporate Culture*, (Chicago Booth School of Business Research Paper No. 13-80, November 13, 2013)

Half, Robert, *12 Ways Bad Bosses Cause Good Employees to Leave*,

(February 19, 2019)

Mayo, T., *Why Don't Leaders Learn From History?*, (Harvard Business Review, September 6, 2007)

Michigan State University, *What are the Qualities of a Visionary Leader?*, (michiganstateuniversityonline.com, December 15, 2020)

Proust, M., *Remembrance Of Things Past / À la Recherche du Temps Perdu*, (Chapter 2 of Volume 5, The Prisoner, 1923),

Rosetta Technology Group, *Yes, Servant Leaders Actually Do Lead*, (WorkBytes, May 4, 2018)

Ryan, R.M., & Deci, E.L., *The 'what' and 'why' of goal pursuits: Human needs and the self-determination of behavior*, (Psychological Inquiry, 11, 2000)

Schleckser, J., *Why Warren Buffet Believes Feedback Is A Gift and You Should Too*, (Inc., March 27, 2018)

Simons, Tony, *The Integrity Dividend*, (Jossey-Bass, 2008),

Stanford Graduate School of Business, *Why Some Managers Won't Let Go*, (Insights, September 1, 1997)

Taylor, B., *The Best Leaders See Things That Others Don't. Art Can Help*, (Harvard Business Review, August 18, 2018),

Tulia, S., Morgan, *Executive Coaching and the American President*, (Article Archive, 2005),

Wampole, C., *In Praise of Disregard*, (The New York Times, February 16, 2014)

Afterword

Holy Bible, (NIV) Romans 11:6

Ong, Y.S., *A Grace-Based Approach to Managing Gen A in the Digital Age*, (Business Ethics and Leadership, Volume 3, Issue 3, 2019)

Index

About the Author

Phillip Kane is a husband, father, and servant leader. He has had a successful business career of more than 30 years in some of the world's best-known corporations. Working for brands like Goodyear, Pirelli, Rothschild, and NAPA, Kane has had the privilege to lead thousands of individuals and has managed billions of dollars in value for stakeholders. Consistently recognized by the leaders of these organizations for excellence, Kane though credits any personal success to those he has led and who have made each win possible. Born in Detroit, the grandson of an International Harvester (now Navistar) truck dealer, Kane has spent a lifetime in and around cars and trucks. An Eagle Scout, Kane has been serving others since he was a young boy. Crediting his father and a Nigerian priest with almost every good thing he has learned about life, leadership, business and the art of storytelling, Kane has been recognized twice by Jim Kouzes and Barry Posner for the impact of his storytelling on teams. Kane lives in Ohio with his wife, Annie, of 27 years, 3 children, Caroline (23), Charlotte (20) and William (17), and the wonderdogs – Moses, Daisy, Eddie and Pete.

BUSINESS
BOOKS

Business Books

Business Books publishes practical guides
and insightful non-fiction for beginners and professionals.
Covering aspects from management skills, leadership and
organizational change to positive work environments, career
coaching and self-care for managers, our books are a valuable
addition to those working in the world of business.

15 Ways to Own Your Future
Take Control of Your Destiny in Business and in Life
Michael Khouri
A 15-point blueprint for creating better collaboration, enjoyment,
and success in business and in life.
Paperback: 978-1-78535-300-0 ebook: 978-1-78535-301-7

The Common Excuses of the Comfortable Compromiser
Understanding Why People Oppose Your Great Idea
Matt Crossman
Comfortable compromisers block the way of anyone trying to
change anything. This is your guide to their common excuses.
Paperback: 978-1-78099-595-3 ebook: 978-1-78099-596-0

The Failing Logic of Money
Duane Mullin
Money is wasteful and cruel, causes war, crime and dysfunctional
feudalism. Humankind needs happiness, peace and abundance. So
banish money and use technology and knowledge to rid the world
of war, crime and poverty.
Paperback: 978-1-84694-259-4 ebook: 978-1-84694-888-6

Mastering the Mommy Track
Juggling Career and Kids in Uncertain Times
Erin Flynn Jay
Mastering the Mommy Track tells the stories of everyday working
mothers, the challenges they have faced, and lessons learned.
Paperback: 978-1-78099-123-8 ebook: 978-1-78099-124-5

Modern Day Selling
Unlocking Your Hidden Potential
Brian Barfield
Learn how to reconnect sales associates with customers and unlock hidden sales potential.
Paperback: 978-1-78099-457-4 ebook: 978-1-78099-458-1

The Most Creative, Escape the Ordinary, Excel at Public Speaking Book Ever
All The Help You Will Ever Need in Giving a Speech
Philip Theibert
The 'everything you need to give an outstanding speech' book, complete with original material written by a professional speech-writer.
Paperback: 978-1-78099-672-1 ebook: 978-1-78099-673-8

On Business And For Pleasure
A Self-Study Workbook for Advanced Business English
Michael Berman
This workbook includes enjoyable challenges and has been de-signed to help students with the English they need for work.
Paperback: 978-1-84694-304-1

Small Change, Big Deal
Money as if People Mattered
Jennifer Kavanagh
Money is about relationships: between individuals and between communities. Small is still beautiful, as peer lending model, micro-credit, shows.
Paperback: 978-1-78099-313-3 ebook: 978-1-78099-314-0

Readers of ebooks can buy or view any of these bestsellers by clicking on the live link in the title. Most titles are published in paperback and as an ebook. Paperbacks are available in traditional bookshops. Both print and ebook formats areavailable online.
Find more titles and sign up to our readers' newsletter at
http://www.jhpbusiness-books.com/
Facebook: https://www.facebook.com/JHPNonFiction/
Twitter: @JHPNonFiction

Sweetening the Pill
or How we Got Hooked on Hormonal Birth Control
Holly Grigg-Spall
Has contraception liberated or oppressed women? *Sweetening the Pill* breaks the silence on the dark side of hormonal contraception.
Paperback: 978-1-78099-607-3 ebook: 978-1-78099-608-0

Why Are We The Good Guys?
Reclaiming your Mind from the Delusions of Propaganda
David Cromwell
A provocative challenge to the standard ideology that Western power is a benevolent force in the world.
Paperback: 978-1-78099-365-2 ebook: 978-1-78099-366-9

Readers of ebooks can buy or view any of these bestsellers by clicking on the live link in the title. Most titles are published in paperback and as an ebook. Paperbacks are available in traditional bookshops. Both print and ebook formats are available online.

Find more titles and sign up to our readers' newsletter at http://www.johnhuntpublishing.com/culture-and-politics

Follow us on Facebook at https://www.facebook.com/ZeroBooks

and Twitter at https://twitter.com/Zer0Books